French Pianism

An Historical Perspective

INCLUDING INTERVIEWS WITH
CONTEMPORARY PERFORMERS

by

CHARLES TIMBRELL

FOREWORD BY GABY CASADESUS

Pro/Am Music Resources, Inc.
White Plains, New York

Kahn & Averill
London

FIRST EDITION

Published in the United States of America 1992 by
PRO/AM MUSIC RESOURCES, INC.
63 Prospect Street, White Plains, New York 10606
ISBN 0-912483-89-X

U.S. School & Library Distribution by
PRO/AM MUSIC RESOURCES, INC.

U.S. Trade & Retail Distribution by
THE BOLD STRUMMER, LTD.
20 Turkey Hill Circle, Box 2037, Westport, Connecticut 06880

Published in Great Britain 1992 by
KAHN & AVERILL
9 Harrington Road, London SW7 3ES
ISBN 1-871082-49-8

To the memory of

MONIQUE HAAS (1909-1987)

whose vivid performances and illuminating teaching

kindled my interest in *l'école française de piano*

Contents

CONTENTS

Please note: Chapter I-V footnotes appear on pages 264-72.

FOREWORD

Following in the footsteps of Rameau and Couperin, the brilliant harpsichordists, the French school of piano seems to have inherited Chopin's technique — a technique of beauty, legato, sonority, and clarity. This rich heritage has been handed down to us through Georges Mathias, the French pianist and pedagogue who was one of Chopin's favorite students.

Francis Planté, born in 1839, was a child prodigy who obtained the first prize at the Paris Conservatory at the age of eleven. From Planté we inherited his beautiful sense of touch, suppleness of wrist, subtle phrasing, not to mention clarity worthy of Mozart. My husband and I heard him play Chopin's Barcarolle when he was ninety, and he performed with a *souplesse* and sonority worthy of the composer.

Like Chopin, Debussy was very conscious of these same pianistic qualities. He hated a style of playing that was brittle and noisy, and he loved the refinement of Chopin's music. Debussy published an edition of Chopin's works, and dedicated his *Douze Etudes* to the memory of his revered predecessor. Ravel, on the other hand, gravitated toward the Lisztian concept of pianism, the outcome of which revolutionized piano playing. He truly embodied our classic ideals of clarity, rhythm, and the musical line as a whole.

Charles Timbrell is surely not only a virtuoso pianist, but a remarkable musicologist as well. His previous publications attest to his interest in the different schools of pianism. In this book, which reflects his interviews with more than fifty French-trained pianists, he has drawn particular attention to the many significant contributions made by French musicians who are too little known in the United States.

Gaby Casadesus
Paris, 29 May 1991
(Translated by Michelle A. Mead)

PREFACE AND ACKNOWLEDGMENTS

Paris was the center of the piano world during the first half of the nineteenth century. The early piano was perfected there, and virtually every great performer of the time played, lived, or taught there. Thus it is not surprising that a distinctive style of piano playing was cultivated in France from about 1810, and that it centered around the Paris Conservatoire. Nor is it surprising, given the nature of French musical education, that this style continued more or less intact until the 1960s. That it differed from German, Viennese, Russian, English, and other styles of piano playing has often been remarked upon, but its history and its characteristics have never received a detailed investigation.

This book, which is equally concerned with historical developments, performance, and pedagogy, is the outgrowth of a long-standing interest in French music intensified by the lessons I had in Paris during several summers in the early 1980s with Monique Haas, Jeanne-Marie Darré, Eric Heidsieck, Gaby Casadesus, Vlado Perlemuter, and Magda Tagliaferro. These pianists — and Yvonne Lefébure and Pierre Sancan in master classes — taught me many things about the French repertoire, but they also taught me that there have been diverse schools within the so-called "French school" of playing.

Much of the substance of this book comes from the interviews I had with numerous French-trained pianists between 1981 and 1991. (A list of these pianists follows this preface.) The oldest, Paul Loyonnet, was ninety-seven at the time. A student of Charles de Bériot and Isidor Philipp, he had an extraordinary memory of musicians and events in Paris during the early years of the century. I was also fortunate to interview a half-dozen other pianists of his generation or slightly later, and these artists, several now deceased, contributed substantially to the picture of French pianism in the 1920s and 30s. Their musical ideas, pianistic advice, and personal recollections document a bygone era.

Interviews with many major pianists and teachers of the postwar period are also included, although their number may not be evident from the

Table of Contents. Some of these interviews had to be excerpted, especially in Chapter III; others were combined for a more effective presentation in a "roundtable" format, as in Chapter II; and still others, which seemed to me of particular interest or which touched mainly on subjects not otherwise dealt with earlier, have been presented in their entirety in Chapter IV. Biographies of these interviewees are found in Appendix I.

*   *   *

I owe debts of gratitude to many people, above all to Karen Taylor, who over several years has generously shared her knowledge of this subject with me, especially regarding the careers of Alfred Cortot, Edouard Risler, and Lazare-Lévy. I am also very grateful to Cecilia Dunoyer and Curtis Stotlar for reading sections of the manuscript and offering helpful suggestions based on their extended study in France, and to Jean-Max Guieu and Jean-François Thibault for assistance with the transcription of some of the taped interviews. Oleg Volkov and Victor Derevianko shared their recollections of piano training in the Soviet Union, and Gustav Heintze did the same for Vienna. Basil Kyriakou gave me insights into French pedagogy of orchestral instruments, and Steven Permut and Kevin Shannon shared their collections of historic recordings. Raymond Donnell made valuable suggestions for the discography, and Michael Yugovich was able to trace numerous live and private recordings.

I am also obliged to helpful staff members of the Bibliothèque Nationale, the Phonothèque Nationale, the Bibliothèque de l'Arsenal (all in Paris), and the New York Public Library. Special thanks are due Michelle Perny-Devarenne, archivist of the Paris Conservatoire, Elmer Booze and Charles Sens of the Music Division of the Library of Congress, Neil Ratliff and Morgan Cundiff at the University of Maryland's International Piano Archive (College Park), and Henry-Louis de La Grange of the Bibliothèque musicale Gustav Mahler (Paris).

I also thank the editors of the *Piano Quarterly,* the *Journal of the American Liszt Society,* and *Keyboard Classics* for kindly allowing me to reprint articles of mine that first appeared, in somewhat different form, in those journals.

My warm appreciation goes to numerous friends and colleagues in France who made my work there easier and more enjoyable, including Randall Blatt, Jeanne-Marie Darré, Thérèse Dussaut, Eric Heidsieck, Dorothy and Henry Kraus, Noël Lee, Joseph Plaskett, Bruno Saint-Germain, and the late Daniel Varsano. Special thanks go to Philippe Rougier, who kindly agreed to do research at several stages during my work.

I am particularly grateful to three other individuals: Stewart Gordon, who suggested that I write this book, and who has served as the best model of a teacher-performer-writer; Maurice Hinson, whose encouragement and practical suggestions were invaluable; and William Kloss, whose patient, knowing advice and constant support have been vital from the beginning.

Finally, I have benefited greatly from the interest and stimulation I have received from my colleagues and students at Howard University, The American University, and the University of Maryland.

Washington, D.C.
March 1992

LIST OF INTERVIEWEES

(with place and date of interview)

Jean-Joël Barbier (Paris, 6 July 1987 and 28 June 1988)
Pierre Barbizet (Marseille, 17 June 1986)
Jacqueline Blancard (Geneva, 27 May 1990)
Yury Boukoff (Neuilly-sur-Seine, 24 February 1991, by letter)
Gaby Casadesus (Paris, 30 May 1986)
Aldo Ciccolini (College Park, Maryland, 22 July 1983)
France Clidat (Paris, 29 May 1986)
Jean-Philippe Collard (Paris, 3 June 1986)
Evelyne Crochet (New York City, 30 March 1983)
Jeanne-Marie Darré (Nice, 22 July 1981)
Jörg Demus (Washington, D.C., 6 April 1981)
Lucette Descaves (Nice, 24 July 1981)
Marylène Dosse (Washington, D.C., 28 November 1986)
François-René Duchâble (Paris, 12 July 1987, by telephone)
Thérèse Dussaut (Paris, 16 July 1981, and by letter)
Brigitte Engerer (Paris, 6 June 1986)
Philippe Entremont (New Orleans, 30 March 1986, by telephone)
Daniel Ericourt (Greensboro, North Carolina,
    1 December 1985, by telephone)
Lélia Gousseau (Paris, 6 June 1986)
Monique Haas (Paris, 15 July 1981)
Eric Heidsieck (Nice, 22 July 1981; and Paris, 31 July 1981 and
    25 June 1986)
Claude Helffer (Paris, 9 July 1981)
Nicole Henriot-Schweitzer (Louveciennes, 13 July 1981)
Jean Hubeau (Paris, 4 June 1986)
Christian Ivaldi (Paris, 8 July 1981 and 9 June 1986)
Grant Johannesen (New York City, 13 December 1987)
Roy Johnson (College Park, Maryland, 11 October 1991)

Geneviève Joy (Paris, 9 June 1986)

Cyprien Katsaris (Paris, 6 July 1988, by telephone)

André Krust (Aulnay-sous-Bois, 13 May 1991, by letter)

Fernando Laires (Washington, D.C., 13 December 1985 and
10 June 1987)

Monique LeDuc (Philadelphia, 16 April 1983)

Yvonne Lefébure (Paris, 5 August 1981 and 3 July 1984)

David Lively (Paris, 7 July 1987 and 3 July 1988)

Yvonne Loriod (Paris, 25 June 1986)

Paul Loyonnet (Montréal, 5 January 1986, by telephone and
later by letter)

Guthrie Luke (London, 20 May 1981)

Robert Lurie (Montclair, New Jersey, 23 February 1987)

Nikita Magaloff (Washington, D.C., 7 November 1985)

Ina Marika (Paris, 1 July 1988)

Barbara English Maris (Hyattsville, Maryland,
15 August 1991, by letter)

Jean-Pierre Marty (Paris, 6 July 1988)

Dominique Merlet (Paris, 2 August 1981)

Marthe Morhange-Motchane (Montclair, New Jersey,
24 November 1985, and by letter)

Cécile Ousset (Paris, 28 May 1986)

Vlado Perlemuter (Paris, 9 July 1981)

Jean-Bernard Pommier (Washington, D.C., 26 January 1989)

Eliane Richepin (Paris, 28 June 1988)

Bernard Ringeissen (Paris, 17 July 1981)

Pierre Sancan (Nice, 24 July 1981)

Jean-Paul Sevilla (Ottawa, 4 June 1991, by letter)

Gabriel Tacchino (Paris, 31 May 1986)

Magda Tagliaferro (Paris, 10 July 1981 and Greenwich,
Connecticut, 9 June 1983)

Jean-Yves Thibaudet (Washington, D.C., 12 August 1987)

Raymond Trouard (Paris, 4 and 7 July 1987)

Jeannine Vieuxtemps (Paris, 27 June 1988)

Daniel Wayenberg (Mandres-les-Roses, 28 May 1991, by letter)
Beveridge Webster (New York City, 8 June 1983)

LIST OF ILLUSTRATIONS

French Pianism

An Historical Perspective

I. The Nineteenth Century

EARLY FRENCH PIANOS

The first public piano performance in France was given at a Concert Spirituel in Paris on 8 September 1768. The event was reported a few days later in *L'Avant Coureur:*

> Mademoiselle Le Chantre played some pieces by M. Romain on a new piano-forte. The novelty of the instrument, its brilliant sounds and the accurate playing of Mademoiselle Le Chantre gave the greatest pleasure.[1]

With this modest, almost offhand account begins the notable history of French pianism.

The instrument used on this occasion was almost certainly not a French one. Although plans for a piano had been submitted to the Académie Royale des Sciences by an inventor named Jean Marius as early as 1716, there is no evidence that his instruments ever got beyond the planning stage. The first regular piano-maker in Paris is thought to have been Johann Mercken, who was producing instruments in 1770. Pianos heard in Paris prior to that time were probably German or English imports, especially ones by the popular London maker Johannes Zumpe.[2]

Not everyone in France was enthusiastic about the early piano. Voltaire wrote in 1774 that it was "a kettle-maker's instrument in comparison with the harpsichord." And the composer Claude Balbastre is reported to have told an early piano-maker not to waste his time: "Never will this newcomer, this bourgeois instrument, dethrone the majestic harpsichord."[3]

Opinion in favor of the instrument was swayed by positive comments in the press and by the pioneering work of Sébastien Erard. This ingenious harpsichord-builder's apprentice made a "square" (really oblong) piano for the Duchesse de Villeroi in 1777, and the instrument was heard at her soirées and deemed the finest piano of its time.

Success then came fast to Erard, who opened a London branch of his firm during the Terror. By 1796 he had returned to Paris and built his first grand piano.

For his early grands, Erard adopted the "English" action, which had a deeper key-dip and a heavier touch than pianos with the "Viennese" action. But around 1808 he seems to have had the idea of combining the better qualities of both mechanisms. In 1821 Erard's nephew Pierre patented in England the invention that has most assured the fame of the Erard family: the repetition or "double escapement" action. The main feature of this mechanism was that the struck hammer remained close to the string until the finger released the key completely. For repeated notes, this meant that the hammer traveled less than half the usual distance. The action was not only lighter than on Erard's earlier pianos (and on English pianos) but it also gave the player greater control over dynamic nuances.

The only French piano firm to offer serious competition to Erard was that of Pleyel. Ignace Pleyel, a successful composer, founded his piano business in 1807 and passed it on to his composer-son Camille, under whom it flourished after 1824. Camille had studied piano-making in London, and he was able to modify the English action and produce an instrument that was less resistent – and also more mellow sounding – than Erard's.

When he took over the business, Camille had the shrewd sense to take on as his partner Friedrich Kalkbrenner, one of the most eminent Parisian pianists and teachers. In addition to benefitting from this prestige-by-association, the younger Pleyel opened a concert hall in 1830, the Salle Pleyel, and this soon rivaled the older Salle Erard. Naturally, the pianists who performed in these halls were expected to play the "house" instrument.

Other piano makers who founded concert halls were the noted pianist-composer Henri Herz, Jean-Henri Pape, and – in the early twentieth century – the successors of Joseph Gaveau. Pape was an indefatigable inventor who held more than 120 patents for piano improvements, the most important of which were for overstringing and the use of felt in hammers.[4]

The fact that important French pianists and composers became piano manufacturers and opened concert halls had obvious effects on the simultaneous development of French piano technique, composition, manufacturing, and public taste.

The influence of Henri Herz was particularly strong in all of these areas, and his attributes as a refined and polished pianist extended to the perfection (and simplification) of the Erard action that he used in his prize-winning pianos. This Herz-Erard action continues to be used by manufacturers throughout the world today.

Pleyel's pianos were subtle-sounding ones preferred by Chopin, Hiller, and Kalkbrenner. Erard's, which had a brighter tone that carried better in larger halls, were preferred by Liszt, Herz, Thalberg, Bertini, and Louise Farrenc. Comparing the two pianos, Chopin is reported to have said: "When I feel out of sorts, I play on an Erard piano where I easily find a ready-made tone. But when I feel in good form and strong enough to find my own individual sound, then I need a Pleyel piano." Chopin cautioned a student against too much practice on an instrument like the Erard, for it could ruin one's touch: "You can thump it and bash it, it makes no difference: the sound is always beautiful . . . ."[5]

Modern recordings made on restored Erard and Pleyel pianos of the 1840s and 50s reveal the Pleyel to be the more delicate-sounding instrument, readily capable of subtle tonal shading. The Erard has a brighter treble and warmer bass. Rapid passagework is effective on both pianos because of the light and fast actions, and clarity is notable — especially in large bass chords — because of the rapid decay of sound.[6]

These characteristics — clarity, delicacy, and precision (often coupled with lively tempos) — have been the predilections of French performers and composers for centuries. It is not surprising, then, that French pianos have tended to reflect these characteristics to a greater degree than pianos from other countries.

After 1800 there were no longer any harpsichord makers in Paris, although that instrument continued to coexist with the piano for a time, as is evident from titles of works such as Etienne-Nicolas Méhul's *Sonates pour le clavecin ou piano-forte* (Paris, 1804).

The date of the "official" demise of the harpsichord in France seems to have been 1816. During the unusually cold winter of that year the harpsichords in the Conservatoire were burned as firewood.

The original Paris Conservatoire (seen today from the corner of
the rue du Conservatoire and the rue Sainte-Cécile)

THE PARIS CONSERVATOIRE
AND FRENCH MUSICAL EDUCATION

Following the Battle of Waterloo and Napoleon's second abdication in 1815, when France lost most of its power and its acquired territories, Paris became the artistic capital of the world. Numerous theatres, orchestras, concert societies, and concert halls were founded or re-established by the early 1830s. These replaced the Concerts Spirituels and the more aristocratic salons of pre-Revolution days, and provided more opportunities not only for operatic productions but also for chamber and solo performances. Foreign composers, performers, writers, and artists flocked to the French capital because it had become a lively center where individuality and creativity were encouraged as nowhere else. As Stendhal observed, "I believe that more witticisms are made in Paris in a single evening than in all of Germany in a month."[7]

During the first half of the nineteenth century, Paris was the center of pianistic activity in Europe, easily eclipsing Vienna and London. Virtually all the greatest pianists active between 1800 and 1850 performed, studied, or taught there, including Dussek, Steibelt, Cramer, Hummel, Field, Zimmerman, Kalkbrenner, Lemoine, Pixis, Hünten, Moscheles, Bertini, Herz, Louise Farrenc, Mendelssohn, Chopin, Hiller, Liszt, Stamaty, Marie Pleyel, Thalberg, Alkan, Heller, Döhler, Henselt, Prudent, Dreyschock, Lacombe, Hallé, Clara Wieck, Goria, Mathias, Rubinstein, Gottschalk, and Saint-Saëns.

When we consider that Paris was the birthplace of the modern piano and its double escapement action, and that by 1847 there were 180 piano firms in the city,[8] it is not surprising that a distinctive style of pianism developed there and was nurtured at its Conservatoire.

The Paris Conservatoire dates from 1783 and the founding of the Ecole Royale de Chant. This school for future opera singers, which began with fifteen children taught by Rameau's former pupil François-Joseph Gossec, was apparently the world's first government-supported national music academy. In 1795 it and the Institut National de Musique (founded as a National Guard school for wind players during the revolutionary era) merged to form the Conservatoire National de Musique et de Déclamation.[9] The Conservatoire thus predated most of the world's major music schools, including those in Prague (1811), Vienna (1817), London (1822), Brussels (1832), Geneva (1835), Leipzig (1843), Munich (1846), Berlin (1850), St. Petersburg (1862), Moscow (1866), and in North America. The aim of all of these schools was of course different from that of the sixteenth-century conservatories in Naples and Venice, which were founded as charitable institutions in which deserted and orphaned children were kept (*conservati*) and given musical instruction.

At first, instruction at the Conservatoire seems to have been offered in both harpsichord and piano, but in 1798 the harpsichord professors switched to piano teaching. New piano professors were also added that year, bringing the total number to eleven. Three of these were especially important: Louis Adam, Hélène de Montgeroult, and François-Adrien Boieldieu. It is with these teachers and their students that the real history of French pianism begins.

The number of students was initially set at 600, with a faculty of 115, but these numbers have varied considerably over the years. Tuition has always been nominal, with acceptance based entirely on competitive auditions. The degree of competitiveness has been high: for example, in 1875, thirty-three pianists were accepted from 201 who auditioned; a century later, in 1978, thirty-seven were accepted from 229.[10] During the nineteenth century auditions often consisted of just a single work of the applicant's choice. Today, however, the entrance examinations are on a very high level and divided into two stages. For the elimination stage, candidates must prepare two Chopin études, a twentieth-century work, and a Classic or romantic work. On the day of the competition candidates draw lots to determine which Chopin étude and which other single work they must play. All who pass this stage are then assigned the same compulsory work (or works) to prepare for the second stage, held one month later. The repertoire for this stage changes from year to year and is not announced ahead of time. (For example, in 1974 the required work was Chopin's Scherzo in B-flat Minor; in 1978 it was Beethoven's Sonata in C, Op. 53, second and third movements.)

Although foreigners, including Franz Liszt, were denied admission during the early years, they were later admitted in such large numbers that by 1888 it was deemed necessary to limit their enrollment to two for each class of twelve students. Presently they are limited to four per class. Classes were segregated by sex until the time of the First World War, when the men's classes were under-enrolled and women were admitted to fill them. Classes have been mixed since then.

Minimum and maximum age requirements have varied over the years. In the nineteenth century it was possible for an especially gifted student to be admitted as early as age six, as was Charles-Valentin (Morhange) Alkan. Today, students are admitted only between the ages of fourteen and twenty-one. Two years is the minimum length of study, five years the maximum. Usually there is a conflict with the French system of free, mandatory education, which includes five years of elementary school and seven years at a *lycée,* culminating in the examination for the *baccalauréat* at age seventeen or eighteen. Because study in the nationalized *lycée* system is as rigorous, competitive, and time-consuming as that at the Conservatoire, serious music students have often dropped out of the *lycée* at the legal age of sixteen, before obtaining the *baccalauréat.* To remedy this situation, young musicians are presently allowed to prepare for their *baccalauréat* by attending special half-day "artist classes" at the Lycée Racine or by taking correspondence courses through the Centre National de Télé-Enseignement.

Piano instruction at the Conservatoire has always been given in classes, with twelve students assigned to each professor. The number of piano professors has varied over the years, ranging from five to eleven.[11] Typically, the class of each professor is divided into three groups of four students, and each group meets once a week for four hours. In addition, each student is given a weekly private lesson with the professor's assistant, who assigns études, drills technique, instills good work habits, and helps the student to prepare the works that will be heard by the professor. The student's progress is assessed entirely by juries, both at regular performance examinations during each year and in the final competition for first and second prizes. These prizes represent categories of accomplishment, and they are not normally reserved for a single individual; in fact, it has been common since the late nineteenth century for a number of first and second prizes to be awarded each year on the same instrument.

The Paris Conservatoire, 1911 to 1990
(at 14 rue de Madrid)

In 1878 the Conservatoire established a preparatory level (discontinued in the late 1970s), and its students competed for first, second, and third medals. The process of advancement from third medal to first prize may be illustrated by tracing the pianistic progress of Joseph Morpain. Born in 1873, Morpain won a third medal in the class of Emile Decombes in 1887, a second medal in 1888, and a first medal in 1889. Then, as an advanced-level student of Charles de Bériot, he won a first *accessit* (honorable mention) in 1891, a second prize in 1893, and a first prize in 1895. The only stage that Morpain skipped was the second *accessit*. Fortunately, this slow progress did not prevent him from later becoming an important teacher and the director of the Ecole Normale de Musique.[12]

The final competitions, one for men and one for women, are open to the public and members of the press. Today's candidates must play one or more required pieces, as well as works representing different historical periods. The latter works are chosen six weeks beforehand from the candidate's repertoire. The musical value of these competitions, with their compulsory pieces and the opportunities for claques and various machinations, has been questioned since the mid-nineteenth century.[13]

The Conservatoire, unlike most of the world's other major music schools, has never tried to offer its students a "rounded musical education." Rather, its objective has been limited to providing the opportunity for talented students to perfect their skills in performance or composition. Thus, even today, pianists at the Conservatoire are required to take only three courses: sight-reading, analysis, and solfège.

These courses are quite restricted in nature. The sight-reading course is confined entirely to piano music because score-reading is another course (not one that is required of pianists). Similarly, the analysis course does not deal with harmony, which is another course (also not required of pianists). Solfège includes the study of intervals, rhythm, clefs, and, of course, singing by solmization. Solfège training usually begins at an early age and is so rigorously taught that a class of pre-Conservatoire students is able to sing, for example, the Overture to Mozart's *Marriage of Figaro* up to tempo with syllables. Students who have gone through this kind of training in their early years are usually able to test out of the Conservatoire's solfège requirement.[14]

The new Paris Conservatoire, in use since 1990
(in the Cité de la Musique in the Parc de la Villette)

Because the Conservatoire has never required performers to take a complete curriculum in theory or music history, the attainment of a performance prize has usually marked the end of a soloist's formal education in music. However, performers have always been able to pursue studies that might lead to prizes in other areas, including harmony, counterpoint, fugue, composition, accompanying, conducting, chamber music, and music history—providing they pass the competitive entrance examinations for those areas.

The present-day performance curriculum at the Conservatoire includes three "cycles" of study. In the first, the student must attain certificates in the areas of solfège, sight-reading, and analysis. Upon receiving these, the student passes into the second cycle, which culminates in the competition for a performance prize. The third cycle, or *cycle de perfectionnement,* is a two-year post-graduate course of study open only to a select number of former first-prize winners. It is designed specifically to prepare musicians for international careers. Teaching in this cycle, unlike the previous ones, is given in private weekly lessons, two hours with the principal teacher and two hours with an assistant. In addition, students at this level have the opportunity to receive coaching from visiting pianists — including, in recent years, Paul Badura-Skoda, Dmitri Bashkirov, György Sebök, Nikita Magaloff, Lili Kraus, and György Sandor.

For nearly two hundred years the Paris Conservatoire has reflected various government designs for a nationalized but centralized education. For this reason it has always been *the* music school in France, and the sixty or more municipal, national, and "branch" schools that were created in various towns and cities throughout the country during the nineteenth century were never intended to compete with it. Most of these schools are still in operation, although a reorganization of the entire national system of music schools, begun in 1969, resulted in classifications of five distinct types: municipal schools, municipal schools approved by the state, national schools, national regional conservatories, and two national superior conservatories: the Paris Conservatoire and (since 1979) the Lyon Conservatoire. The national schools (such as those at Troyes and Bobigny) and the national regional conservatories (such as those at Nantes, Marseille, and Versailles) have specific programs that prepare students for the entrance examinations at the national superior conservatories.

Finally, mention should be made of three independent music schools in Paris. The earliest of these, the Ecole Niedermeyer, was founded in 1853 to train church musicians, although in due time it broadened its scope. Saint-Saëns was its most distinguished piano professor and Fauré its most famous graduate.

Next came the Schola Cantorum, founded in 1896, which soon became a center of scholarship and a place for training complete musicians rather than mere virtuosos. Still in existence today, its professors have included Isaac Albeniz, Gaby Casadesus, Alexandre Guilmant, Vincent d'Indy, Edouard Risler, Albert Roussel, Blanche Selva, and Louis Vierne; and its students have included Bohuslav Martinu, Erik Satie, Déodat de Séverac, and Edgar Varèse.

From the standpoint of piano training, however, the most important of the independent schools has been the Ecole Normale de Musique. Founded in 1919 by Auguste Mangeot and Alfred Cortot, its aim has been to provide a fuller musical education than was available at the Conservatoire. Intermediate *diplômes* and advanced *licences* are offered in two fields, performance and teaching, with obligatory lessons in solfège, harmony, form, sight-reading, chamber music, and music history. The faculty has included Nadia Boulanger, Lucien Capet, Pablo Casals, Alfred Cortot, Claire Croiza, Paul Dukas, Marcel Dupré, Henri Dutilleux, Arthur Honegger, Wanda Landowska, Lazare-Lévy, Isidor Philipp, Igor Stravinsky, and Jacques Thibaud. Notable pianists who studied there have included Idil Biret, Hélène Boschi, Thierry de Brunhoff, Samson François, Reine Gianoli, Eric Heidsieck, Dinu Lipatti, and David Lively.

Each of these schools has played a significant role in the musical life of Paris, and each has offered a more well-rounded education than has the Conservatoire. But the fact remains that for a performing musician to have a successful career in France, a first prize from the Paris Conservatoire has almost always been *de rigueur*.

COMPOSERS, PERFORMERS, TEACHERS, AND METHODS

Paris was the scene of the revolution of piano technique in the 1830s. There Chopin published his Etudes, Opp. 10 and 25, Liszt completed the first version of his Paganini Etudes and the second version of his Transcendental Etudes, and Thalberg performed his flamboyant fantasies on *God Save the King* and Rossini's *Moïse*. But such works could not have received notable early performances, except in the hands of their composers, for they required a liberation of the arm that was then quite new.

Before 1830, piano composers in France were influenced partly by opera composers and partly by the styles of visiting pianists such as Clementi, Dussek, and Cramer. The result was a large body of derivative-sounding sonatas, fantasies, variations, caprices, and battle-pieces composed in an early-Classic vein characterized by attractive tunes, regular phrases, ordinary harmony, Alberti basses, hand crossings, scales, and broken octaves. The main early piano composers active in France were:

Johann Gottfried Eckard (1735-1809)
Johann Friedrich Edelmann (1749-94)
Nicolas Joseph Hüllmandel (1756-1823)
Louis Adam (1758-1848)
Etienne-Nicolas Méhul (1763-1817)
Ignaz Ladurner (1766-1839)
Louis Jadin (1768-1853)
Hyacinthe Jadin (1769-1802)
François-Adrien Boieldieu (1775-1834)
Friedrich Kalkbrenner (1785-1849)
Alexandre-Pierre-François Boëly (1785-1858)

From both a pianistic and a compositional view, the most interesting of these were probably Hüllmandel, Adam, Méhul, and Kalkbrenner. As the historian François-Joseph Fétis expressed so well in 1830, "nature labored in vain to give birth to a Haydn or a Beethoven in France."[15]

A harpsichord technique would have sufficed for most of the piano works performed in France before Erard's 1821 patent for double escapement action. Indeed, much of the technical advice of Couperin and Rameau is reflected in what pianists preached more than a century later.

For example, in *L'Art de toucher le clavecin* (1717) Couperin urged "holding the fingers as close to the keys as possible," and he placed a high premium on "suppleness and great freedom of the fingers."[16] Rameau was more explicit in his essay *De la Mechanique des doigts sur le clavessin*, published with his *Pièces de clavecin* (1724):

> The wrist must always be supple. This suppleness, which spreads to the fingers, gives them freedom and all necessary lightness; and the hand is, as it were, lifeless, only serving to guide the fingers to places on the keyboard where they might not reach by themselves. ... A large gesture [of the hand] must only occur when a smaller one is not sufficient: and, as long as a finger can reach a key without more than stretching or opening the hand, be careful not to exceed the necessary movement. Each finger must have its own action, independent of the others: even when the hand must move to a [different] point along the keyboard, it is still necessary that the finger falls on the key by its own independent action.[17]

Later, in his *Code de musique pratique* (1760), Rameau wrote:

> In all positions, and the largest jumps, the hand obeys the fingers, the wrist-joint obeys the hand, and the elbow obeys the wrist; the shoulder must never have anything to do [with playing].[18]

These comments by Couperin and Rameau about well-schooled, independent fingers staying close to the keys, with a quiet hand (and arm and torso), and an avoidance of force, could well summarize the approach of most of the early piano schools. Clementi, Mozart, and others advocated these basically Baroque notions during the Classic period; and Cramer, Hummel, and Moscheles — and their French colleagues — held onto them well into the nineteenth century. Even as late as 1893 Hugo Riemann advised pianists to follow Rameau's advice, and Teresa Carreño — the fiery pianist who died in 1917 — maintained that one should be able to play with a glass of water balanced on the wrist.[19]

An examination of French keyboard exercises and methods from Michel de Saint-Lambert (1702) to Marguerite Long 250 years later confirms that the French have been preoccupied with "pure" finger technique to a greater extent than pedagogues of any other country. The main features of a few of these methods are noted in the following consideration of the most prominent pianists and teachers active in Paris during the nineteenth century.

* * * *

The first important professor of piano at the Conservatoire was Louis Adam, an Alsatian who was largely self-taught. His tenure at the Conservatoire for forty-five years contributed significantly to the development of native pianism. In his first piano method (1798, co-authored with Ludwig Lachnith) he advocated a technique in which tone was "drawn out" of the keyboard by finger pressure only, with the arm motionless. Goals were good fingering habits, the development of strength, precision, and lightness in the left hand (to equal that of the right), smooth passage of the thumb, and the independence of curved fingers. Scales in single and double notes were followed by the study of octaves, chords, and exercises with held notes (*tenues*) — but arpeggios were not mentioned. In Adam's *Méthode* of 1804, which was adopted by the Conservatoire for some years, there is a new insistence on the importance of tone production. Different touches — using fingers only — are explored in order to sensitize the player to the inflections that a singer might employ in shaping words or phrases. Some attention is given to enhancing musical effects through the use of the pedals. As far as the exploration of touch and tone are concerned, Adam's method goes beyond the important earlier ones by C.P.E. Bach and Türk. Adam's most notable students were Kalkbrenner and Henri Lemoine.

Friedrich Kalkbrenner was, along with Henri Herz, the most important pianist in Paris before Liszt and Chopin. His playing was said to have been clear, neat, very close to the keys, with an especially charming touch and ringing tone, and with octaves played from the wrist. He was concerned, above all, with developing the widest variety of finger touches —

and, like his teacher Adam, he emphasized that these must serve the widest variety of expression. A touch not frequently dealt with before his 1830 *Méthode* is that for "caressing" the keys—that is, sliding the finger from the middle to the edge of the key with a gentle pressure.

Kalkbrenner also advocated a device known as the *Guide-Mains,* consisting of a rod attached to the keyboard and on which the forearm rested so that the fingers alone could work on touch and tone production. His music, like his method, reflects the pianism of Clementi and Cramer rather than that of his younger contemporaries. He is primarily remembered for having taught Charles Hallé, Georges Mathias, Camille Stamaty, Sigismond Thalberg, Arabella Goddard, and Marie Pleyel—and for advising Chopin that he needed a three-year course of study with him (advice not taken, although Chopin had great admiration for his playing and dedicated his Concerto in E Minor to him).

Kalkbrenner is important because it is to him that we can trace the French style of playing known as the *jeu perlé*: rapid, clean, even passagework in which each note is bright and perfectly formed, like each pearl on a necklace. This style, which requires the utmost equality of touch and an unforced tone that is controlled entirely by the fingers, has been a prime concern of the French school from Adam to such later pianists as Saint-Saëns, Marguerite Long, Isidor Philipp, and their students.

Pierre Zimmerman may be considered the great-grandfather of the French school, for his influence was more far-reaching than Adam's. Zimmerman studied piano with François-Adrien Boieldieu and graduated from the Conservatoire in 1800 with the first prize (Kalkbrenner won second that year). His success as a teacher at the Conservatoire for more than thirty years was such that he virtually stopped performing. In 1842 he rejected Louis Moreau Gottschalk, soon to become the first great American pianist, with the remark that America was a "country of railroads but not of musicians."[20] His *Encyclopédie du pianiste* contained his method, and his principal pupils included Antoine-François Marmontel, Alexandre Goria, César Franck, and the first three native French pianists to have major careers: Emile Prudent, Louis Lacombe, and Charles-Valentin Alkan.

Another early figure of importance was Johann Peter Pixis, who studied with his father in Germany before coming to Paris in 1825 and establishing himself as a performer and teacher. He must have been accomplished, for he was one of the six virtuosi who contributed variations for the showy work known as *Hexameron* — the others being Liszt, Chopin, Herz, Czerny, and Thalberg. Pixis was the dedicatee of Chopin's *Grand Fantasy on Polish Airs*, Op. 13, and his principal student was Thalberg.

Henri Herz graduated from the Conservatoire at fifteen. Although he studied with Louis Pradher (who had studied with Hélène de Montgeroult, a former pupil of Dussek) his mature style seems to have been influenced most by his brief contact with Moscheles. Herz performed his own works almost exclusively — concertos, fantasies and variations on opera themes, potpourris, and the like — and many of these became very popular despite the condescending attitudes toward them by Schumann, Mendelssohn, Moscheles, Rubinstein, and other musicians. His playing style, ideally suited to his music, was characterized by a rapid, pearly finger technique, highly developed wrists, and a shallow tone.

Herz was also an immensely popular teacher, sometimes having to schedule lessons as early as six o'clock in the morning. In 1838 a writer for *Le Corsaire* jokingly described his pedagogy:

> M. Henri Herz, No. 38, Rue de la Victoire, is quite an eccentric professor. His lesson generally lasts half an hour — ten minutes for arranging the large curls and the cravat of M. Henri Henz; ten minutes more to draw his watch — his showpiece from Bréguet — out of his fob, which he hooks with ceremony on the piano; the last ten minutes for the instruction and advice which M. Henri Herz, No. 38, Rue de la Victoire, invariably gives while arranging his curls. . . .[21]

From 1842 to 1874 Herz taught a women's class at the Conservatoire. His teaching was interrupted by a five-year tour of the United States, Mexico, and the West Indies, part of which is amusingly recounted in his book, *Mes voyages en Amérique*. Following Herz's New York performance of his Second Concerto, *Lucia* Fantasy, and *Otello* Variations, a critic wrote in the *Tribune*:

> His execution is the very perfection of grace, delicacy, lightness, elasticity, equality . . . . [Another journal] spoke of Herz as a "musical pyrotechnist." The epithet was brilliant but inappropriate. We should rather compare his execution to the most delicate flower-work which the frost fairies draw upon the window-pane in their frolicsome hours of winter moonlight. His harmonies and combinations are so symmetrical, and his fingering is so rapid and precise, that one would think a bird had escaped from his fingers and went undulating and singing through the air. But we must confess that we were not excited by his playing; nor did it seem to be any part of the effect at which he aimed to rouse his hearers — rather to subdue, delight and soothe them with such fairy-like speech as would have stayed Shakespeare himself to hear.[22]

Herz is remembered for advocating the once-popular "Dactylion," a device that was intended to strengthen the fingers by inserting them into individual rings attached to springs that lifted them high. Three of his students became important pedagogues themselves: Emilie Réty, who taught a preparatory or *clavier* class at the Conservatoire from 1856 to 1888; Louise Aglaé Massart, who taught an upper-level class at the Conservatoire from 1874 to 1887; and Marie Jaëll, who is remembered as the first French pianist to perform the thirty-two Beethoven sonatas (in 1893) and as the author of pioneering studies on touch and the role of psycho-physics in music training.[23] Another Herz student, Berthe Marx-Goldschmidt, was an active performer in Berlin around the turn of the century, specializing in such un-Herzian repertoire as the late sonatas of Beethoven and the major works of Bach, Chopin, and Schumann.

Félix Le Couppey was a contemporary of Herz who studied with Pradher. He began as a harmony teacher, then took over Herz's class while the latter was on tour, and later was given a class of his own. Like Herz, he was preoccupied with the idea of perfect independence of the fingers. His *Célèbre Cours de piano* and books of studies such as the Czerny-like *L'Agilité* are still in wide use in France today. Among Le Couppey's bet-

Henri Herz
Lithograph by Achille Devéria (1832)
(University of Michigan Museum of Art, Acc. No. 1956/1.55)

ter-known students were Cécile Chaminade, Caroline (Fanny) Montigny-Rémaury, Léontine Bordes-Pène, and Sophie Chéné. Chaminade, a popular composer, was among the first French pianists to make recordings. Bordes-Pène was the dedicatee of d'Indy's *Symphonie sur un chant montagnard français* and Franck's *Prélude, aria et final*, both of which she premiered. Sophie Chéné, who taught at the Conservatoire for fifty years (1870-1920, first as an assistant teacher and then as professor of a preparatory class), influenced the formation of many French pianists who themselves became active teachers in Paris between 1900 and the mid-1960s, including Marguerite Long, Germaine Alem-Chéné, Lucie Léon, Lucie Caffaret, Blanche Selva, Blanche Bascourret de Guéraldi, and Jean Doyen.

Ignaz Moscheles arrived in Paris in 1820 and created quite a stir by his first concert. Although he was among the most important pianists after Hummel and before Chopin, his crisp touch, sparse pedaling, and restricted arm movements placed him closer to the older tradition. Liszt and Chopin, however, played and taught his music regularly for two decades, and his Etudes, Opp. 70 and 95 are still of some pedagogic interest today. In 1839, after hearing Chopin play, Moscheles commissioned his *Trois nouvelles Etudes*; and at about the same time he ordered an etude from Liszt (the one later re-worked as *Ab Irato*). These were published — along with études by Cramer, Döhler, Henselt, Thalberg, and Moscheles himself — as part of the Fétis-Moscheles *Méthode des méthodes* (1840). Although Moscheles lived and taught mostly in London and Leipzig, he had two important Parisian students, Elie Delaborde and Marie Pleyel.

Franz Liszt arrived in Paris in 1823 at age twelve, after studying piano with his father and with Czerny. He was denied admission to the Conservatoire because he was a foreigner, so his incredibly fast development was due to his own hard work and intelligence — plus the influence of Paganini's violin virtuosity. Liszt performed, lived, and taught in Paris off and on for twenty-four years (until 1847), during which time Thalberg was considered his only real rival. A well-publicized pianistic "duel" between them in 1837 produced a diplomatic verdict from the Princess Belgiojoso, who sponsored the event: "Thalberg is the first pianist in the world — Liszt is the only one."[24] Among Liszt's students during his Paris years — which were not his greatest teaching years – were Wilhelm von Lenz and Valérie Boissier. An interesting account of the latter's twenty-some lessons was left by her mother, who attended them during the winter of 1831-32.[25] It would seem that Liszt did not pass on many secrets of his bravura playing during his Paris years – or, if so, they did not rub off on the French school, which remained fixed on wrists and high fingers long after he left. Although some of his pedagogy was reflected in the teaching of his later French students, Marie Jaëll and Théodore Ritter, Liszt's major influence in France was to come indirectly through Edouard Risler, who studied in Germany with three of his most important students.

Frédéric Chopin came to Paris in 1831, at age twenty-one. He was already a fully formed pianist who, like Liszt, was largely self-taught, his only piano teacher having been the violinist Wojciech Zywny. His unique brand of playing – refined, expressive, and as close to the keys as possible – has been documented many times over. Here it suffices to note that some elements of his approach were passed on by two of his many Parisian students: Georges Mathias (whose students at the Conservatoire later included Raoul Pugno, Isidor Philipp, Santiago Riera, and Georges Falkenberg); and Emile Decombes (perhaps more of a Chopin disciple than an actual student, whose own students at the Conservatoire later included Alfred Cortot, Edouard Risler, Victor Staub, and Joseph Morpain).

Mathias studied with Chopin for approximately five years, beginning around 1838. Clara Wieck heard him play in Paris in 1839 and wrote her father that "he outshines all the keyboard strummers around here."[26] Marmontel later remarked on Mathias's agile fingers, transparent clarity, and unexaggerated expression – all hallmarks of good Chopin playing, then and now. However, Mathias was also a student of Kalkbrenner, so it is difficult to ascertain to what degree his teaching really reflected Chopin's. To judge from his method and the approach of some of his students, it is possible that Mathias did not quite grasp the core of Chopin's approach, in which the mechanics of playing were not divorced from interpretive considerations.

Daniel Ericourt, in an interview for this book, described his study at the Conservatoire with two of Mathias's students, Georges Falkenberg and Santiago Riera. The former, a professor of a preparatory class, taught in a very detailed way, patiently taking us through a piece measure by measure, with very precise advice about every aspect of playing. He taught the works of Mozart and Mendelssohn especially well, and he emphasized the importance of a good, clean technique. He insisted on our learning a lot of Czerny, especially from the *School of Velocity* and the *School of Finger Dexterity*. I can't say that he was much concerned with our development as interpreters, but we were just children of eleven or so.

Riera, on the other hand, was an excellent teacher of an advanced class. Unlike Falkenberg, his emphasis was very much on interpretation—color, emotion, dash, and the over-all effect of a work. He had a hot Latin temper and no patience with unprepared students. When I studied with him [1916-19] he was no longer performing, and I don't remember that in class he ever demonstrated more than a phrase or two, always with just one hand in the upper part of the keyboard. Earlier he had been famous for his spectacular octaves, and this was a technique that he emphasized a lot at lessons. I remember learning with him Liszt's *Mephisto Waltz,* Beethoven's Op. 57, and many of the Chopin études, the B-flat Minor Sonata, and the Fantasy. I studied with him for three years, but I never heard him tell a student that he needed to relax or to use more forearm or shoulder. And neither did Falkenberg. What they taught was primarily high finger articulation.

Whether or not they passed on Chopin's teaching, Mathias's students—and their students—exerted a strong influence in France. Mathias, Decombes, Pugno, Philipp, Falkenberg, Cortot, Risler, Staub, and Morpain all taught at the Conservatoire, and most of them published significant pedagogical works.

Chopin's sketch for a piano method, unfinished at his death, stressed several important points: the most natural hand position is that in which long fingers are placed on black notes and short fingers on white notes (as for the scale of B Major); the study of "piano mechanism" is divided into three parts: 1) scales and trills, 2) arpeggios and chords, and 3) double notes, including octaves; a good technique is one that allows the player to control and vary a beautiful sound; each of the fingers is differently formed and has its own characteristic touch — therefore one should not aim to make these fingers equally strong; and, because the hand, wrist, forearm, and upper arm are all involved in playing, "one cannot try to play everything from the wrist, as Kalkbrenner claims."[27] The most original of these points are the last two, which, interestingly enough, have not been emphasized by too many subsequent pedagogues in France.

Another source for Chopin's thoughts on technique is the short set of exercises that he devised for his niece, Ludwika Jedrzejewicz. These are based on the same five-note diminished-seventh chord that Stamaty and Philipp were to use as the basis for so many of their own exercises.[28]

Kalkbrenner's protégé was Camille Stamaty, who made a notable Paris debut in 1835, studied briefly with Mendelssohn in Leipzig, and then became a much sought-after teacher in Paris. To judge from his exercises in *Le Rythme des doigts*, his approach was not an overly musical one. The development of strong and flexible fingers is achieved while the hand is kept in a fixed position. Various rhythms are applied, and the use of a metronome is an integral part of his method. Stamaty also advocated his teacher's *Guide-Mains,* and required its use by his own most gifted students, Gottschalk and Saint-Saëns.

Sigismond Thalberg, a student of Hummel, Moscheles, Pixis, and Kalkbrenner, created a sensation by his first Paris performances in 1835. He was noted for his round and beautiful tone, his nearly motionless control and crystal-clear passage work, and his ability to create the illusion of three hands by the division of melody between alternating-hand arpeggios — a technique used by Liszt, notably in *Un Sospiro* and some of his opera fantasies and paraphrases. His piano works suggest that he was a more musical and imaginative artist than Herz or Kalkbrenner. The metaphor of "pearls" to describe rapid, clean, and even passage-work, as in the *jeu perlé*, was used to describe Thalberg's playing in 1836 — and it may have been the first time that a French writer used the term.[29]

Thalberg was opposed to high fingers and summarized his thoughts on singing tone in the preface to *L'Art du chant appliqué au piano* (c. 1860), a collection of his transcriptions. His advice for obtaining the best tone in declamatory music was to "catch" and press the keys from a close position, rather than striking them from above. But for playing simple, graceful melodies he said that one should "knead the keys [as though] with a boneless hand and fingers of velvet."

The most influential of Thalberg's Parisian students was Charles de Bériot, son of the famous Belgian violinist. Like Thalberg, he attached great importance to critical listening, refinement of touch, singing tone, slow practice, and meticulous use of the pedals. This very musical approach is reflected in his two books of exercises, *Mécanisme et style* and *La Sonorité du piano*. The most famous products of Bériot's class at the Conservatoire were Ricardo Viñes, Maurice Ravel, Joaquin Malats, Enrique Granados, Lucien Wurmser, and Paul Loyonnet.

A towering pianist of the mid-nineteenth century was Charles-Valentin (Morhange) Alkan, who graduated from the Conservatoire in 1824 at age ten. Although he was reclusive and never enjoyed the fame of Liszt or Paganini, he was regarded as belonging in that company by those who heard his regular recitals at the Salle Erard. Among Alkan's most demanding piano works are the Twelve Etudes, Op. 39, which include a four-movement Symphony for Piano Solo, a three-movement Concerto for Piano Solo (with a first movement of seventy-two pages), and a brilliant set of twenty-five variations known as *Le Festin d'Esope*. At times the massive, quasi-orchestral style of writing, the use of several staves, and the long pedal indications — coupled with the music's often diabolic, almost manic character — seem to justify references to Alkan as "the Berlioz of the Piano." When his piano writing is compared with that of his friends Chopin and Liszt, we find that Alkan's approach is much drier, almost severe, and certainly less legato and less idiomatic. As a performer, Alkan also favored the "drier" literature, and as late as the 1870s his programs included the works of Hummel, Weber, and Baroque composers over those by Chopin, Mendelssohn, and Beethoven. This tendency toward a *style sévère* is a characteristic of certain French performers that can be traced from Alkan's teacher Zimmerman to Saint-Saëns and into the early twentieth century.

During the Second Empire (1852-70) Paris was no longer the dominant musical center of Europe, and although notable foreign pianists performed in the city, few of them settled there. Thus it was that during this time a distinctive French style of piano playing developed without much outside influence, building on the style of Saint-Saëns and at the same time reflecting the ideals of the clavecinistes: clarity, elegance, and sobriety of expression. These ideals were in opposition to the interpretative "excesses" of the Liszt and Rubinstein schools. The major figures who helped shape this style included Saint-Saëns, Francis Planté, and Raoul Pugno, all of whom are discussed in the following section on historic recordings.

Eriam-Miriam (Elie) Delaborde was Alkan's most important student and probably his illegitimate son. He also studied for a time with Moscheles, and was praised as a performer with strong, agile fingers and a serious, unexaggerated style. By the standards of the time, his recital programs were unusually weighty: in 1872, for example, he played a program that included Bach's Concerto in D Minor, works by Heller, Schubert, Weber, and Schumann, études by Chopin and Liszt, Beethoven's Sonata, Op. 111, Saint-Saëns's transcription of the fugue from Beethoven's Quartet, Op. 59, No. 3, and works by French contemporaries. After tours of England, Germany, and Russia, he became a successful teacher at the Conservatoire, where his pupils included Marie Poitevin (who became the dedicatee of Franck's *Prélude, choral et fugue*), Aline van Barentzen (the first American to obtain a first prize in piano at the Conservatoire), Germaine Alem-Chéné (who later taught a preparatory class at the Conservatoire for many years), and Marthe Dron (who later taught at the Schola Cantorum, championed the works of Franck and d'Indy, and played the cycle of Beethoven's thirty-two sonatas).

A most important woman of the mid-century was Louise Farrenc, who was successful on four musical fronts: as an active composer (she studied with Reicha and composed three symphonies, some chamber music, and more than thirty published piano works); as a performer (she worked with Hummel, was highly praised for her subtle playing of Beethoven and other "serious" composers, and in 1840 gave what may have been the first Paris

Louise Farrenc
(Engraving by J. B. Laurens)

performance of Beethoven's Sonata, Op. 109); as a dedicated and successful teacher (she was the third woman ever to head an upper-level piano class at the Conservatoire, where she taught for thirty years); and as a scholar (she compiled with her husband Aristide a famous anthology of twenty-three volumes, *Le Trésor des pianistes*). In 1838 an anonymous critic praised her in *La France musicale*:

Mme. Farrenc is not only a pianist of subtleness and delicacy, with a performing style that is brilliant as well as accurate, but also a composer whose productions — full of grace, talent, and variety — demonstrate thorough musical preparation . . .[30]

One of her students, Hortense Parent, became a noted pedagogue, establishing a school for piano teachers in Paris in 1882.

The next woman-professor at the Conservatoire was Louise Aglaé Massart, primarily a chamber-music player whose students included Aimée-Marie Roger-Miclos, Clotilde Kleeberg, and Marie-Jeanne Riss-Arbeau. Roger-Miclos had a distinguished career and was among the earliest to make recordings. Kleeberg impressed some listeners with her clean way of "pearling" — but when she played Beethoven's Fourth Concerto in London in 1892 George Bernard Shaw described her as "running her hands daintily up and down the keyboard without once awakening the work."[31] Riss-Arbeau was the first French pianist to perform the complete works of Chopin, which she did in eight recitals in Paris in 1908.

If Zimmerman was the great-grandfather of the French school, his pupil Antoine-François Marmontel was the grandfather — even though his appointment as head of the Conservatoire's piano department in 1848 was considered disgraceful by Alkan and his supporters. (Alkan wanted the job badly and was considered a much finer pianist.) Marmontel knew all the pianists of his time, and wrote about most of them in flattering terms in his books, *Les Pianistes célèbres* and *Virtuoses contemporains*. In lauding Delaborde as a teacher, Marmontel gives us some insight into his own views about teaching:

[Delaborde] believed, with good reason, that the possession of a good mechanism, backed by study of the independence of the fingers and of good, firm articulation, should always precede education in phrasing, taste and style. The truth of this becomes evident in the case of students hoping to be admitted to the advanced class. There is confusion and danger in shaping young students too early to a style that, for them, is abnormal, the parody of feelings that they can neither understand nor explain. [It] incites

Louis Diémer

them to affectation, to mannerism . . . [and to] exaggerating the advice of the teacher. It is much better, during the first years, to have them study special exercises and etudes . . . .[32]

Marmontel often taught eleven hours a day, but he also found time to edit many piano works for the firm of Heugel and to write some important methods (notably *Le Mécanisme du piano* and *L'Ecole de mécanisme et d'accentuation*, the latter consisting of five volumes of short exercises of every kind, in all keys and rhythms). Marmontel's teaching career at the Conservatoire was an illustrious one that lasted forty years and made him famous throughout the world. His pupils included his son Antonin, Henri Fissot, and Victor (Alphonse) Duvernoy (all of whom become teachers at the Conservatoire); Théodore Lack, Léon Delafosse, and the composers d'Indy, Thomas, Bizet, and Debussy; and especially Francis Planté and Louis Diémer, two of the most accomplished French pianists at the turn of the century.

If Marmontel was the grandfather of the French school, Louis Diémer was the father. By all accounts he must have been a finer performer than either Marmontel or Zimmerman, and he recorded a number of impressively played pieces around 1905. He was the dedicatee of Franck's *Variations symphoniques*, Saint-Saëns's Fifth Concerto, Tchaikovsky's Third Concerto, concertos by Lalo and Massenet, and the Twelfth Barcarolle by Fauré; and he played the premières of Franck's *Variations symphoniques* and *Les Djinns*. He edited and fingered the complete piano sonatas of Beethoven, Mozart, and Weber, as well as numerous works by Chopin and four volumes of pieces by French *clavecinistes*. At the Paris Exposition of 1889, Diémer gained attention by playing a series of harpsichord recitals on new instruments made by Pleyel and Erard — and five years later he helped to found the Société des Instruments Anciens. His activity as a champion of the harpsichord predated Wanda Landowska's first public performance on the instrument by fourteen years.

Against these achievements, we must weigh some unflattering observations, including one by the Leschetizky-trained pianist Mark Hambourg, who dismissed him as "a dry-as-dust player with a hard rattling tone."[33] Alfredo Casella, who studied with Diémer from 1896-99, described him thus:

> [He was] invariably thirty to forty minutes late . . . very sensitive to adulation . . . [and] a very mediocre teacher. This is strange, as his fame was great. For many years the most brilliant new French

pianists, including Cortot, and many foreign ones had come from
his class. When a piece did not go well, he never knew how to explain the cause, but told the student only to study it again and to
practice many exercises, especially scales.

From three years in his class, I do not remember ever having
heard from him one of those observations which solve a problem
for the pupil and disclose a new horizon to him.

His technical instruction was thus negative. He was no more interesting in matters of interpretation, where his remarks were
colorless and banal. His tastes were reactionary: he infinitely
preferred Gounod to Wagner.[34]

Along these same lines, Joseph Morpain told his former student Clara
Haskil that Diémer "never gave a single piece of advice, not one sugges-
tion . . ."[35]

The list of Diémer's best-known students during his thirty-some years
of teaching at the Conservatoire is a very distinguished one, including Jean
Batalla, Joseph Benvenuti, Georges Boskoff, Robert and Gaby Casa-
desus, Alfredo Casella, Marcel Ciampi, Alfred Cortot, Henriette Faure,
Armand Ferté, Marius-François Gaillard, Henri Gil-Marchex, Gabriel
Grovlez, Léon Kartun, Georges de Lausnay, Lazare-Lévy, Robert Lortat,
Yves Nat, Edouard Risler, Elie Robert Schmitz, Sigismond Stojowski, and
Eugène Wagner.

As performers and teachers, Diémer's students constituted a
remarkably heterogeneous group. Nine of them became piano professors
at the Conservatoire, and they in turn taught a number of the artists interviewed in this book.

* * * *

The charts on the following two pages (31 and 32) summarize the
teacher-student lines of some major pianists and teachers active in France
before 1925. The first chart shows a "pure" line of French teaching that
extends from Adam, Montgeroult, and Zimmerman through Diémer and
his students. The second chart shows some (usually brief) links that

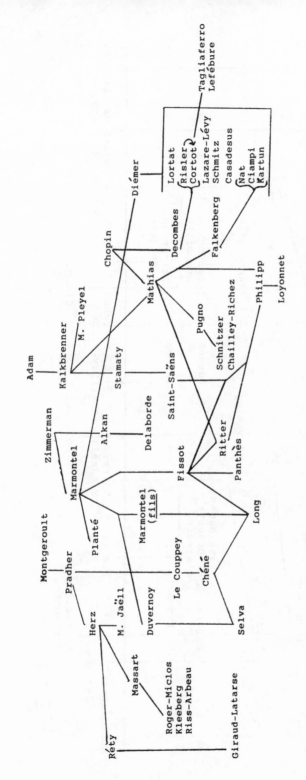

CHART ONE: SOME MAJOR FRENCH PIANISTS AND TEACHERS ACTIVE BEFORE 1925

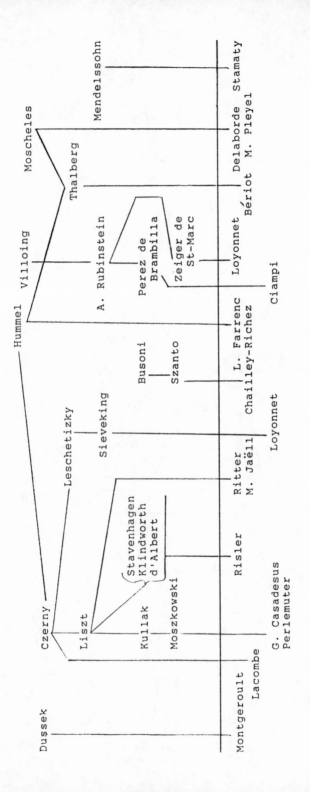

CHART TWO: SOME FOREIGN TEACHERS OF FRENCH PIANISTS BEFORE 1925

French pianists had with foreign teachers such as Dussek, Hummel, Czerny, Moscheles, Liszt, Thalberg, Rubinstein, and Busoni.

HISTORIC RECORDINGS

An important part of the history of French pianism is documented on recordings of artists whose formal musical education was completed in the nineteenth century. Two of the oldest recorded pianists were Camille Saint-Saëns and Francis Planté, each of whom had a completely formed style of playing by the mid-1850s and lived to make some quite remarkable recordings more than sixty years later. Other influential pianists who were trained in France during the nineteenth century and made recordings include: Louis Diémer, Raoul Pugno, Isidor Philipp, Aimée-Marie Roger-Miclos, Cécile Chaminade, Marie Panthès, Céliny Chailley-Richez, Joaquin Malats, Ricardo Viñes, Victor Staub, Edouard Risler, Marguerite Long, Alfred Cortot, Blanche Selva, and Lazare-Lévy.[36]

Saint-Saëns, who used Kalkbrenner's *Guides-Mains* as a student, cultivated a very precise, fast, clear finger technique that we can take as the epitome of the *jeu perlé* style. Although this glittery, shallow-keyed approach should not be thought of as characteristic of all French pianists — anymore than it is characteristic of all French piano music — it is certainly reflected in numerous works by Saint-Saëns, notably the *Etude en forme de Valse*, several of the Etudes, Op. 111, and the finales of the five piano concertos. From a technical standpoint, Saint-Saëns's 1904 recording of an improvised cadenza for his "Africa" Fantasy is a fine display of the old French school's perfection of finger and wrist techniques. Arpeggios, repeated notes, and scales in single and double notes are tossed off with lightning speed and clarity. Equally fast octaves are played from the wrist and close to the keys — and consequently rather thin sounding. Similarly, in a 1904 recording of his *Valse mignonne*, we hear very precise, clean playing of filigree and repeated notes, with just minimal dabs of pedal. In keeping with his clean, chaste style, Saint-Saëns was known for his playing of Baroque music and for his performances of Mozart's concertos, seven-

Camille Saint-Saëns

teen of which he played in a cycle in Paris. The writer Adolphe Boschot has left an account of a concerto performance by Saint-Saëns in 1920:

> In spite of his eighty-five years, his playing, from memory . . . was always pure, clean, rhythmic, and elegantly phrased. His left hand had a lightness that would be the envy of young pianists. In powerful passages . . . he bounced on his chair to accent and underline chords. This man still has marvelous vitality.[37]

Although his performing style was very influential in France in the late nineteenth century, Saint-Saëns had surprisingly few actual students.[38]

Louis Diémer is precisely in line with the Saint-Saëns style in his c. 1904 recording of his own *Grande Valse de Concert*. The tone is dry, scale passages are light and extremely fast, octaves are from the wrist, and the large left-hand leaps are negotiated swiftly and accurately. A more complete sense of Diémer's musicianship is obtained from his 1903 recording of Chopin's (slightly truncated) Nocturne in D-flat, Op. 27, No. 2. The interpretation is rather free and nicely inflected, with voices carefully balanced and a fine projection of long-lined melody, without a sense of the bar line. Although the right hand occasionally anticipates the left and there are some extra arpeggiations and octave doublings, the recording is of particular interest because the approach is so different from Diémer's characteristic style in notey salon pieces or in the French harpsichord repertoire (which he championed on both the piano and the harpsichord).

Francis Planté was considered, along with his friend Saint-Saëns, the foremost French pianist at the end of the century. Like Diémer, he studied with Marmontel (*père*), and also like Diémer his style of playing shared many of the attributes of Saint-Saëns's, although his approach apparently was grander and his sound more cushioned. His friendships with Liszt, Thalberg, and Anton Rubinstein undoubtedly influenced these latter aspects of his playing. Planté's programs were long and taxing, and usually included important works by Schumann and Chopin. His only recordings were made in his country home in 1928, when he was eighty-nine years old, but in them we hear a pianist with spontaneity, a wide tonal palette,

Francis Planté

and confident if not always reliable fingers. The most impressive playing is of Mendelssohn's *Spinning Song* and Chopin's Etudes, Op. 10, No. 5 and Op. 25, No. 9. We can also admire his control of some very charming, shimmering sounds — the "floating tone" for which he was especially noted—in works such as Mendelssohn's *Spring Song* and the middle section of the Scherzo, Op. 16, No. 2. Had Planté been willing to record earlier, we would undoubtedly have really memorable examples of the pianism that was so universally admired by his colleagues.[39]

Raoul Pugno was a pianist with as much dexterity as Saint-Saëns or Diémer, but with a more highly cultivated approach to sound. This is evident in his series of recordings made in 1903, despite the vibrato-like tone quality caused by the studio's wavering turntable. In Chopin's Nocturne in F-sharp, Op. 15, No. 2, the tempo is perhaps the slowest on records—and Pugno defended this by referring to the advice of his teacher Georges Mathias, who was Chopin's pupil.[40] The opening section is played in a most intimate, coloristic, and elegant manner. This approach is in sharp contrast with the *jeu perlé* style for which he was more noted, as heard in Massenet's *Valse folle*, Scarlatti's Sonata in A (Longo 495), the central part of Liszt's Eleventh Hungarian Rhapsody, and in Chopin's Waltz in A-flat, Op. 34, No. 1. In all of these works, the *jeu perlé*—whether in scales, passage work, repeated notes, or trills—is so fast that it can only have been possible with close-to-the-key pressure, rather than with high fingers. This approach is therefore much like that heard in the recordings of Saint-Saëns and another Mathias student, Isidor Philipp. But contrary to some other French pianists, Pugno's *jeu perlé* is almost always pedaled, and rather generously. When a larger technique is called for, as in the ending of the Liszt Rhapsody, Pugno can combine great wrist control with a degree of temperamental abandon that was uncommon among his French contemporaries.

Céliny Chailley-Richez received her first prize in Pugno's class in 1898. She made a number of recordings with the great violinist-composer-conductor Georges Enesco and she founded her own piano quintet in 1940. Chamber music seems to have been Chailley-Richez's chief interest and strength, and her recording of Beethoven's Sonata, Op. 47 ("Kreutzer") with Enesco shows her in fine form. The outer movements are played in a strong and virtuosic manner, with a sure sense of the music's drama and a deep-keyed technique that one suspects she did not acquire from her study with Pugno. In the second movement she is a refined and alert partner, matching the fine detail and nuances of Enesco's playing – as she does throughout the very exciting and colorful recording of Enesco's own Third Violin Sonata. Her recording of the Schumann Concerto (with Robert Heger conducting the Austrian Symphony Orchestra) is less impressive, especially in the finale, where her playing lacks clarity and animation. This may be due in part to the orchestra, which often sounds overly prominent and under-rehearsed. Of all Pugno's students – including André Benoist, Camille Decreus, Ernst Levy, Germaine Schnitzer, and Andrée Vaurabourg – it seems that Chailley-Richez was the most active soloist and recording artist.

Isidor Philipp studied with Marmontel's pupil Henri Fissot and won a first prize in the class of Mathias in 1883. He was much more active as a teacher than as a performer, especially after 1903, the date of his appointment to the Conservatoire. He had a highly polished technique based on fingers and wrists, and this – together with his emotional restraint – made him an ideal performer of the music of Saint-Saëns, to which he was devoted. His 1935 recording of Saint-Saëns's Violin Sonata in D Minor (with André Pascal) is characterized by moderation, clarity, grace, and refinement of detail. In the outer movements he is shown to be the equal of any of the pianists mentioned so far in his absolute control of touch and his clear, fast octaves, scales, arpeggios, and passage work. But for all the professional qualities of his playing, it seems musically disengaged and lacking in warmth. The same must be said for his recording of Mozart's Concerto in F, K. 459 (never officially issued) and an album of his arrangements of pieces by early Italian masters.

Aimée-Marie Roger-Miclos was not only a fine technician, but also an unusually interesting musician – and the only student of Henri Herz to make recordings. That she went beyond the Herz influence (and possibly beyond that of her other teacher, Louise Massart, also a Herz student) can be heard in her 1905 versions of Mendelssohn's *Rondo Capriccioso* and Chopin's Waltz in D-flat, Op. 64, No. 1. Although she avoids the overly fast and overly light approach with which some French pianists of this period can be charged, the passage work is nonetheless very clean and with little pedal, even in the right-hand arpeggio sections of the Men-

Raoul Pugno

delssohn piece. Interestingly, she is able to achieve quite a degree of color and shape in both of these works despite her sparce pedaling. What further sets her playing apart is its sense of spontaneity and utter conviction, including some quite personal rubato in the Chopin Waltz and some daring, if flawed, virtuosity in the Mendelssohn piece. To judge from these and other recordings, and from a published list of her repertoire, Roger-Miclos was an atypically "big" pianist with a technique that used more arm and shoulder than was common in France at the time. She was an active champion of modern composers and of such virtuosic works as Falla's *Fantasia Baetica*, Tchaikovsky's First Concerto, and Anton Rubinstein's Fourth.

Smaller-scaled but refined playing is revealed in the few recordings made of her own pieces by Cécile Chaminade, a pupil of Le Couppey. *Pierrette,* recorded in 1901, is played in a clean and rhythmically precise way, but also with some stylish rubato in places, and with rather generous pedaling. Although she had no influence as a teacher of piano, Chaminade's works were once performed by many major artists.

A much grander pianist was the Russian-born Marie Panthès, a student of Massart and Fissot who received a first prize at the Conservatoire in 1888. Her Paris concerts in the 1920s and 30s included Beethoven's Fifth Concerto, Schumann's Sonata in F-sharp Minor, and—on one program—Beethoven's Sonata, Op. 57, Liszt's Sonata, and Chopin's Sonatas, Opp. 35 and 58. Unfortunately, she made only a few recordings. In Albeniz's *Granada* she plays with considerable warmth and color, bending the beats just enough to project the melodic lines freely and naturally across the bar lines. In a *Pastorale variée* that was once attributed to Mozart her sensitive phrasing and good contrasts of touch and texture hold the attention throughout.

Joaquin Malats and Ricardo Viñes studied in their native Spain before completing their training at the Conservatoire under Charles de Bériot. Malats recorded a few works in 1903, the year he won the Conservatoire's prestigious Prix Diémer. In Liszt's Thirteenth Hungarian Rhapsody and in a truncated version of the Wagner-Liszt *Liebestod* we hear playing that balances technical polish with tremendous vitality and temperament.

Ricardo Viñes is remembered as a champion of new French, Spanish, and Russian music. His recordings, done in 1930 and 1936, demonstrate fine attention to color and texture, charming rhythmic pointing and insouciance in pieces by Albeniz and Turina, and a technique that is very much on the surface of the keys — whether in Scarlatti, Falla, or Debussy. The latter's *Poissons d'or* is played in a masterly way, very fast and light, with shimmering pedal effects and contrasting degrees of clarity. The piece also seems less sectionalized than in the hands of many modern players, including Robert Casadesus. *Soirée dans Grenade*, however, is much less effective. Possibly because of the time limits of recording at 78 rpm, the tempo is rather fast and suggests swagger rather than languor. (On the other hand, one recalls Ravel's comment about Viñes in a letter to M. D. Calvocoressi: "He assured me that *Le Gibet* would bore the audience if he observed all the shadings and tempi I wanted." Debussy, in a letter to Jean-Aubry, similarly accused Viñes of "distorting the expression" of the second book of *Images*; and, in a conversation with Victor Segalen, of being "too dry".)[41]

Victor Staub, who studied with Marmontel (*père*) and received his first prize in Diémer's class in 1888, was appointed professor of an advanced class at the Conservatoire in 1907. His students included José Iturbi, Hélène Pignari, Raymond Trouard, Germaine Devèze, and Madeleine Giraudeau. He recorded several short works, including Chopin's Waltz in F, Op. 34, No. 3, Debussy's *Minstrels*, and Schumann's *Des Abends*. These reveal him to have been a capable if rather prosaic miniaturist, well attuned to contrasts of touch and dynamics.

Edouard Risler was perhaps the first truly great French-trained pianist after Saint-Saëns. Born in Baden-Baden, he studied in Paris with Emile Decombes and later with Diémer, from whose class he won a first prize at the Conservatoire in 1889. Subsequently he studied for several years in Germany with three of Liszt's best-known students: Eugen d'Albert, Bernard Stavenhagen, and Karl Klindworth. Returning to France, he became the first pianist to forge a synthesis of Liszt's ideals and concepts — such as singing tone, romantic breadth, and spiritual qualities — with the best aspects of the old French tradition, such as clarity, taste, and discretion. Risler was able to pass this legacy on to a number of French-trained pianists, especially his younger friend and colleague, Alfred Cortot, who wrote a tribute to him in *Le Monde musical* (June 30, 1930):

Edouard Risler

We haven't stated often enough how much we owe [Risler], we, the pianists of his time and country. . . . For a long time, French pianists had not set their sights very high . . . [and merely] affirmed the qualities of a school of piano playing still devoted to the principles of Herz, Kalkbrenner, and Stamaty—elegance and verve, the charm of a phrasing replete with clever effects, the polish of an irreproachable mechanism. . . . At once he imposed his artistry, and remedied the situation. He undertook, with the calm courage of a Siegfried of the piano, to educate both the public and his fellow musicians.[42]

Risler's repertoire was large and comprehensive. He performed the complete *Well-Tempered Clavier*, the complete solo works of Chopin, and at least a dozen performances of Beethoven's thirty-two sonatas as a cycle. Arthur Rubinstein wrote of his Beethoven playing: "To this day, I have never heard anybody play these sonatas as beautifully and movingly as Risler."[43]

Risler's few recordings, made around 1917, are inferior in sound and barely suggest the wide range of dynamics for which he was noted. Beethoven unfortunately is not very well represented. The last movement (only) of the Sonata in A-flat, Op. 26 is often rushed, though with well-contrasted dynamics; the second movement (only) of Op. 31, No. 3 is steady and humorous, with a wonderfully controlled staccato touch; and the second movement of the Fourth Concerto (in which he plays both solo and orchestral parts) is a beautifully unaffected example of his control of pianissimo dynamics. Weber's *Invitation to the Dance* demonstrates Teutonic vigor in chordal attacks and immaculate *jeu perlé* elsewhere. Liszt's Eleventh Hungarian Rhapsody includes some re-writing, but it compares well with Pugno's version in all respects, including bravura abandon and light filigree.

In arrangements of pieces by Couperin, Rameau, and Daquin, Risler's playing is light and cleanly articulated, but the sound is never dry, even in the repeated notes of *Le Tic-toc-choc*. His Chopin playing is more straightforward and monochromatic than Pugno's or Cortot's.

Marguerite Long and Alfred Cortot—two very different pianists and personalities—were among the most influential musicians in France from about 1910 to 1950. Long had studied with Sophie Chéné, Henri Fissot, and Antonin Marmontel. From 1906 she taught a preparatory class at the

Conservatoire, and in 1920 she was awarded an advanced class that she kept until her retirement in 1940 — afterwhich she continued to teach at her own school. Her digital approach was much like Philipp's (they had both studied with Marmontel's student, Fissot), and for tonal variety they both relied — as did Kalkbrenner and Saint-Saëns — more on varied finger weight than the use of arm or pedals. Her thoughts on technique are summed up in the foreword of her method, *Le Piano*, where she stresses acquiring good, clear finger articulation by lifting and releasing the fingers vigorously, just as runners or dancers might exercise their legs; and building tempo from slow, musical practice, always with an ideal of beauty in mind. She was a strong advocate of Czerny's études and of held-note exercises, and she took a dim view of the weight and relaxation schools:

> The terms 'to relax' and 'to let go' are overused ones that I condemn [because] they are contrary to the action of playing the piano. . . . If one has fingers, one doesn't need 'to let go'. To be supple is sufficient.[44]

Her most successful recordings are those in which she is partnered by other musicians, as in the two Piano Quartets and Ballade by Fauré (her second recording of the latter, with André Cluytens conducting), Chopin's Concerto in F Minor (her first recording, with Philippe Gaubert conducting), and Ravel's Concerto in G (her first recording, with Pedro de Freitas Branco conducting — not the composer, as stated on the record label). In impetuous, dance-like, or sparkling music, as found especially in the finales of the two concertos, she is completely at home and an ideal interpreter.

Long felt almost duty-bound to uphold French musical traditions and the ideals of clarity, grace, moderation, and elegance. This she achieved perfectly in her recordings of Debussy's *Deux Arabesques* and Fauré's Fourth Nocturne. She was less successful, however, in works that call for a large sound or a grand conception. In the first movement of her 1946 recording of Beethoven's Fifth Concerto (with Charles Munch conducting) her approach is notey and her sound is thin, with little pedal. Her shallow-keyed playing is also inappropriate in Chopin's Fantasy, which often sounds uneventful or merely graceful. Debussy's *Jardins sous la pluie*, at exactly three minutes, is possibly the fastest on record. While the dynamics are well scaled, the excessive clarity seems foreign to the nature of the work. (In her book on Debussy's music, Long seems to exaggerate the extent of her friendship with the composer. She was closer to Ravel, who told her that only she should be allowed to play the *Prélude* from *Le Tombeau de Couperin* as fast as possible, "because with you, one is sure of hearing all the notes.")[45]

Alfred Cortot was a grander pianist, and a musician with broad cultural interests and stylistic understanding. Although his repertoire was immense — from Purcell to *Petrouchka* — he had a particular affinity for the music of Chopin and Schumann, most of whose major works he performed and recorded. Like Risler, he studied with Chopin's disciple Emile Decombes, and also with Diémer, in whose class he won a first prize in 1896. After successful Paris concerts, he went to Bayreuth for two years as a vocal coach and assistant conductor under Felix Mottl and Hans Richter. This important experience, and his exposure to German pianos and pianists, undoubtedly altered his French outlook. He taught an advanced class at the Conservatoire from 1907 to 1923 and helped found the Ecole Normale de Musique, where he taught into the 1950s. He also published a large number of study-editions and several important books.

Cortot's playing and teaching differed from most of his French contemporaries by a much greater use of the arms and shoulders, a non-percussive and often flat-fingered approach to melody playing, a precise projection of moods and of the composer's imagined orchestration, and a coloristic use of both pedals. The musical force of Cortot's best recordings can still rivet one's attention and astonish one's ears. Contrary to popular opinion, he had a very big technique in his prime, and his variety of touch and unique combination of eloquence and elegance have often been compared with Chopin's own style of playing.

Cortot's recordings are more numerous than those of any pianist of his era except perhaps Arthur Rubinstein. Certainly his finest ones include (with dates in the cases where he made more than one version of a work):

Chopin's twenty-four Preludes (1926), four Ballades (1929), Sonata in B Minor and the Fantasy (both 1933), and the twenty-four Etudes (1933-34). Among his recordings of Schumann, the outstanding ones are the Concerto (1934, with Landon Ronald conducting), *Kreisleriana*, and *Papillons*. On the same high level are Debussy's twelve Preludes, Book I (1931), Franck's *Prélude, choral et fugue* and *Variations symphoniques* (with Landon Ronald conducting), Saint-Saëns's Fourth Concerto (with Charles Munch conducting), Weber's Sonata in A-flat, and all of the chamber works recorded with Jacques Thibaud and Pablo Casals.

Blanche Selva was one of the very few important French pianists who did not study in an advanced class at the Paris Conservatoire. Instead, she left that school at age eleven, after winning a first medal in the preparatory class of Sophie Chéné. After studying harmony in Geneva, she began her distinguished performing career at age thirteen. She taught at the Schola Cantorum from 1901-21, and also in Strasbourg, Prague, and Barcelona (where she founded her own school). Her students Lucienne Delforge and Libussé Novak had major careers in Europe.

Selva specialized in contemporary music and the music of Bach, whose complete keyboard works she played in seventeen recitals in 1904. Among the works she premiered were Albeniz's *Iberia* (different books in 1906, 1907, 1908, and 1909, with Book II dedicated to her), d'Indy's Sonata (1908, dedicated to her), Roussel's Suite, Op. 14 (1910, dedicated to her), d'Indy's Piano Quintet (1925), and some pieces by Séverac.

Like Cortot and Risler, Selva adopted a style of playing that went beyond the limits of the old French school. This is evident from her repertoire, with its emphasis on big, "muscular" pieces, including the major works of Franck and the late Beethoven sonatas, which she played often. It is most tellingly evident, however, in her sequence of books on technique, *L'Enseignement musical de la technique du piano*, in which she gives very detailed and systematic exercises in touch that involve each muscle and joint in the fingers, hand, arm, shoulder, and back. She was familiar with the Russian school, and in 1919 published preparatory exercises for sections of Vassily Safonov's *Nouvelle Formule*. Her adoption of weight-playing, "free fall" of the arm from the shoulder, rotary action of the

Blanche Selva
(Lithograph by Carlos de Castera)

forearm, and related ideas may well have come from her study of the
methods by Rudolf Breithaupt and Friedrich Steinhausen. In any case, in
France these ideas had not been dealt with previously except by Marie
Jaëll.

Her recording of Franck's *Prélude, choral et fugue* is very close to Cortot's expansive and coloristic conception, especially in the opening section, which is played quite freely and nobly. In the chorale her rubato is minimal, and this adds welcome architectural shape. By contrast, in the fast transition to the fugue she plays in long-lined surges that go across the bar lines, and the fugue builds with real urgency even as the voices are kept unusually clear. The recording remains one of the finest versions of this work.

Her 1928 recording of Bach's Partita in B-flat displays a degree of purity and restraint that was unusual among pianists playing Bach at that time. Her more overt pianism is heard in a very colorful account of Séverac's *Baigneuses au soleil* and in Franck's Violin Sonata (with Joan Massia). In the second movement of the latter work Selva plays with a remarkable combination of speed, drive, lightness, and color.

Lazare-Lévy, a first-prize winner in the class of Diémer in 1898, concertized widely at first, and then sporadically after being appointed to the Conservatoire's faculty in 1923. His technical approach seems to have developed along different lines from that of his teacher — something we have noted about several other of Diémer's students. He advocated slow, deep-into-the-key practice, as well as participation of the arm and shoulder. His few recordings include a remarkably "modern" interpretation of Mozart's Sonata in A Minor. In the outer movements the approach is fiery, although the rhythm is always steady and the sound not too dry or too big. The slow movement flows naturally, with judicious inflections but without the "romanticisms" that were common in Mozart playing of this period.

Lazare-Lévy, Cortot, and Yves Nat all made recordings of Schumann's *Kreisleriana*, and a comparison is particularly instructive because all three pianists studied with Diémer. In the lengthy second piece, Cortot's version features strong contrasts of mood, long lines, warm sound, and interesting voicing. Lazare-Lévy's playing, while musically thoughtful, is characterized by less marked contrasts, less rubato, and less pedal. Nat plays each section with a heavier touch, less attention to voicing, and less strong contrasts than either of the other pianists. In the difficult seventh piece, Nat's playing is the cleanest, although Lazare-Lévy's benefits from better contrasts and a more febrile approach. Nat is more colorful than Lazare-Lévy in the trio of the fifth piece, but not elsewhere — and never as coloristic as Cortot. Throughout *Kreisleriana*, Lazare-Lévy links up contrasting sections without the little pauses that Cortot tends to insert. Cortot's playing of this work seems the most consistently interesting, while Lazare-Lévy's is straight-forward and musical, and Nat's is more erratic than was the norm for him.[46]

As a postscript to this section, mention should be made of Robert Lortat and Magda Tagliaferro, who completed their training very shortly after the turn of the century. Lortat, a first-prize winner in Diémer's class in 1901, was particularly noted as a Chopin player. On a series of six recitals in Paris in 1912 he played Chopin's complete works — "except for the rondos, ecossaises, and some posthumous mazurkas and polonaises," according to the unusually honest advertisement. Of his many Chopin recordings, the 1931 issue of the complete etudes shows him to have had an extraordinary virtuoso technique and a musical personality nearly as strong as Cortot's. In Op. 10, No. 4 and Op. 25, No. 11, the flair and even some details of the musical rhetoric — including caesuras, rushes, and a tendency to "bunch" fast notes — anticipates the style of Cortot's versions made two years later. The two artists also bring similarly subtle rhythmic and coloristic inflections to Op. 10, No. 6. Lortat's very clean Op. 10, No. 5 is one of the most musical and least mannered interpretations on record.

Tagliaferro began her studies in her native Brazil, moved to Paris in 1906, and won a first prize in the class of Antonin Marmontel in 1907, at age fourteen. In 1910 she toured with Fauré, playing his Ballade (with him at a second piano) and several of his solo pieces. By the time of her 1908 Paris recital debut, Cortot had become her mentor, and she studied and performed with him regularly for many years. Her early recordings reflect his influence, especially in the generous sound, flexible rhythms, and occasional impulsiveness that she brought to her 1934 recording of Schumann's *Faschingsschwank aus Wien*. Her Mozart playing was elegant and remarkably chaste for the time, as heard in the 1931 recording of the

Concerto in D (K. 537), with Reynaldo Hahn conducting the Orchestre Pasdeloup, and in the somewhat later recording of the Violin Sonata in B-flat (K. 454), with Denise Soriano. Finally, mention should be made of her exquisite 1929 recording of Fauré's Ballade, with Piero Coppola conducting. It was her first recording, and also the first recording ever made of this work. Her last recording, made in 1981 at age eighty-eight, was also of this work, and it provides not only some remarkable musical congruity with the earlier version but also a valuable point of reference, drawing us back over the decades to the very beginning of this century.

II. LEADING ARTIST-TEACHERS,
1900-1940

F ollowing a crushing defeat in the Franco-Prussian War, France went through a period of intense nationalism that extended to all the arts. In music, perhaps the most positive achievement of the time was the formation in 1871 of the Société Nationale de Musique. The aim of this important organization, whose founders included Saint-Saëns and Fauré, was to promote the music of contemporary French composers. This was achieved even though many leading musicians remained for decades under the strong influence of German (especially Wagnerian) music and aesthetics — as evidenced by the operas of Chabrier, the mature works of Lalo and Franck, and the music of d'Indy, Duparc, and Chausson.

German influences waned as French composers became fascinated with Russian and Oriental music, especially as heard at the Exposition Universelle of 1889. In the early 1890s Erik Satie asserted that Wagnerism went against the natural aspirations of the French, and he urged his fellow composers to create music "without sauerkraut." Debussy achieved this definitively in 1894 with his *Prélude à "L'Après-midi d'un faune"*.

From then until the mid-1920s Paris was unrivaled as an international center of the arts. Writers, painters, and musicians flocked to the city from all corners of the world, creating an extraordinary melting pot. A list of a few of the artistic achievements for the decade from 1910 to 1920 serves as a reminder of the wealth of activity. In literature, those years saw the publication of such diverse works as Marcel Proust's *Swann's Way*, Paul Claudel's *Five Great Odes*, Guillaume Apollinaire's *Breasts of Tiresias*, André Gide's *Caves of the Vatican*, Paul Valéry's *Young Fate*, Jean Cocteau's *Cock and Harlequin*, Gertrude Stein's *Tender Buttons*, Romain Rolland's *Jean-Christophe*, and Colette's *Chèri*.

Painting styles ranged from primitivism to fauvism, cubism, and Dadaism, including such masterworks as Henri Rousseau's *Dream*, Henri Matisse's *Red Studio*, Pablo Picasso's *"Ma Jolie"*, Marcel Duchamp's *Nude*

Descending the Staircase, Georges Braque's *Musical Forms*, and Fernand Léger's *Card Players*.

In music, the decade's diversity of styles was at least as wide as in the other arts, including Jules Massenet's *Don Quixote*, Vincent d'Indy's *Legend of Saint Christopher*, Stravinsky's *Rite of Spring*, Ravel's *Daphnis and Chloë*, Satie's *Parade*, Fauré's *Penélope*, Poulenc's *"Le Bestiaire"*, and Debussy's *Twelve Etudes*.

Great figures in the Parisian dance and drama worlds during that decade included Isadora Duncan, Ida Rubinstein, Tamara Karsavina, Serge Diaghilev, Michael Fokine, Vaslav Nijinsky, Léonide Massine, Sacha Guitry, Sarah Bernhardt, and Réjane.

By the mid-1920s Sergei Prokofiev and Bohuslav Martinu had moved to Paris, along with a number of young American composers who came to study with Nadia Boulanger, including Aaron Copland, Virgil Thomson, Roy Harris, and Walter Piston. Other noted American musicians and writers who had settled there by this time included George Antheil, Walter Morse Rummel, Josephine Baker, Gertrude Stein, Ernest Hemingway, and Djuna Barnes.

Regular symphonic concerts were provided by the four leading Parisian orchestras – the Lamoureux, Pasdeloup, Colonne, and Conservatoire. Major halls included the Châtelet, Théâtre des Champs-Elysées, Palais de Chaillot, Opéra (also used for concerts), Opéra-Comique, and Théâtre de l'Etoile. Recitalists regularly appeared at the Conservatoire, Théâtre des Champs-Elysées, Théâtre Mogador, Salle Gaveau, Salle Pleyel, Salle Erard, and Salle des Agriculteurs. Other organizations sponsoring concerts included the Concerts Spirituels de la Sorbonne (founded 1898), the Société Philharmonique de Paris (founded 1902), and the Société Musicale Indépendante (founded 1909). The latter, which became internationally important for more than three decades, was initiated by Ravel and had Fauré as its first president. It promoted a much wider repertoire than that featured by the Société Nationale, which by then mainly represented the conservative ideals of the Schola Cantorum.

Pianists, too, were affected by the Schola Cantorum's views, which at the turn of the century included an active campaign against solo virtuosos, virtuosic music, and the ideals of the Conservatoire. Performances of

Baroque music and religious music were favored by the followers of d'-Indy, the leader of this campaign, and a determined movement was made against performances of concertos. In addition, playing from memory, which had been most strongly advocated in France in the 1880s by Le Couppey, was now frequently frowned upon as a symptom of virtuosity. Thus some virtuoso pianists, including Selva, Viñes, and occasionally Risler, did not hesitate to perform with the music in front of them.

Pianists of all persuasions thrived during this period when old-school French salon playing gradually gave way to the higher artistic standards of Risler, Cortot, Selva, Long, and others. During the first decade of the century a pianophile might have attended these events in Paris:

1901 Edouard Risler's première of Dukas's Sonata
1903 Ossip Gabrilowitsch's recital at the Salle Erard
       Marguerite Long's orchestral debut with Camille Chevillard
              conducting Franck's *Variations symphoniques*
       Emil von Sauer as soloist in one of his own concertos
       Teresa Carreño's performance of Grieg's Concerto with the
              Lamoureux Orchestra
1904 Blanche Selva's seventeen recitals of Bach's keyboard works
       Arthur Rubinstein's debut
       Ricardo Viñes's première of Debussy's *Estampes*
1905 Performances by the newly-formed trio of Alfred Cortot,
              Jacques Thibaud, and Pablo Casals
       Risler's performance of Beethoven's thirty-two sonatas
1906 Viñes's première of Ravel's *Miroirs*
1907 Sergei Rachmaninov's debut
       Cortot's performance of Fauré's Ballade with the
              Lamoureux Orchestra
1908 Selva's premières of d'Indy's Sonata and Albeniz's *Iberia*,
              Book II
       Two-piano performances by Raoul Pugno and Nadia
              Boulanger
       Yves Nat's performance of Liszt's *Don Juan* Fantasy
1909 Long's all-Fauré recital at the Salle Erard

Despite the war, the next decade included some particularly significant piano concerts. Isidor Philipp performed concertos by Bach, Mozart, and Widor (1911), the "complete" works of Chopin were played on six recitals by Robert Lortat (1912), Alfredo Casella played the première of Ravel's Piano Trio (1915, with Gabriel Willaume and Louis Feuillard), Cortot performed the Paris première of Fauré's *Fantaisie* (1919), Long played the première of Ravel's *Le Tombeau de Couperin* (1919), a concert for two and four pianos was given by Cortot, Risler, Selva, and Viñes (1919), and Ferruccio Busoni played a recital that included two of his own sonatinas, Bach's "Goldberg" Variations, and Chopin's four Ballades (1920).

The 1920s saw the blossoming of the career of Marcelle Meyer, a remarkable pianist whose style seems to have reflected all the best qualities of her three mentors, Long, Cortot, and Viñes. Her recordings of Rameau, Ravel (especially *Alborada del gracioso* and *Le Tombeau de Couperin*), and Chabrier (especially the *Bourrée fantasque* and *Idylle*) show a real flair for sharply contrasting timbres and insouciant rhythms. An ardent champion of "*Les Six*", she premiered Milhaud's *Printemps, L'-Automne* and *Scaramouche* (and recorded the latter work with the composer), and was the dedicatee of Poulenc's *Cinq Impromptus*. She also was a great supporter of Stravinsky, taking part in the first performance of *Les Noces* in 1923 and programming his major solo works in 1926, including the *Trois Mouvements de Petrouchka*, *Piano Rag-Music*, the Sonata, and the then-new *Sérénade en La*. In some ways Meyer stands alone in the history of French pianism, and unfortunately she had no well-known students.

During the 1930s many young French-trained pianists whose names appear often in this book enjoyed international careers. They included Aline van Barentzen, Robert and Gaby Casadesus, Marcel Ciampi, Jeanne-Marie Darré, Lucette Descaves, Ania Dorfmann, Jean Doyen, Daniel Ericourt, Jacques Février, Youra Guller, Clara Haskil, José Iturbi, Léon Kartun, Yvonne Lefébure, Paul Loyonnet, Yves Nat, Guiomar Novaes, Vlado Perlemuter, Elie Robert Schmitz, Magda Tagliaferro, Madeleine de Valmalète, and Beveridge Webster.

As always, the most important piano training continued to be provided by the Conservatoire, although advanced students were also taught at the Schola Cantorum, the Ecole Normale de Musique, and the American Conservatory at Fontainebleau. The last-named has functioned as a summer school since its founding in 1921, when its piano instructors were Philipp, Camille Decreus, and Robert Casadesus. Also worth mentioning is the short-lived Conservatoire Femina-Musica, where the piano faculty in 1911 included Pugno, Roger-Miclos, de Lausnay, and Boulanger.[47]

The professors of advanced piano classes at the Paris Conservatoire during the forty-year period covered in this chapter were:

> Raoul Pugno (until 1901)
> Charles de Bériot (until 1903)
> Alphonse Duvernoy (until 1907)
> Elie Delaborde (until 1913)
> Louis Diémer (until 1919)
> Antonin Marmontel (1901-07)
> Isidor Philipp (1903-34)
> Edouard Risler (1907-09)
> Alfred Cortot (1907-23)
> Victor Staub (1909-40)
> Santiago Riera (1914-37)
> Lazare-Lévy (1923-53)
> Marguerite Long (1920-40)
> Yves Nat (1934-56)
> Magda Tagliaferro (1937-39)

The first six of these, whose careers were mainly in the nineteenth century, have been mentioned earlier. Of them, Pugno was undoubtedly the greatest pianist, and Diémer and Bériot the most influential teachers. Of the others, Risler, Staub, and Tagliaferro were certainly important performers. But, like Riera, their teaching at the Conservatoire did not yield a large number of pianists who achieved international reknown.

The remaining four — Philipp, Long, Cortot, and Lazare-Lévy — were not simply by default the most influential artist-teachers in France between 1900 and 1940. The dual nature of their achievements – as leading performers as well as great teachers – set them apart from other active French pianists of the time. Today, their ideas and ideals have been transmitted to thousands of pianists and teachers throughout the world.

● ● ● ●

ISIDOR PHILIPP

. . . was born in Budapest on 2 September 1863 and moved to Paris with his family when he three years old. He entered the Paris Conservatoire in 1879 and won a first prize in piano in 1883 in the class of Georges Mathias. He also received the pianistic advice of Henri Fissot, Camille Saint-Saëns (whom he knew for forty years), Stephen Heller, and Liszt's student Théodore Ritter. After a decade or so of concertizing, including with his own trio as well as with the *Société des Instruments à Vent* and orchestras in France and England, he was appointed professor of an advanced class at the Conservatoire in 1903. He held this post until his retirement in 1934. Philipp was also a founder of the American Conservatory at Fontainebleau, where he taught piano in the summers from 1921 to 1933.

After 1920 Philipp's rare performances were usually as a chamber musician, often in the works of Saint-Saëns. In 1933 he was joined by Cortot and Lazare-Lévy in the performance of his own Concertino for Three Pianos (without orchestra). In 1940 he moved to the United States, where he taught until he returned to Paris in 1955. His farewell appearance in New York that year, at the age of ninety-one, was at Carnegie Recital Hall, where he performed Franck's Violin Sonata with John Corigliano. Philipp died in Paris on 20 February 1958.

His prolific publications include dozens of volumes of exercises, many original pieces and transcriptions, and numerous editions, including works by French *clavecinistes*, English virginalists, Mozart, Debussy, Fauré, Albeniz, Scriabin, and Bartók. He also wrote several short books on piano technique, and many articles in *Le Ménestrel, Le Courrier musical, The Musician*, and other magazines. His best-known pedagogical

Isidor Philipp

works are *Exercises for Independence of the Fingers*, *Complete School of Technic for the Piano*, and *Exercices de tenues*.

Philipp's students included (roughly chronologically): Maurice Dumesnil, Paul Loyonnet, Cella Delavrancea, Madeleine Grovlez-Fourgeaud, Emma Boynet, Youra Guller, Marcelle Herrenschmidt, Guiomar Novaes, Ania Dorfmann, Madeleine de Valmalète, Germaine Thyssens-Valentin, Genia Nemenoff, Jeanne-Marie Darré, Beveridge Webster, Jacqueline Blancard, Nikita Magaloff, Jean Françaix, Phyllis Sellick, Monique de la Bruchollerie, Rena Kyriakou, and Fernando Laires.

* * * *

Six of Philipp's students were interviewed: JACQUELINE BLANCARD, JEANNE-MARIE DARRÉ, FERNANDO LAIRES, PAUL LOYONNET, NIKITA MAGALOFF, and BEVERIDGE WEBSTER.

How would you summarize Philipp's technical approach?

JACQUELINE BLANCARD: He had a real genius for teaching suppleness, firmness, rhythmic exactitude, and articulation. One heard all the right notes from Philipp's students. He said, "Play fast, but never to the point that a note doesn't have time to say its name in passing." Isn't that superb! Everything is contained in that. He was stern, but musically wonderful. His technique included developing a sense of respiration: for example, inhaling before a chord and exhaling on the chord. Articulation had to be very clean and clear, even in Brahms, but this of course didn't mean that you sacrificed the beauty of the music. He had a respect for sound. If you played a fast run, he might say, "The B-flat was ugly." He said the hand should be held like a conch shell – although for different hands he adapted this advice. He wanted his exercises played always with great suppleness. For articulation he had us do a lot of the *exercices de tenues* (held-note exercises). The fingers should strike well, but with great attention to suppleness and to the use of different nuances – not always just forte. The attack he wanted was firm, but not *marcato*. He would have us play one note perhaps twenty times, trying each time to get a different sound. This kind of practice can lead to a nice, velvety sound in pianissimo passages.

JEANNE-MARIE DARRÉ: It was really Philipp who put a stamp on my technique. His approach was in line with Madame Long's, with less arm and shoulder than Cortot taught. He gave me some stretching exercises that were excellent, because my hand was small. Philipp taught octaves from the wrist, with a motionless arm. He also gave exercises for raising the hand high from the wrist when you play slowly.

NIKITA MAGALOFF: He was very strict about what the composer wrote. He told us to study every nuance that the composer wanted, to respect it, and to play simply, directly, and in tempo. He was very severe about the direct way of playing, and he didn't like the freer approach of Cortot, for example. Naturally, he wanted everything to be clean. He couldn't stand to hear a pianist bang the piano. He often said *"Ne cognez pas!"* ("Don't thump!") That was his expression, and I often think of it.

I must say that I now consider Philipp's teaching old-fashioned. It was very much finger technique – and especially independence of the fingers, using an open, stretched [diminished-seventh] position. It was exactly the opposite of Leschetizky's teaching. I completely changed my way of playing after I stopped studying with Philipp. But I have always appreciated what he did for me enormously. He gave me finger technique. He was not in favor of the idea of weight playing – passing the weight of the hand from finger to finger, with a closed hand position. But I think it is one of the great secrets – except, of course, when the movements must be quick.

Philipp always had us practice in dotted rhythms. But I never do that now. I believe that the best way to practice is to play very slowly, like Rachmaninov recommended, learning all the positions and knowing exactly every movement that you must make. Then gradually you work with faster motions, section by section. If the motions are not ingrained in this way, you can become flustered at a concert, and that can be disastrous. You have to try fingerings at a fast tempo, to make sure that they will work. You can't just practice slowly all the time. I remember

Jeanne-Marie Darré

that Turczynski, a Busoni pupil who edited the Polish Chopin edition, told me that he always practiced slowly, and that fast tempos always came naturally after that. But the performance I heard him give of Chopin's Sonata in B Minor disproved his theory! I think you must practice slower than you want to perform, but also much faster. You must be able to play faster than you want to.

FERNANDO LAIRES: Philipp never advised me to practice in dotted rhythms. Maybe there was something about my playing that suggested I didn't need to, I don't know. I am sure that each student got a small part of what he could offer, not everything. Like Leschetizky and some other great teachers, he didn't have a "system". He gave you what he thought you needed at a particular time. I remember that he had me practice the Chopin Etude, Op. 25, No. 2 without using the thumb, then without using the index finger, then without the third finger, and so on.

PAUL LOYONNET: I remember that at the very first lesson I had to play for him some of his *Exercices de tenues*. He wanted us to articulate vigorously, with fingers curved from the tip and with each phalange contributing to a hollowed hand-position. He also had us do scales in different rhythms and [black-key scales] with the C Major fingering. He had us transpose difficult passages, and of course this gave us better facility in accurate lateral motions. His chief merit was his guidance in choosing the right progressive order of works that a student should study—but not in interpreting them. His ideals were velocity, sobriety of expression, and the *jeu perlé* style.

He was not concerned with interpretation. He felt that his students should have that already, from their previous professors, so that his only task was to make a kind of "final judgment." Often he was content to say, "That's good," or "Re-work that," or "The sound is too hard," or "Too weak," or, often to me, "It's too heavy." If one asked him to explain these basic criticisms, he would often respond with something sharp, like *"Mettez votre tête au bout de vos doigts!"* ("Put your head in charge of your fingers!")

BEVERIDGE WEBSTER: I had been well-trained before I came to Philipp, and he didn't emphasize technique with me. I played a great deal of music for him—much Liszt, some Weber, Henselt, Hummel,

and a lot of Clementi. He fed my capacity for covering a lot of repertoire, and for that I am very grateful. I learned a lot, but in my case he
was not overly critical. Once I remember playing three or four pieces
for him at a private lesson in his apartment. He remained in another
room, where he had a huge table on which he wrote many letters during
my lesson. At the end, he came in and circled a note in a Chopin nocturne, and said, "That note is not quite right." And that was just about
all he said on that occasion. I think he trusted me, and I'm glad he did!
As far as I know, he was not a "terror" in any way. When I left his apartment that day, he reminded me again: "Be sure not to forget that note
in the nocturne."

I don't think Philipp's teaching was particularly different from that
of other teachers in France at the time. Philipp was famous because his
teaching was good and important. But unfortunately a legend was built
around him, having to do with his exercises, especially the ones using
tenues. It annoys me very much to see these exercises used in a belit-
tling way by certain teachers – even ones at Juilliard. Some students
are told simply to play each note at a certain tempo for one week, and
then to shove the metronome marking up each week thereafter. That
was not Philipp's idea at all.

LAIRES: A fast tempo goes against the nature of the *exercices de tenues*,
which are about feeling depth and pressure, about probing the instrument. During my first three months with Philipp I worked exclusively
on these exercises! In this way you could really see and understand his
point of view thoroughly. Only after that did I get some music to work
on, a Mozart concerto. Gradually I discovered that something really
fundamental and important was happening to my playing, because of
these exercises. My tonal control had grown immensely, and my understanding and handling of it became more refined.

If I may, I would like to say more about these exercises, because I
think there is some misunderstanding about them today. First of all,
Philipp never meant for students to practice any of his exercise books
from the first page to the last. He meant for the teacher and student to
pick and choose what was needed. During my first three months with
him, he had me do just Series 1, 4, 14, and 18 from Part I of the Schirmer

edition of *Exercises for Independence of the Fingers*. His words at the beginning of this volume are often ignored: "Practice slowly, with a very supple arm, and strong finger-action, depressing each key to the bottom with a full, round and even tone." Philipp was a man of very few words, so these are important. (He told me that he once said to Matthay, "It takes you 800 words to say what I say in eight!")

I like to tell my students to start with the idea of a full, round tone, depressing each key to the bottom with strong finger action while keeping the arm supple. Keep the key down until just before it has to play again. Keeping the key down doesn't mean pushing; just have a sense of weight, so that the finger feels strong. The playing is done through the *first* stage of the key-descent, not the second. This is the most refined aspect of his exercises: to play through the first stage, and then land by natural means at the bottom of the key, with the wrist flexible and the hand not stiff. In working this way we, perhaps paradoxically, develop an exceptional awareness of the second stage of the key descent — and this is a vital skill in artistic playing.[48]

When the key comes up, the finger should still be resting on it. Debussy said that the fingers must be attracted to the keys like a magnet, and this is what Philipp's exercises do. The finger becomes so relaxed that the key pushes it up. It stays relaxed until it must flex again to put the next note down. The striking is never from high up, *marcato*, as one might practice, say, Hanon. This is the most refined use of Philipp's exercises — to feel that you are an extension of the keyboard, not that you are hitting and missing as you go along! "Independence" doesn't mean the Hanon-type forcing the fingers to work on their own by articulation, separating the fingers one from the other. By the time you get to Philipp's exercises your fingers should already be able to do that.

This is not to denigrate Hanon's exercises. Although Philipp called them "*peu intéressant*", he never suggested that they were useless. It depends on how you practise them. With Philipp's exercises the fingers will gain their independence by having complete control, complete relaxation on the part of those fingers that are touching the keys but *not* pressing them down, versus those that *are* pressing them down. For example, imagine that all five fingers are down on a chord and I ask you to gradually relax the index finger. Slowly, the key will come up, with the finger on it. You will have controlled relaxation of that finger *independently* of the other four. That is independence.

One often hears the warning that too much practice of the Philipp exercises can lead to stiffness. Do you agree?

LAIRES: Too much practice of anything might lead to stiffness! It depends on the level of the pianist. After practising the independence exercises for a certain amount of time, one should switch to an entirely different kind of work, such as scales. That was Philipp's advice to me. Some people have complained that the diminished seventh position is too stressful for the hand. Well, Philipp would never assign those exercises to students whose hands were not ready for them. Everything that he taught was *physically natural*. It is hardly conceivable that anyone incapable of handling that hand position could harbor expectations of playing the literature . . . .

Did he demonstrate much at the piano during your lessons?

WEBSTER: It's a striking thing — and I think an important thing — that in all my years of study with him I never heard him really play the piano! In his studio at the Conservatoire there was usually just one piano. He would sit next to the student and illustrate certain things in the highest register, usually with one hand, occasionally with two. But I never actually saw Philipp seated at the piano during those years. And I don't know of anyone else who did at that time. Not until years and years later did I hear him perform — here in New York, some chamber music. This certainly in no way denigrates him. But I think it is an interesting point to make.

LAIRES: He didn't play pieces for me, although he was often practicing them before I arrived for my lessons. But I recall distinctly that he would illustrate exercises for me, so that I would see exactly how his hands were being used. His hands were the most extraordinany ones that I ever saw, even to this day. They were extremely strong, extremely stretched, and extremely flexible, in an extraordinary combination. He never said "Pass the weight from finger to finger," but as I think about it, it seems that that is what he was showing me.

Is it too much of a generalization to say that the Russian school has been oriented mostly toward arm and shoulder, while the French school—especially the students of Philipp and Long—has been preoccupied with fingers and wrists?

LAIRES: Some people have that impression today, and I wish that I could correct it regarding Philipp. Certainly the needs of most students start with the fingers—with the point of contact with the key and how to approach it. And Philipp emphasized those basic needs. But when I played the Liszt Sonata for him, he never said, "Oh, please play it all just with your fingers!"

Did Philipp give you a daily technical regimen?

DARRÉ: I always did hours and hours of technique every day, when I was a student and even today—Czerny, Moszkowski, Kessler, Moscheles, Alkan, and so on, and lots of scales in single and double thirds, sixths, and octaves. Finger technique is what Long and Philipp were about. Very clear articulation was gotten from exercises with high fingers that strike fast into the keys. Of course, it is very important to have a relaxed wrist.

WEBSTER: I didn't get much of a daily technical regimen with Philipp. He gave me a few exercises here and there, but he wasn't against my getting technique from difficult pieces. He had walls and walls of books containing his own exercises, études, and transcriptions. One day I asked him how he found the time to write so much and also teach so much. He said, "Haven't I told you that I suffer from insomnia?!" I had visions of this old man getting up in the middle of the night, unable to sleep, and writing more and more exercises, études, and transcriptions—which I guess is exactly what he did.

At lessons, though, surely he had technical ideas that were based on the music you played?

LOYONNET: No. Never did he invent on-the-spot exercises that were based on the music. Instead me referred me to his published exercises for such-and-such a problem. Also, he never asked me to try things out in front of him. To experiment on the spot was not his way.

Can you summarize his technical advice?

LOYONNET: At my very first lesson he summarized it strongly — and he never again repeated it. He said, "You must listen to yourself when you are working, repeat passages until you have them in your fingers, work the difficult parts in different rhythms, transpose them with the same fingering, and make up exercises in which you find the same type of difficulty." This was concise and wonderful advice that I have never forgotten.

LAIRES: He was concerned with teaching the instrument — to know it as deeply as possible: touch, sonorites, pedaling, the idea of ten fingers playing instead of two hands. He did not try to enforce an interpretation. It seems that at master classes we always want to know how to play a Beethoven sonata better, or a Chopin Ballade, or whatever. But instead we should want to know how to play the piano better!

What repertoire did you study with Philipp?

LOYONNET: I remember especially Liszt's Paganini Etudes, in the early [1839] version that is nearly unplayable. That made me make great progress! Also, Philipp introduced me to Schumann's *Humoreske*, which I recorded. He also had me do some Scarlatti, Schubert's Sonata in A, Op. 120, and a new Chopin etude and a new Bach prelude and fugue each week.

BLANCARD: Philipp wanted us to play everything. He had me learn
three of Liszt's Hungarian Rhapsodies, even though I was never excited by Liszt's music.

MAGALOFF: We covered a huge amount of repertoire in Philipp's class
at the Conservatoire. For instance, he would say, "For next week's lesson learn the Chopin Preludes." Of course it takes years, a lifetime, to
master this music, but we had to learn the notes on short notice — "as
you can," he would say. He gave us two weeks to learn the Tchaikovsky
First Concerto. Today's young pianists have a terribly limited repertoire. They know a few pieces very well, and can sometimes play them
to perfection, but they don't know the repertoire inside out. With
Philipp we played all the Beethoven sonatas, all the *Well-Tempered
Clavier*, lots of Schumann, Scarlatti . . . everything.

Did Philipp have any unusual ideas about pedaling?

MAGALOFF: No. Philipp and Long used "careful" pedaling — just the
usual kind. I must say that most of my ideas about pedaling, including
half-pedals and flutter pedals, came from listening to Gieseking and
Horowitz.

Did Philipp give you exercises other than his own?

MAGALOFF: Oh, yes. I remember that he gave me a lot of Pischna and
Tausig.

LAIRES: I remember that Philipp advocated the extension exercises by
Pietro Floridia [published by Carl Fischer, 1915]. He said that these
offer the best concept of how to develop stretching. Liszt, in his master
classes at Weimar, commented that most piano playing is *leggiero*,
which means he wanted the same thing as Philipp did when he talked
about playing through the first stage of the key descent. Of course, Liszt
could get the biggest sound, too. But the point is that by playing, as
many do today, with such pressure into the keys, one loses fluency, and
therefore loses the grace, elegance, and facility for the arabesques,

cadenzas, filigree, and so on, that romantic music requires. Remember that Philipp studied with Mathias, a student of Chopin.

Did Philipp ever refer to his study with him?

LAIRES: No, I don't remember that he talked to me about Mathias. He did mention many great figures — Saint-Saëns, Bartók, Busoni, Cortot, and many others.

MAGALOFF: Philipp told me that Mathias said that Chopin wanted all arpeggiated figures in small notes to begin *on* the beat. Philipp also taught us to use a sliding thumb, from a black note to a white one, as Chopin did. Also, I remember that he had us practice Chopin's Etude Op. 25, No. 8 [in sixths] using only thumbs on the inner notes — no index fingers. Perhaps that was Chopin's advice to Mathias . . . ?

● ● ● ●

MARGUERITE LONG

. . . was born in Nîmes, in southern France, on 13 November 1874. After early piano studies in her native city, she continued her training at the Paris Conservatoire in the preparatory class of Sophie Chéné and in the advanced class of Henri Fissot, winning a first prize in 1891. Subsequently she studied privately with Antonin Marmontel. Her first real acclaim came after her orchestral debut in 1903, when she played Franck's *Variations symphoniques*, with Camille Chevillard conducting the Lamoureux Orchestra. The performance earned the highest praise from Fauré, then a critic for *Le Figaro*, who singled out qualities that would apply even much later to her style: "One could not play with better fingers, more clarity and taste, [or] a more natural and charming simplicity . . . ." (*Le Figaro*, 23 November 1903). She maintained an active concert career during her many years of teaching at the Conservatoire, first as professor of a preparatory class from 1906 to 1920, then as head of an advanced class from 1920 to 1940.[49]

Marguerite Long

In 1914 Long performed three works in one evening with the Lamoureux Orchestra: the Saint-Saëns Third Concerto, d'Indy's *Symphonie sur un chant montagnard français*, and Fauré's Ballade. The latter work was long associated with her, as was Ravel's Concerto in G, which was dedicated to her. She studied many French works with their composers, and was known primarily as a champion of this music, along with that of Chopin and Mozart.

In 1941 she opened her own school in Paris, the Ecole Marguerite Long—Jacques Thibaud. At this school, and in branches of it in other cities, she supervised teaching that was done principally by her assistants, who were her former students. Thus her teaching spread to the extent that during almost any month in the early 1950s as many as 500 young pianists in France could claim to be a "student of Marguerite Long." In 1943 she and Jacques Thibaud founded the competition that continues to bear their names and to attract international pianists and violinists. Her tours took her from Brazil to Moscow, although she never performed in the United States. Marguerite Long died in Paris on 13 February 1966.

Her publications include *Au piano avec Debussy*, *Au piano avec Fauré*, *Au piano avec Ravel* (with Pierre Laumonier), and her method, *Le Piano*. Her editions include Mendelssohn's *Songs Without Words*, the complete Mozart sonatas, and Mozart's Concertos Nos. 20, 23, 24, and 27.

Long's students included (roughly chronologically): Aline van Barentzen, Janine Weill, João de Souza-Lima, Rose-Aye Lejour, Jacques Février, Gaby Casadesus, Jeanne-Marie Darré, Lucette Descaves, Carmen Guilbert, Jean Doyen, Paul Doguereau, Germaine Leroux, Ina Marika, Annie d'Arco, Eliane Richepin, Nicole Henriot-Schweitzer, Samson François, Marie-Thérèse Fourneau, Vasso Devetzi, Daniel Wayenberg, Philippe Entremont, Gabriel Tacchino, Bernard Ringeissen, Thérèse Dussaut, André Gorog, and Bruno-Leonardo Gelber.

* * * *

Seven of Long's students were interviewed: GABY CASADESUS, JEANNE-MARIE DARRÉ, THÉRÈSE DUSSAUT, PHILIPPE ENTREMONT, NICOLE HENRIOT-SCHWEITZER, GABRIEL TACCHINO, and DANIEL WAYENBERG.

Marguerite Long began her career at the Conservatoire teaching a preparatory class. May we begin with your memories of those classes? Was there a great emphasis on technique? What repertoire did you learn at that early age?

JEANNE-MARIE DARRÉ: I was just ten years old, but I remember that we did a great deal of technique. Madame Long always said that the fingers should articulate from high up when practicing slowly, but close to the keys when playing rapidly. She also stressed the importance of the wrist for a good sonority in melodic passages. We always had to play études in class, and I remember especially doing Kessler's, which aren't well known today. And, of course, Clementi, Czerny, Stamaty, Pischna, and Philipp. I have always worked hard on all these études and exercises, which she got us to do at an early age. The repertoire I remember working on included quite a bit of Mendelssohn, Liszt's *La leggierezza*, Hummel, Weber, and Fauré, but not very much Chopin.

GABY CASADESUS: Madame Long really formed me, as far as finger technique is concerned. We did a lot of Hanon, Czerny, and Clementi, and all of it had to be memorized. She said, correctly, that if technical studies are worked on in the right way they will be memorized automatically. She was a very good teacher for clear finger technique. But we never did double notes. And scales were played just with the fingers, never with any wrist movement. As far as repertoire was concerned, Madame Long knew how to make you work on the things that she herself knew best. Unlike Risler [with whom I later studied], she did not have a comprehensive view of the literature. I did Fauré with her, some Mozart, Mendelssohn, a Hummel sonata . . . .

The so-called "pearled" style of playing is very much associated with Long. Can you describe it?

NICOLE HENRIOT-SCHWEITZER: Madame Long's playing exemplified the *jeu perlé*, and she passed it on to her students — though perhaps not consciously. The *jeu perlé*, however, is really just a mirage, not a technique. Yes, in certain passages in Mozart, and above all in

Saint-Saëns, one must play fast finger-work very close to the keys, so that a series of equally-sounded notes reminds us of uniformly shaped pearls on a string. But I can't think of an entire piece that requires this technique from beginning to end, even among the French show-pieces.

DARRÉ: It's true that Long had a wonderful, pearly finger technique. She was a fine player, very good in Mozart, but maybe not too powerful, because she used mostly her fingers. Like Philipp, she taught technique basically from the knuckle and wrist. For me, Philipp was an extension of Long's technical outlook, and I got even more from him.

THÉRÈSE DUSSAUT: Her playing was extremely precise and clean. Of course, compared with Cortot, who remained the greatest interpretive genius in France, Long had the reputation of being a bit cold. But this was a false reputation. I assure you that there was nothing more moving than the second movement of Ravel's Concerto in G played by her, or the slow movement of Chopin's Concerto in F Minor. It was a moment of restrained emotion, of magical sounds suspended in the air, of equilibrium, of modesty that ended up bowling you over! During all the years that I knew her, she always received an ovation starting at the beginning of a concert and it was so impressive to see crowds standing up to show their respect.

What factors made her teaching so successful?

DUSSAUT: She taught the piano like a doctor making a diagnosis — and she had all the remedies, too! She could completely change a piece in ten minutes. From beginners to professionals taking master classes, she was able to work marvels with each student. By the time I knew her she had retired from the Conservatoire and was the director of her own school, which included students who were preparing to enter the Conservatoire. I played for her assistant, Rose-Aye Lejour, once or twice a week in preparation for a lesson once each month with Madame Long. One needed that preparation, because at age eight you can imagine what a tremendous and sometimes rather frightening experience it was to have a lesson with Madame Long! Sometimes we hid behind one another if we didn't feel that we were ready to play. But I think I

Nicole Henriot-Schweitzer

was lucky to know her in her old age, when she had mellowed, because she had somewhat traumatized some pianists of earlier generations, such as Jean Doyen. I was astonished, as an adolescent, to see fifty-year-old men trembling in front of her!

DANIEL WAYENBERG: She paid attention to many of the problems that are generally treated, including all aspects of musicality and technique, phrasing, dynamics, touch, the use of the pedal, and especially the execution of crescendos and diminuendos. I must add to these that she inculcated an unconditional respect for the text. These aspects indicate that her teaching certainly was not devoted entirely to technical concerns. But work on technical refinement was essential with her. She demanded daily work on scales, arpeggios, études (Czerny), and exercises (Hanon). She could hear immediately if this work was neglected, and if that was the case she would correct us without pity, often in public. Precision in piano playing was one of the most important elements that she gave us. If you read what she wrote in the preface to her book *Le Piano*, you will know all the main ingredients of her teaching. It is all there.

PHILIPPE ENTREMONT: I must say that Madame Long was a very impressive figure. We had what might be called a love-hate relationship. I was a very undisciplined student, really very rebellious. And she was a very strict, very didactic teacher — it had to be her way and nobody else's. This kind of teaching was partly a reflection of the times. One couldn't teach that way today. Today students are ready to slap you! But I must say that it could be a humbling experience to work with some monsters of that old school! You arrived for a lesson and were made to wait awhile; then you started to sweat, your hands became cold, and finally sheer terror set in!

Her emphasis was on clarity. She didn't like a muddy sound, and of course she was right. She always wanted very elegant playing. I must say that I got some very good practice techniques from her, things that I still do today — especially very slow practice, deep into the keys with high fingers. I owe how I practice to her — even though my musical thinking today is totally different.

HENRIOT-SCHWEITZER: She was what we call a *grand personnage* — extraordinarily intelligent, a really fascinating woman, not beautiful but very charming. And she worked very hard, not only as a performer and teacher, but also socially. We did a lot of technical work — the whole gamut. I remember that she was not against assigning works that were perhaps too difficult, if a student loved them. For example, I begged for and got the Chopin Concerto in E Minor before I was twelve.

She had great respect for the score, and was a perfectionist in this and in every other way. I would say that her technical ideas could always be used as a base, to add to or subtract from other methods — unlike the technique that Philipp taught, which had to be taken entirely or not at all. But I must say that one thing that Madame Long did not have was a sophisticated idea of pedaling. She used to say, "The pedal is for hiding problems." Even today, many French pianists don't pedal very imaginatively, and the three French pianists in the most recent [1981] Van Cliburn Competition, which I judged, used poor pedaling.

I think the pedal can create miracles. I don't really believe in the old French school. I use more weight. Why should the use of weight be restricted, not involving the wrist, arm, or shoulder? All weight ends in the fingers, but the fingers should never be one's "end," if you know what I mean. The idea of high fingers, fast into the keys does not appeal to me. I believe in very, very slow practice, deep into the keys, without pedal, close and not brusque. I like to think of slow-motion films, with absolutely smooth and hypnotic movements — and I recommend this regardless of what the final tempo must be.

GABRIEL TACCHINO: My contact with Madame Long was very important because of her ideas on Debussy and Ravel, whom she knew. She gave public master classes at her school, and these were most valuable, although she tried to foist a "definitive" way with certain works. Her technique was the opposite of the Russian school — not much weight, not much sound. But she gave some very penetrating advice about playing French composers.

Her strong personality was almost legendary, and it led to many anecdotes about her, some of them less flattering than others. But she seems to have been a most generous teacher . . . .

DUSSAUT: Yes, I must say that she was a very generous woman — she taught me for free throughout my childhood. I loved her like a grandmother — a grandmother who could sometimes be a general! The last lesson I had with her was on Chopin's Concerto in F Minor, and it

was extraordinary. For three hours this aged woman used her last energy to give me as many things as she could, getting so out of breath that
I feared for her health.

WAYENBERG: She had a strong personality, expressing her thoughts
always very frankly, and not wasting time with small talk. But at lessons
she was most generous with both her time and her energy, and often
without asking the least remuneration. She called us her "children," and
since I was for a long time the youngest in her class, she called me "mon
bambino."

I remember that a few days before her death we spoke on the
telephone and she said that, since she was feeling better, I should come
to her house with my recent recording of Jolivet's two sonatas, so that
we could listen to it together. Unhappily, this meeting never took place.

TACCHINO: If she thought you were interesting, she wouldn't charge a
penny. I didn't have much money as a student, and I remember that
once she gave me money before the Long – Thibaud Competition, and
said, "Go to a restaurant and have a good steak, because the Russians
are coming and they play very well, and you'll need your strength!"
Once she told me, "Don't worry about paying me. I have some rich students without talent, so in effect they're paying for you!" She was a most
gracious and generous teacher.

●   ●   ●   ●

ALFRED CORTOT

. . . was born in Nyon, Switzerland, to a French father and a Swiss mother
on 26 September 1877. He began his piano studies at an early age with his
elder sisters, and at nine was admitted to the Paris Conservatoire's
preparatory class taught by Emile Decombes. In 1896 he graduated with
a first prize in the advanced class of Louis Diémer. After successful Paris
recital and orchestral debuts (Beethoven's Concerto in C Minor), Cortot
began to realize his conducting ambitions in Bayreuth, where for two years
he was a vocal coach and assistant conductor under Felix Mottl and Hans

Richter. This training in Germany, together with his friendship and lessons with Edouard Risler (who had recently studied with Liszt's students Stavenhagen, Klindworth, and d'Albert) gave him a perspective that many French pianists of the time lacked.

Returning to France in 1902, he conducted *Tristan und Isolde* and the first Paris performance of *Götterdämmerung*. In the same year he founded the Société des Festivals Lyriques and led the Paris premières of many works by young French composers. In 1905 he established with Jacques Thibaud and Pablo Casals a trio that was for a quarter of a century the finest of its kind.

In 1907 Cortot was appointed professor of an advanced class at the Conservatoire, a position that he kept until 1923, when be resigned because of his busy concert activities. In 1918 he made the first of six acclaimed tours of the United States, of which the second was particularly notable: forty-nine concerts in three months, including four different recital programs, the five Beethoven concertos on two programs at Carnegie Hall, the Saint-Saëns Fourth and Schumann Concertos, and the Rachmaninov Third Concerto.

In 1919 he founded, with Auguste Mangeot, the Ecole Normale de Musique, an institution with broader aims than the Conservatoire's and a prestigious faculty that attracted students from throughout the world.

The period between the two world wars found Cortot at the peak of his activity. During those twenty years he made more than 150 recordings, gave 183 public master classes at the Ecole Normale, gave 282 concerts in the United States, 292 in England, and 1425 in Europe, Russia, and South America.[50] During World War II, Cortot made the mistake of accepting the post of High Commissioner of the Fine Arts in the Vichy government. For this, and especially for playing concerts in Germany in 1942, Cortot was found guilty by a French purge committee that suspended all his professional activities for one year (April 1945 to April 1946).

During the 1940s and 50s, Cortot played as many as 130 concerts a season. His last Paris recital was a triumphant success: an all-Chopin program played at the Salle Pleyel on 17 October 1949, the exact 100th anniversary of Chopin's death. A tour of Japan followed, and a series of "farewell" recitals throughout Europe and South America. His last public appearance was in Prades, in recital with Casals in July 1958. His last master classes were held at the Ecole Normale in November 1961. He died in Lausanne, Switzerland, on 15 June 1962.

Cortot's immense number of publications include *La Musique française de piano* (three volumes); *Aspects de Chopin*; dozens of study-editions of the major works of Chopin, Schumann, Liszt, Mendelssohn, Schubert, Weber, Brahms, and Franck; and his method, *Principes rationnels de la technique pianistique*.

Cortot's students included (roughly chronologically): Magda Tagliaferro, Henri Gil-Marchex, Yvonne Lefébure, Clara Haskil, Marcelle Meyer, Marthe Morhange-Motchane, Janine Weill, Jeanne Leleu, Simone Plé, Blanche Bascourret de Guéraldi, Franz Hirt, Madeleine La Candela, Tatiana de Sanzévitch, Vlado Perlemuter, Juliette Durand-Texte, Gina Bachauer, Reine Gianoli, Dinu Lipatti, Ruth Slenczynska, Samson François, Jean-Pierre Marty, Thierry de Brunhoff, Eric Heidsieck, Guthrie Luke, Thomas Manshardt, and Dino Ciani.

* * * *

Six of Cortot's students were interviewed: ERIC HEIDSIECK, YVONNE LEFÉBURE, GUTHRIE LUKE, MARTHE MORHANGE-MOTCHANE, VLADO PERLEMUTER, and MAGDA TAGLIAFERRO.

Cortot's recordings and editions have had a strong influence on pianists all over the world. I know that he had a powerful, inspiring effect as a teacher. Could we begin with some of your recollections of his teaching and his personality?

MAGDA TAGLIAFERRO: Cortot was such a fabulous man, with total culture. He could talk with you for hours and hours on any subject you might raise. He was truly exceptional as a musician, and of course all his students were in love with him! As a teacher, he wasn't interested in technique per se – and his students usually had it already. His inter-

Alfred Cortot

est was in interpretation, and the images that he conjured up for us were absolutely visionary. He was a true poet, and his playing always came from the heart. Even in the fastest and most difficult passages, the sense of the music was always his first concern.

YVONNE LEFÉBURE: Certainly he was a terrific inspiration by the force of his personality and his example as a pianist. He was never what one would call a "professor." He was a master, an inspirator. When you listened to Cortot play, you realized that what he was doing at the piano was not like what other people were doing.

VLADO PERLEMUTER: Even now, after all these years, I have the most vivid memories of his teaching and playing! You simply couldn't forget a lesson with Cortot. He played and taught absolutely everything, and what an impact it had on us! I especially remember his lessons on Chopin's Fantasy and Sonata in B-flat Minor, and Schumann's *Kreisleriana*, which he taught and demonstrated in such a way that all the details have remained to this day a part of my thinking. Even now his advice is always in my mind when I play and teach.

MARTHE MORHANGE-MOTCHANE: Cortot's was unique artistic teaching. Without thinking of our age, he threw us straight into a bath of music, forming our taste and enthusiam for all things beautiful. His teaching was a mixture of pianism, aesthetics, and history—the same mixture that you find in his editions. After you played in class, he would make comments and then play your piece himself, stopping to explain things along the way. I must say that the greatest playing we ever heard from him was in class—not in public or on recordings. He opened a whole generation of French pianists to new ways of thinking about music, ways that went far beyond the usual considerations of good fingers and good rhythm. By 1920, Cortot was the top pianist in France, above—not along with—anyone else, and not only by his artistry, but also by his intellect and his magnetic charm and young romantic appeal. People lined up for his concerts like I have never seen since except for Horowitz.

What were some of the principal tenets of his teaching?

TAGLIAFERRO: Cortot didn't care for the technique of his teacher, Diémer. At that time, Diémer and the Marmontels [father and son] had firmly established the notion of fast, super-articulated playing; light, transparent sounds produced with minimal wrist and arm motion. The fingers were high, but they never really felt the bottom of the keybed! Marguerite Long inherited and passed on that style: fast, digital playing that was semi-legato and without much pedal. The sound was thin and uninteresting. Cortot's conceptions involved much more arm, and also more legato — a really more harmonious approach in every way.

ERIC HEIDSIECK: The French have traditionally been concerned with clarity, and Long certainly exemplified this in her playing and teaching. In some circles here in France it is still the prime concern. Recently a visiting Soviet pedagogue attended the piano classes of three teachers at the Conservatoire, and he told me later that the main admonition of each teacher was "more clarity, more clarity." But Cortot taught the need for textural contrasts, and that shadows are as important as light. Another major concern of his was the importance of a supple wrist. Time and again he stressed this, and I know I learned from him the idea of playing broad, singing melodies not only with a relaxed wrist but also with flat, cushioned fingers. Naturally for fast, brilliant passages a more arched position is necessary. But this other kind of cantabile style was one of his real hallmarks.

GUTHRIE LUKE: How to use the hand and wrist was more often the question than how to use the fingers. He often played melodic notes with outstretched fingers, to avoid percussiveness. For him, melody playing was really hand playing. Even when "pure" technique was used, it was the *hand* that gave the impulse to the fingers. The result was a kind of "drop-and-throw" motion. I remember him saying that "the pianist's fingers on the keys should be like the violinist's bow on the strings." This image is good for understanding the idea that the fingers don't "shock" the keys, but rather they leave a "digital impression" on them. Melodic inflection then came from varying pressure of the hand brought to the fingers, with the fingers usually poised quite close to the keys—not "raised for attack," as other teachers have advocated. Of course, for declamatory passages he could get a terrific sound by the opposite means, dropping his hand from a considerable height, as I remember in the finale of Saint-Saëns's Fourth Concerto.

LEFÉBURE: I definitely got from Cortot the idea of the fingers leaving deep impressions on the keys, as if "kneading" them rather than attacking them. This is what I try to convey to my students. But the fingers must always be firm. Relaxation and mobility are concentrated in the wrists and arms—and, believe me, there are no great pianists without great wrists! So for me it is very important that the sound (which often originates in the lower back) is transmitted from relaxed muscles in the shoulder, arm, and wrist to, finally, firm fingers.

PERLEMUTER: It's true that Cortot's playing was close to the keys and not as over-articulated as some other French pianists and teachers advocated. But he really could play wonderfully articulated and sparkling Saint-Saëns as well as anyone. Unlike some pianists then, he didn't just have one kind of technique. He constantly adapted his technical approach to the music. My own technique was established by Moszkowski, with whom I studied for four years before I entered the Conservatoire. Also, I owe a lot to Madame Giraud-Latarse, a marvelous teacher who was one of Cortot's assistants.

MORHANGE-MOTCHANE: He always had us working on an étude by Chopin or Liszt—always. A major concern of his was a "bouncing" wrist, for lightness. An exercise for this was to have the hand attack an octave from high up and then rebound on it lightly several times from the wrist. The idea was to avoid short, stiff movements, which sometimes characterized French pianists of that time. Possibly Cortot was influenced by some of Leschetizky's ideas. But he didn't talk much about technique—which of course was what we worked on in our private lesson with the assistant once each week. (At the time of my study, Cortot had three assistants. They taught you Czerny and other études, and drilled the notes of your pieces.) Cortot constantly asked, "What is the *character* of this piece?" He stressed this more than any other teacher of the time. I remember that students from other classes would come up to me and ask, "What did Cortot have to say about such-and-such a piece? My teacher only talked about fingering." His color-ful, vivid, often very poetic images went to the very heart of the style and character of a piece, and it was especially helpful for the new music that he had us play—music for which there was not yet a performing tradition, like Ravel's *Scarbo*, Dukas's Sonata, and Granados's *Goyes-cas*. Cortot was not interested in people who just "played the piano." Often he would say to us, "Oh, that's good playing, excellent playing. But it's nothing. Artistically, you didn't do a thing, you just played the piano!"

In his editions, Cortot gives some rather special advice about the use of the soft pedal, even in passages that might be marked forte. I believe he had some strong ideas about how this pedal should be used?

HEIDSIECK: Oh, definitely. For color, this pedal is one of our best resources, maybe even in fortissimo passages. For example, if you want to cry "Help" from a distance, you can play softly without the soft pedal and get a sound that has no urgency. But if you cry "Help" playing mezzo-forte and *with* the soft pedal, then your distant sound will also be one that conveys urgency and is interesting, different, and not just quiet. Of course, you don't use that pedal as a crutch, to cover up your bad control! And it depends on the piano and the acoustics, so don't decide on it in the practice room.

PERLEMUTER: It's a simple fact that the modern piano is often too harsh without the soft pedal but too timid with it. So Cortot would often prefer the sound that one got by playing strongly with the soft pedal, if he wanted a sonorous soft sound. It's a sophisticated concept that is not well understood in some quarters even today. When I judged the Van Cliburn Competition a few years ago, so many pianists played either too harshly or too timidly—hardly ever in between, and hardly ever with the soft pedal.

LUKE: Cortot's use of the soft pedal reflects the fact that he always started with the sound. With him, it was necessary to decide on the character of the sound for every passage, to be able to put it into words. The sound — in other words, the ear — dictated for him the technique.

MORHANGE-MOTCHANE: I remember that he told me to play strongly using the soft pedal in Chopin's Barcarolle, where he wanted a vibrant, expressive sound that wasn't thin.

Cortot's ideas about touch and sound make so much sense to us now. But at the time they must have seemed quite advanced, or at least outside the norm in France. Would you agree?

PERLEMUTER: Yes, he always fought against the dry, high-fingered brilliance and the notey playing that one frequently heard at that time. He detested it. So in addition to his ideas about wrist and arm, he would help the sound by using a lot of fancy half-pedal and flutter-pedal.

LEFÉBURE: Since it is color that gives personality to interpretation, touch and pedal are of paramount importance. Often I repeat to my students the maxim, "The pedal is the third hand" — whether it is short, rhythmic pedals on the beat for Bach or Mozart, or after the beats to connect the harmonies, or fast shallow flutters. For a controlled flutter, by the way, I think it is best to keep your knee against the underside of the keyboard, so that the foot touches the pedal but not the floor. You know, after Debussy it became necessary to pedal differently, because from him we learned that the piano could make new sounds.

LUKE: I remember that at my lessons Cortot would often pedal for me, using quarter, half, and flutter pedaling. Also, in a pedaled work that began with an anacrusis he would always press the pedal down before playing. He got a wonderful effect this way in the opening of Chopin's Concerto in F Minor, first movement, by putting the pedal down for the measures just before the piano's entry — thus picking up overtones from the orchestra and setting the piano strings in vibration.

Many people are under the impression that subtle pedaling is at the heart of French pianism . . . .

HEIDSIECK: Until a few years ago it certainly was not! Maybe when people think of French pianism they are thinking of Gieseking, but he was a German trained in Germany. No. Very clean finger work has always been at the heart of the French school, and only sparse use was made of the pedal. But now the tendency here is to make much wider use of all three pedals. I even use the middle pedal at times in Beethoven, when I think he would have wanted it for certain types of orchestral effects. In the Sonata in E Minor, Op. 90, first movement, a magical difference in sound can be made at bar 84 if the soft pedal is used in the previous bars and then released at that point. The effect is even better if the right pedal is used on the single B-naturals in bars 82-84 but *not* on the preceding ones (when they are the tops of chords). I always try to imagine the composer's orchestration, and that is definitely a concept that I got from Cortot.

TAGLIAFERRO: Cortot often asked for "Flutes here . . . cellos there . . . horns here." He opened up horizons by this emphasis on sound, for it gave us, all at once, a taste for contrasting touches, textures, and the polyphonic style. You know, he did not have a good pianist's physique. He had big hands with big joints, and he didn't have really good arms. Sometimes he missed notes in jumps because he wouldn't go straight for notes. But I must say that he had a natural sonority that was celestial! Always his sound was pure enchantment, whether the music was soft or loud . . . . You know, Gieseking's sound was also very ravishing, and there was a time when everybody wanted to play like him. But Gieseking really played everything alike—the same beautiful sound and touch whether it was *Bruyères* or *General Lavine*! To have a uniform approach to sound isn't, for me, interpretation.

LUKE: I don't remember that Cortot used the word "color," but often he would say, "Never do the same thing twice"—and by this I think he meant a different color, a different sound, a different character, something different each time a theme returns. It's important in a piece with many returns, like the second piece in *Kreisleriana*.

The idea that sensitivity to sound and color leads to polyphonic awareness is an interesting one that I would like to pursue.

HEIDSIECK: Well, Cortot taught us to be in the habit of thinking of the piano as a "little orchestra." Or at times maybe a big one! When you think in those terms, then you are thinking about texture: maybe strong fingers for a "horn melody," with weaker ones doing a staccato "wind accompaniment" while the left hand provides a firm harmonic "cello support." That is why finger independence is so important. Not for its own sake, but for the music — to be able to switch gears and textures easily, with complete control of lines, whether you are playing Bach, Chopin, Hindemith, Fauré, or whatever. Pianists must play music that is conceived horizontally with vertical motions. That is sometimes difficult.

LEFÉBURE: A horizontal conception of music was always implicit with Cortot. It is an absolute essential for a pianist, and it's my first concern as a teacher. They say I have a reputation as a *polyphoniste*, but I believe in this approach not only in fugues. For example, when you play just a succession of four-note chords you should be able to have separate dynamics that follow through for each voice.

Did Cortot have some special ideas about relaxation?

LUKE: He never used the term "relaxation" with me, and I think he was intuitively right not to. How can you get a big sound if you are always thinking of relaxation? He preferred the word "suppleness," and that usually in regard to the wrist.

PERLEMUTER: When the sound was bad, Cortot invariably found it to be caused by a stiff wrist. And he was right!

TAGLIAFERRO: One of my main complaints about young pianists today is that their arms are almost always held close to their sides. This means that the elbow has virtually no role in their playing, which is terrible! I find it helpful in chord playing to think of the arm *pushing* the wrist up rather than thinking of just lifting the wrist. By pushing the wrist up simultaneously with playing the chord, there will be *souplesse* in the entire arm, including the elbow, and that will help both the sound and the control.

MORHANGE-MOTCHANE: Cortot didn't explain "how" very often — that was the assistant's task. In his own playing he kept a still position, using normal, discreet movements, never showy ones. He had a natural, beautiful tone, and, as he explained in *Principes rationnels*, for that you have to go deep into the keys and relax. When he said "relax," it meant to lower the wrist to keep it supple.

This leads me to ask about some of Cortot's recommended procedures for practicing. To begin with, did he stress the value of practicing in different (often dotted) rhythms, as he recommends in his editions? I ask because there are some pianists today who don't believe in it.

TAGLIAFERRO: Are there? Well, I don't know of a better way to drill and secure your reflexes. That kind of practice wasn't something that was new with Cortot, you know. I remember that my first important teacher, Antonin Marmontel, had me work exactly in that way. So dotted-rhythm practice goes back pretty far, and probably not just here in France.

MORHANGE-MOTCHANE: I advocate dotted rhythms, but you must play the short note very rapidly, holding the long note fully and then making the next finger go fast to the next long note. I think that it is important not to practice just in one dotted rhythm. If you do the reverse rhythm as well, then the final result will be evenness.

LEFÉBURE: For difficult passages I make a *petite cuisine* of all possible rhythms and touches. It includes practicing with overlapped notes (each note held beyond its written value) to ensure legato; practicing in various new rhythms for speed and rhythmic sureness; and practicing with finger staccato to develop precision and brilliance. Once the

Magda Tagliaferro

text is mastered, I think the best tempo for practice is moderato. That way, it is possible to work on technical difficulties and interpretation simultaneously. Cortot's book is especially good for the first two chapters, about fingers. But after that, I think you must pick and choose the exercises, for they can be too strenuous — or just plain tedious!

LUKE: For me, the types of rhythmic exercises that Cortot recommended are a help for guaranteeing a smooth-working mechanism in fast running passages. Also, they help to guarantee the accuracy of leaps, such as in the coda of Schumann's Fantasy, second movement. But he didn't talk much about practice habits with his students. Once I overheard him practice for quite a while, and I remember that it was more or less in tempo and not with special rhythms. But there was much repetition, seemingly to perfect the various movements of fingers, wrists, or whatever. Although he advocated practicing with high fingers, in performance he rarely lifted them more than a quarter of an inch above the key — depending of course on the speed and volume of the piece.

PERLEMUTER: I think that Cortot may have advised different students differently, depending on the student and the passage. By and large, he recommended slow practice, and without pedal. So do I. And, as you may know, so did Chopin — according to the recent book about his students [Jean-Jacques Eigeldinger's *Chopin vu par ses élèves*]. Maybe Cortot got this advice from his first main teacher, Decombes, who studied with Chopin. Yes, I think that Cortot's rhythmic exercises are useful. But to do all of them for each Chopin étude, as he suggests, would take months and months! I have worked up all twenty-four études as a unit three different times in my life. First, when I was young, I studied them all and just did my best, sometimes with a teacher, sometimes not. Many years later I re-worked them all, using *all* of Cortot's exercises — a major project. And recently I've re-worked them all again, using *none* of Cortot's exercises. I think that sometimes they go beyond the point of solving the problem, so you have to know when to stop using them.

HEIDSIECK: For myself, I don't use rhythmic exercises very often. Maybe there is a certain *psychological* value in practicing every hard passage in every conceivable way? But I prefer to work hard passages at a moderato tempo and in strict time. Once the notes are learned and secure, what is the point of backtracking to zero and practicing in slow motion all day? Undoubtedly it's good for the memory, but not for the technique. My advice is to find the right motions for the passage and then stick with them. A fast, accurate performance of Ravel's *Scarbo* is not going to happen by practicing slow reflexes! To gain accuracy in leaps, I find it is sometimes helpful to practice landing on a note beyond the one desired. And from Cortot I think I got my preoccupation with positioning, with trying to find ways of avoiding wasted motion, finding fingering that reduces the number of angular, left/right wrist movements.

In his editions Cortot sometimes recommends redistributions between the hands. Did he often suggest them at lessons?

PERLEMUTER: Sometimes, but just as suggestions. He never imposed them. If you observed the musical intentions of the composer, he didn't really care which hand or finger played which note. But I remember that he hated to see and hear the opening octaves of Beethoven's Op. 111 played by two hands. Those octaves are a single musical gesture — just as are those that follow, which cannot be played by two hands. I agree with him. The sound is quite different.

LUKE: One of Cortot's favorite maxims was: "Find the right gesture and the passage will play itself."

I would like to close by referring to another principle of Cortot's that I have heard several of you mention in lessons: the idea of strictness versus freedom.

HEIDSIECK: This was one of his key precepts — the need for the player to attain rhythmic flexibility of the small metric units while maintaining the larger units quite strictly. For example, if you are playing in four-four time with frequent sixteenth notes, you keep the four beats even and regular while the sixteenth notes are freer in relation to each other, melodically expressive even if fast. What he asked for, always, was a balance between sobriety and fantasy.

LEFÉBURE: This concept of freedom within strictness was one of the secrets of his playing. It was exactly related to a central character of his style: to create a beautiful expression within formal simplicity. Or, one might say, to be inwardly romantic while outwardly classical.

● ● ● ●

LAZARE-LÉVY

. . . was born in Brussels, of French parents, on 18 January 1882. After study in his native city with an English woman, a Miss Ellis, he entered the Paris Conservatoire at age twelve and received a first prize four years later in the class of Diémer. He also studied harmony with Albert Lavignac, and fugue and counterpoint with André Gédalge. He appeared regularly as a recitalist while teaching advanced classes for eleven years at the Conservatoire as a *professeur-intérimaire* (temporary-professor). In 1923 he was awarded his own advanced class, succeeding Alfred Cortot, and he held this position — except during the war years — until his retirement in 1953. (It was during the 1920s that Lazare-Lévy chose to hyphenate his first and last names, a form that he used for the rest of his life.) He also gave master classes at the Ecole Normale and taught for a time at the Schola Cantorum.

He performed throughout Europe, as a recitalist, concerto soloist, and chamber musician. During the 1925-26 season he toured the Orient, performed Bach's Triple Concerto with Cortot and Landowska, and also played solo concertos by Mozart and Pierné. His playing was summed up well by a critic for *Le Monde musical* (31 March 1920):

> The dominant quality of M. L. Lévy's playing is its clarity. This comes not only from a very sure technique, but above all from a remarkable musical comprehension and a very precise sense of proportion and design that knows to assign to each part of a work its exact place. The performances of Liszt's Variations ("*Weinen, Klagen*"), *Murmures de la forêt*, and *Mephisto Waltz* were magisterial; but it was above all in Mozart's Fantasy in C Minor and Sonata in A, and in Schumann's *Fantasiestücke*, that he showed himself to be a cultivated and perceptive musician.

Lazare-Lévy died in Paris on 20 September 1964.

Lazare-Lévy

His editions include Schubert's Impromptus, Op. 142, Chopin's complete mazurkas and polonaises, and several collections of Czerny études. He wrote numerous piano preludes, études, and sonatinas, as well as two string quartets and a cello sonata.

Lazare-Lévy's students included (roughly chronologically): Sophie Svirsky, Clara Haskil, Solomon, Jacques Dupont, Louise Clavius-Marius,

Lélia Gousseau, Alexander Uninsky, Monique Haas, Jean Hubeau, Jules Gentil, Jacqueline Robin-Bonneau, Ginette Doyen, Jean-Joël Barbier, Jacques Genty, Yvonne Loriod, Monique Deschaussées, France Clidat, Désiré N'Kaoua, André Tchaikovsky, and Nicole Eysseric.

* * * *

Six of Lazare-Lévy's students were interviewed: JEAN-JOËL BARBIER, FRANCE CLIDAT, LÉLIA GOUSSEAU, MONIQUE HAAS, JEAN HUBEAU, and YVONNE LORIOD.

How would you characterize Lazare-Lévy's technical approach? Was it similar to that of his contemporaries?

MONIQUE HAAS: No, I think it was different from that of almost all other French teachers. Like Cortot, he really was ahead of his time here in France because he used more arm and back for strength. His teaching wasn't founded on the digital, quasi-harpsichord technique of his teacher, Diémer. You really can't play something like the first movement of Beethoven's Op. 111 just with your fingers! Of course the fingers are very important, but with Lazare-Lévy the whole body was used. His regular hand position tended to be rounded at the knuckle and much less curved at the first and second phalanges. In this way the cushions of the fingers rather than the tips were in contact with the keys. Of course, his assistants were the ones who really drilled us on technique, using especially the Brahms Exercises.

LÉLIA GOUSSEAU: His technique was certainly different from the older school in France. You might say that it was Russian-like, but really it was his personal blend of arm use, a relaxed body, and firm fingers. He did a lot of work within the context of the music, when problems arose. Decontraction of the muscles was an important point with him, but he didn't really have a method. What he taught was just a musical/technical way of drilling to find the right gestures.

Monique Haas

FRANCE CLIDAT: I would say that his teaching was somewhere between the romantic and modern schools. In some respects, I think it was similar to Heinrich Neuhaus's, from what I have read. For Lazare-Lévy, technique was the means, not the end. One studied music through the piano, not just the piano. The musical considerations of touch, legato, phrasing, and so on, came first. Then he found the means to achieve them. He had an arm technique, but with solid fingers. It was not the *petite technique* of Madame Long. He had a grand sound, and really expressive color in his playing.

Would you say it was more a technique of pressing than of striking?

GOUSSEAU: Oh, yes. It had *souplesse*, natural weight, and a real legato. The fact that he didn't like the fingers to be too curved made his approach similar to Cortot's. Certainly you can't play a beautiful, long phrase if your style is like a typist's . . . .

JEAN HUBEAU: With Lazare-Lévy the fingers were literally an extension of the hand. But he also cared about the arch at the knuckle. He would often put his fingers under a student's hand and press up hard, forcing the knuckles to stand out. His playing involved more hand and arm technique than pure finger technique, with the cushioned part of the finger going deeply into the key. I remember that he used to place his hands under the piano keyboard and say, "Play so deeply that I can feel it through the wood!"

JEAN-JOËL BARBIER: He certainly hated a thin sound, and he wanted us always to go to the bottom of the key whatever the dynamic level. He was an extraordinary teacher as far as touch was concerned, and he also had a wonderful sense of what was good fingering. He had a large hand, and could stretch an octave between the second and fifth fingers. So he could play the eleventh of Brahms's Paganini Variations, Book II, with an open hand!

YVONNE LORIOD: He had a very intelligent technique of the arm. His advice essentially was this: find the best fingering, liberate the hands, use the thumb correctly, and, above all, use the weight of the arm. He had great reflexes for extending the arms out and back very quickly. He played with force but without hardness or stiffness. He made us work to get the arm to absorb the shock of the attack, using natural, not forced, weight.

Did he talk about the "pearled" style of playing?

HAAS: Oh, never, never! His technique was the opposite of that, and through his teaching he helped to change that old French school of playing. Robert Casadesus, with whom I later studied, was also not a typical French pianist of his generation, though the clarity of his sound was as common to the old school as it was to Lazare-Lévy's.

CLIDAT: Lazare-Lévy's playing was always clear, with very little pedal. He said that the pedal must be used to give color and shading, but that it must be used sparingly and precisely. He liked the idea that it could give flashes of light.

What other memories do you have of his teaching or playing?

BARBIER: He was very nervous as a performer. I was told that once at a concert he just stopped playing, closed the piano, and left the stage! But I can say this: of the pianists I heard play before 1940, he was one of the very few who never played a wrong note. As a personality he was unpredictable. One day he would love your playing, the next day he wouldn't like it at all.

HUBEAU: I remember that he played Schumann often and wonderfully, especially *Kreisleriana* and the *Fantaisiestücke*. Also much Mozart, some Liszt, and *Le Tombeau de Couperin*.

CLIDAT: Lessons were sometimes difficult, because the student always had to come up to his level of teaching—he never went down to the student's level. He constantly said, "*Listen!* Your *ears* are your best teacher!" Concentrated mental work at the keyboard was what he wanted.

HAAS: I had an affectionate teacher-student relationship with him after I won my prize and continued studying with him privately for a year. The older I get the more I realize the value of his suggestions. The idea of getting the hands equally dexterous is something that I still work at, even in doing everyday things away from the piano, like opening doors, using scissors, and so on. Also, I must thank Lazare-Lévy for encouraging me to learn the widest variety of repertoire — Bach, Beethoven sonatas and variations, Liszt's Transcendental Etudes, Debussy, Ravel, Stravinksy, and other music that was quite modern at the time. He taught the importance of knowing very thoroughly the style of each composer you played — and this is something that doesn't seem of much concern to young pianists today, who tend to play everything too loud and in a competition-like manner. For me the most important lesson from Lazare-Lévy was that every sound we make at the piano must come from the arm participating with the fingers.

III. Major Figures of the Postwar Period, 1945-1985

Musical life in Paris returned to its former vivacity fairly soon after the war. By 1946 most concert organizations had fully recovered, major journals such as the *Revue musicale* and the *Revue de musicologie* had been revived, and important new periodicals such as *Contrepoints* and *Jeunesses musicales de France* were being published. In certain areas, however, progress was slow. In an interview, pianist Geneviève Joy recalled a significant aspect of postwar conditions: "The latest works of Prokofiev, Bartók, Stravinsky, and others were completely unknown in France after the war, because the Germans had suppressed them. So one of my tasks for the Orchestre National, for which I was appointed choral conductor for several years, was to play through these scores and calculate their timings for the principal conductors, Roger Désormière and Manuel Rosenthal. It was an important and extraordinary time for all of us then, to finally get to know this music that we had lived for but had not yet heard, and often I would be sight-reading these scores until four in the morning."

France's leading younger composers, Olivier Messiaen, André Jolivet, and Pierre Boulez, produced some of their most important and challenging piano works between 1944 and 1950, and young French pianists emerged to champion them. The Marguerite Long—Jacques Thibaud Competition, which had begun during the war, expanded to international scope in 1946. The Orchestre Radio-Symphonique assumed an increasingly important role in musical life beginning in 1945 under its conductor, Eugène Bigot, while the Orchestre National became the country's leading touring orchestra. The Orchestre de la Société des Concerts du Conservatoire began making long-playing recordings under André Cluytens's direction during the early 1950s.

Some pianistic highlights of the decade 1945-55 in Paris included:

1945 Yvonne Loriod's première of Messiaen's *Vingt Regards sur l'Enfant-Jésus* at the Salle Gaveau

1948 Raymond Trouard's Chopin-Liszt recital at the Théâtre du Châtelet

1949 Alfred Cortot's last Paris recital, at the Salle Pleyel on the 100th anniversary of Chopin's death

Magda Tagliaferro's performance of three concertos on one program at the Théâtre des Champs-Elysées: Mozart's K. 537, Saint-Saëns's Fifth, and the Schumann

1950 Paul Loyonnet's recital at the Salle Pleyel

1952 Monique Haas's performance of Stravinsky's *Capriccio*, with the composer conducting, at the Théâtre des Champs-Elysées

1953 Yves Nat's first performance in public in twenty years, at the Théâtre des Champs-Elysées

1954 Samson François's performance of three concertos on one program at the Salle Pleyel: Liszt's E-flat, Chopin's E Minor, and Prokofiev's Third

French-trained pianists who enjoyed active international careers as soloists and recording artists during the period from 1945 to 1970 included Jacqueline Blancard, Monique de la Bruchollerie, Robert and Gaby Casadesus, Jeanne-Marie Darré, Philippe Entremont, Reine Gianoli, Lélia Gousseau, Monique Haas, Grant Johannesen, Dinu Lipatti, Yvonne Loriod, Nikita Magaloff, Vlado Perlemuter, Raymond Trouard, and Beveridge Webster. Two others, Jean Doyen and Samson François, who receive only passing reference elsewhere in this book, deserve special mention here.

Jean Doyen was born in Paris in 1907 and studied at the Conservatoire in the preparatory class of Sophie Chéné and in the advanced class of Marguerite Long, winning a first prize in 1922. He was a frequent champion of French music, and a sampling of his programs during the 1930s reveals his devotion to works by Saint-Saëns, Chausson, d'Indy, Chabrier, Hahn, Fauré, Debussy, and Ravel. His recordings of Chopin's complete waltzes, Ravel's two concertos, and numerous works by Fauré reveal a facile pianist who tended to generalize dynamics, favor a dry sound, and often lapse into a mechanical approach to rhythm. Warmth, charm and *esprit* are sorely lacking in his Fauré readings.

In 1941 Doyen succeeded Long as professor of an advanced class at the Conservatoire, a post he held until his retirement in 1977. His students included Idil Biret, Thérèse Dussaut, Philippe Entremont, Jean-Rodolphe Kars, André Krust, Arthur Moreira-Lima, Dominique Merlet, and Françoise Petit. Many of Doyen's students felt the need to study with other, often foreign, teachers after graduating from his class. In an interview, Thérèse Dussaut praised him as a performer, but observed that "unfortunately, he was not a gifted teacher. He did not know how to transmit what he knew how to do. He sat at the piano, illustrating, and we took what we were able to. Fortunately he had a wonderful assistant, Rose-Aye Lejour." André Krust added that "Doyen was a purely French pianist whose technique was limited to fingers only, with great articulation. His teaching revolved around respect for the text, the pulse, and strictness."

Samson François was quite a different musician. Born in 1924 in Frankfurt, he had a succession of early teachers because of his father's career in the diplomatic service. After settling in Paris, he studied for two years at the Ecole Normale with Cortot and his assistant, Yvonne Lefébure, receiving the *licence de concert* at age thirteen. The following year he passed the entrance examinations to the Conservatoire by playing Liszt's *Don Juan* Fantasy and Brahms's Variations on a Theme of Paganini. He studied at the Conservatoire for two years with Marguerite Long and won a first prize in 1940.

François seems to have been one of the few pianists to have studied with both Cortot and Long and then to have been able to grasp the best that each had to offer. To judge from his recordings, his playing was much closer to Cortot's, for he had a real coloristic sense, a big sound, a technique that must have involved much arm and shoulder, and a very large, romantic vision of music and of the interpreter's role. From Long he certainly got a feeling for French music, as well as some needed discipline.

In 1943 François won first prize in the first Marguerite Long—Jacques Thibaud Competition. During the 1945 season he performed four concertos in Paris: Prokofiev's Third, Liszt's E-flat, Ravel's G Major, and the

Schumann. For his American debut in 1947 he played Prokofiev's Fifth Concerto with Leonard Bernstein and the New York Philharmonic. His performances in Russia in 1956 were the first ones given by a French artist under official Franco-Soviet exchanges. In 1959, with André Cluytens and the Orchestre de la Société des Concerts du Conservatoire, he set something of a record by playing four concertos in one evening: Bartók's Third, Chopin's F Minor, Liszt's E-flat, and Ravel's Left-Hand. In the same year he made his successful New York recital debut at Carnegie Hall. Tours of China, Japan, Mexico and the Soviet Union followed.

Although sometimes criticized for his musical liberties (in the 1960s Eugene Ormandy and Pierre Monteux vowed never to perform again with him), François was a much adored figure in France. His large following admired not only his pianism but also the aura of individuality, even iconoclasm, that he projected. His colorful off-stage life, which included recording with the accordianist Yvette Horner and haunting Parisian jazz clubs sometimes until six in the morning, no doubt added to his mystique. He died in Paris on 22 October 1970.

François's recordings include virtually the complete works of Chopin, Ravel, and Debussy, Liszt's two concertos and fifteen Hungarian Rhapsodies, Prokofiev's Third and Fifth Concertos and Seventh Sonata, and various works by Schumann, Scriabin, Hindemith, Mendelssohn, and others.

The most successful of these, which capture his mercurial temperament, sophisticated coloristic sense, and superb technical command, are Chopin's four Scherzos, Debussy's *Estampes* and *Pour le piano*, Liszt's Concerto in E-flat, and Ravel's Left-Hand Concerto. (The Ravel, made in 1959, still ranks among the finest versions.) François was not inclined to pedagogy (the young Bruno Rigutto was his only disciple) but his playing inevitably influenced a generation of French pianists.

In the following pages, numerous pianists who are active today provide portraits of some of the major artist-teachers of the postwar era. In doing so, they help explain how and why piano playing in France changed by the 1960s.

● ● ● ●

ARMAND FERTÉ

. . . was born in Paris on 22 October 1881. At the Paris Conservatoire he studied in the preparatory class of Emile Decombes, and in 1898 received a first prize in the class of Louis Diémer. He also studied harmony with Xavier Leroux and composition with Henri Duparc. He made his debut at the Concerts Colonne in 1900, and his career thereafter combined performing, teaching, conducting, and editing. In 1907 he founded a concert society, the Concerts Symphoniques Populaires de Grenoble, which he directed until 1914. He then became conductor of the Orchestre du Casino in Dieppe (1919-28). At the Paris Conservatoire Ferté taught a preparatory class (1927-42) and an advanced class (1942-53). Ferté died in 1973.

His influence as a pedagogue is evident from his numerous publications, including editions of Beethoven's thirty-two sonatas, Bach's *Well-Tempered Clavier*, and works by Liszt, Schumann, and Chopin. He also published a method and numerous anthologies of études.

Ferté's students included Pierre Barbizet, Joseph Benvenuti, Monique de la Bruchollerie, Jean-Michel Damase, Fabienne Jacquinot, and Monique LeDuc.

* * * *

MONIQUE LEDUC studied in Ferté's preparatory and advanced classes at the Conservatoire and received a first prize in 1946.

¶After early lessons with a neighborhood teacher, my mother took me to see Ferté, who at that time was teaching a preparatory class at the Conservatoire. I worked with his assistant, Madame LeDu, and at age ten I was admitted to his class. All told, I studied with him for eight years — four in his preparatory class and four in his advanced class. In addition, I took Ferté's chamber music class, which was held outside the Conservatoire, and after that I studied chamber music with Pierre Pasquier.

French training at that time could be very demoralizing, especially if you were the kind of person who needed encouragement.

Armand Ferté

You simply could never do enough music well enough. The competition was fierce, and we had to learn things quickly. For example, Ferté would give us one week to learn a Debussy étude, including a performance in class from memory. Famous musicians such as Stravinsky would sometimes visit his class, so you can imagine the tension we were under.

We had to have a full program ready for the competitions at the end of the year, and for part of this we had to prepare eight preludes and fugues from the *Well-Tempered Clavier*, picking one of them out of a hat the day before the competition. In preparation for this, Madame LeDu would hear a fugue and say "Stop!" after a few measures. We then had to be able to start again right on the note that we had stopped on, not the one before or the one after. We knew those fugues backwards and forwards, let me tell you! This was most valuable training.

Another rigorous aspect of our training was the required sight-reading examination, as part of the final competition for prizes. The piece, in manuscript, was composed just for this occasion. We were led into the examination room one at a time and given the music. The director would say, "All right. Here's the tempo: one, two, *three*!" And you were looking at something you had never seen before, often in a modern style with no key signature. If you didn't pass this part, you could not get your prize in piano.

There were other stresses. Sometimes I was scheduled for a private lesson at two o'clock, but was not admitted until six o'clock. During those four hours I would study every crack on Ferté's dining room wall while my mother did endless embroidery! It wasn't healthy for an eleven-year-old to have to go through that and then have to function on cue at the lesson. But we had to do it.

Ferté's training was terrific, and it really got results. Madame LeDu taught his method, which revolved around independence of fingers, with equally matched sound for all fingers. He had complete freedom of the hand, with a low but not stiff wrist, with finger tips on the keys. Each joint of the finger was developed, to be able to play deeply and softly at the same time. When needed, strength came from the shoulders, stomach, or back. He taught that each joint of the body should participate when necessary. I remember him saying, "You have a joint there, why don't you use it?" Once he had me walk without bending my knees, to prove the point that natural movements use all the joints. Also we drilled dropping the arms from a height and landing softly. He felt that playing too close to the keys for certain attacks gave you less command of the instrument. He put no great emphasis on speed. He said, "Every note in music is meaningful, even grace-notes and the little notes in Chopin's fastest figures." He was a great believer in very slow practice: "Play it slowly nine times, and up to tempo once. Not the reverse!"

Ferté was a very strong teacher of technique. Sometimes he would say that he wanted a certain effect, but would leave it up to us to figure out how to get it. I think that was good, forcing us to think for ourselves. He had a beautiful touch that always intrigued me. It seemed to "talk" to the instrument. Ferté may not have been a world-renowned performer, but he was a very wonderful teacher.

● ● ● ●

YVES NAT

. . . was born in Béziers, in southern France, on 29 December 1890, and began his studies with an organist in that city. At an early age he knew the *Well-Tempered Clavier* from memory and attracted the attention of Fauré and Saint-Saëns by conducting his own *Fantaisie pour orchestre*. He continued his studies in Toulouse, and then attended the Paris Conservatoire, receiving a first prize in piano in 1907 in the class of Louis Diémer. He enjoyed an immensely successful concert career, performing in New York in 1911 and throughout Europe and in Russia during the 1920s. Although he frequently performed Bach, Chopin, Debussy, and certain modern composers, his real identification was with the music of Beethoven and Schumann. He was the first French pianist to record all thirty-two Beethoven sonatas. At the height of his career he decided to retire from concert life, and in 1934 accepted an appointment as professor of an advanced piano class at the Conservatoire, a position which he held until his death. In 1953, after not performing in public for twenty years, he played a recital at the Théâtre des Champs-Elysées that was a tumultuous suc-

Yves Nat

cess. The following year he gave his last public performance, as soloist in his own Piano Concerto (composed in 1952). His other compositions include a set of preludes, a sonatine, and a symphonic poem, *L'Enfer* (1942). He died in Paris on 31 August 1956.

Practically all of Nat's recordings were made at the end of his life, between 1952 and 1956. That he remained a virtuoso and first-class musician to the end is clear from his recording of Brahms's Variations and Fugue on a Theme by Handel, one of the most striking versions ever made. He meets the work head-on, and brings to it all the requisite color, fire, intellectual rigor, musical continuity, and dexterity. His recording of Chopin's Fantasy is also very fine, a large-scale interpretation that is almost on the level of Cortot's passionate and colorful one. Nat's strong sense of architecture, which he had developed as a composer, contributes to the success of much of his Beethoven cycle. The most convincing interpretations are of the larger works, especially Opp. 57, 106, and 111, which are played with dramatic sweep in the outer movements and contained eloquence in the slow movements — even when the latter are not quite as slow as one might prefer. A favorite recording is Op. 31, No. 2, which receives a virile, nicely contrasted, and perfectly controlled performance. Of Nat's many recordings of Schumann, the *Etudes symphoniques* and the Fantasy are particularly communicative and controlled. Nat's very first recording (1933) was of Schumann's Concerto, with Eugène Bigot conducting, and it still ranks among the finest versions.

Nat's students included: Yuri Boukoff, Theo Bruins, Jörg Demus, Jacqueline Eymar, Gérard Frémy, Reine Gianoli, Fabienne Jacquinot, Roy Hamlin Johnson, Geneviève Joy, Claude Kahn, André Krust, Jacques Loussier, Jean Neveu, Jean-Bernard Pommier, Pierre Sancan, Robert Veyron-Lacroix, and Jeannine Vieuxtemps.

* * * *

GENEVIÈVE JOY studied with Nat at the Conservatoire from 1935 to 1941, the year she won a first prize in his class.

¶Nat's assistant was Lucette Descaves, who was wonderful for teaching technique. With her I did a lot of Czerny, especially *School of the Virtuoso*, and études by Anton Rubinstein and, of course, Chopin. It was wonderful to work with Nat and Descaves at the same time, because they complemented one another perfectly. The works that we brought to Nat were already polished and memorized with Descaves, so he did not have to offer us much technical advice. But he was very insistent on special fingering, including reversed fingers for trills (in the right hand, for example, the thumb on D and third finger on C). He put a lot of attention on the thumb and on the fifth finger, and he had us do trill exercises with the thumb and each other finger successively, and then with the fifth finger and each other finger successively. This helped to equalize the sound among the fingers and to stabilize the playing. When he taught at his house, lessons sometimes lasted two or three hours, with much talking. But not about technique, although I know that he himself practiced five-finger exercises in the morning—often while reading Simenon or other mystery writers!

In his teaching he stressed the left hand, perhaps because he was a composer. He played deep into the keys, and had a wonderful *parlando* sound. He always talked about orchestration in his teaching, and I remember that he liked to do a lot of half-pedal with vibrations. In *L'Isle joyeuse*, for example, he spoke about layers of sound, different colors, different instruments. He also had a very orchestral approach to Beethoven, mentioning specific instruments in Op. 57 and Op. 111. He was a great artist, a genius, a dreamer. He used to say, "The heart is the only metronome you need."

* * * *

The American pianist ROY HAMLIN JOHNSON studied with Nat on a Fulbright fellowship in 1952 and 1953, after receiving an Artist Diploma under Sandor Vas at the Eastman School of Music.

¶I remember that at my first lesson I played Beethoven's Sonata, Op. 81a, and Nat said, "It's too German!" This seemed an odd response, but I think that by that he meant "too academic." It was also then that I got the Great Fingering Lesson—because he had noticed that I hadn't written any of my own fingering into the Schnabel edition I was using. He showed me his copy of the Bach-Busoni Chaconne, with all the recent fingerings that he'd put in— and they covered every *inch* of the pages! He said that this was a fundamentally important thing to do, and explained that the choice of fingering was not just for comfort, but for added brilliance or for a particular voicing. He often avoided a thumb on a black note of a chord (unless to voice it out) but preferred it for single black notes in the bass. All this was important for me, and it caused me to think a lot about all the options for any passage.

He redistributed notes between the hands to a greater degree than I had done before, and I found that some of this advice really worked – for example, in the coda of Chopin's Ballade in G Minor, which he demonstrated with a huge sound and great accuracy.

Nat never had me bring a work in for more than one lesson, so I was always working up new pieces for him. When he made suggestions for improvements, he would always end with a polite, "Si vous voulez . . . ." ("If you want . . . .") He told me, "Improve your ear and work on your concept" – but he never explained how I should do those things. It wasn't until I played Ravel's *Le Gibet* and *Scarbo* for him that he seemed really pleased, and he had me play all of *Gaspard de la nuit* for his class at the Conservatoire.

I liked many of his suggestions in Schumann's Fantasy. For example, in the opening of the second movement he used thumb/thumb on the two top notes of each left-hand rolled chord. He said, "In this movement you must imagine an army of a million men!" and he marched around the room like a soldier. He occasionally exchanged the hands in this movement, for a fuller and more secure tone – and also because some of the hand crossings were difficult for him because of his stocky build. I remember that he pedaled this piece lavishly. He played it on his "comeback" recital in March 1953, with Beethoven's *"Appassionata"*, Schumann's *Kinderszenen*, and Chopin's Sonata in B-flat Minor. It was terrific playing, maybe not with the cleanest technique, but so exciting that you never thought about that. The response was stupendous. The three recitals that I remember most vividly that season were by Nat, Edwin Fischer, and Wilhelm Kempff.

* * * *

JEAN-BERNARD POMMIER worked privately with Nat from 1954 to 1956, and won a first prize at the Conservatoire in 1966 in the class of Pierre Sancan, Nat's protégé.

¶I started my studies with my father, a professional organist, and in 1948 he took me to a wonderful Russian pianist, Mina Kosloff, who was living in my native city of Béziers. She had studied in Kharkov and had much the same background as Horowitz, whom she knew. I worked with her three hours every day for seven years. It was fabulous. I can't imagine getting better teaching for that period of my life. She didn't just tell me what to do, but how to practice, how to really organize my time, and especially how to know what you want to do at the piano and whether you're achieving it or not. After these years of intensive work I was ready to study privately with Nat for two years.

Studying with Nat at that time seemed to me rather like sharing *moments musicaux* with a distinguished grandfather. His physical approach was one of weight, with articulation *on* the key always — not like Long's, where the finger was like a little hammer that came down from above the key. Nat's approach was similar to that of the Russian school. It makes a big difference where you start to articulate from — it can be from above the key, with very curved fingers; or from close to the key, with only slightly curved fingers and small movements. Nat prepared me for my audition at the Paris Conservatoire, where he suggested that I study with his former student, Pierre Sancan. Sancan's teaching turned out to be very complementary to Nat's. It was influenced by the writings of Marie Jaëll, with a real emphasis on the role of the whole body in playing, and on a complete physical analysis of how one plays.

● ● ● ●

MARCEL CIAMPI

...was born in Paris on 29 May 1891. His principal teacher for many years was Marie Perez de Brambilla, who had studied with Anton Rubinstein and Liszt's pupil Théodore Ritter. In 1909 he received a first prize in Louis

Diémer's class at the Conservatoire. Numerous concerts soon followed, as soloist and as the partner of Casals, Enesco, Thibaud, and other leading artists. In 1938 he played the première of Enesco's Third Piano Sonata, which is dedicated to him. He was appointed professor of an advanced piano class at the Conservatoire from 1941 to 1961, and he also taught at the Ecole Normale and at the Yehudi Menuhin School in England. Ciampi died in Paris on 2 September 1980.

He was at his best in big, romantic works, and reviewers frequently praised his broad, free style and subtle approach to sound. His few solo recordings include pieces by Debussy and Chopin's Nocturne in C Minor. The latter seems to reflect a Russian influence from his first teacher. Certainly it is one of the slowest and most orchestrally conceived interpretations, with singing lines, resonant bass notes, and a big, rich sound at the climactic moments. It is playing of great conviction, and it shows Ciampi to have been a striking Chopin stylist. He was also a convincing interpreter of Debussy's music. His playing of *Les Collines d'Anacapri* is very rapid and clean, with careful differentiation of foreground and background material, a most seductive middle section, and a wide dynamic range. The same qualities, and a projection of real spontaneity, make his recording of *La Sérénade interrompue* a complete success. Ciampi also recorded Franck's Piano Quintet, with the Capet Quartet. His publications include an edition of Beethoven's Fourth Concerto.

Ciampi's students included: John-Paul Bracey, Philippe Corre, Nicole Eysseric, Marcel Gazelle, Eric Heidsieck, Tania Heidsieck, Jean-François Heisser, Stanislav Knor, Yvonne Loriod, Jean-Marc Luisada, Hephzibah Menuhin, Jeremy Menuhin, Yaltah Menuhin, Sylvie Mercier, Cécile Ousset, Denyse Rivière, and Jean-Paul Sevilla.

* * * *

JEAN-PAUL SEVILLA, who won first prize in the 1959 Geneva Competition, studied with Ciampi at the Conservatoire from 1948 to 1952.

¶Ciampi's technical regimen required three or four hours daily— which at age thirteen or fourteen seemed severe to me. But now, of course, I am very thankful to have had it. It consisted of held-note exercises using patterns in whole tones [they were rather like Philipp's exercises, except for the size of the intervals], chord exercises that required pressure as well as ones involving jumps (with and without stopping before landing), exercises for rebounding that used the weight of the arm without contracting, and so on. I don't recall that he had a particular way of teaching scales, except for insisting that the thumb move under immediately after playing. He called the thumb the "snake finger" because of how it should glide along the keyboard. He was also concerned with free elbows and a perfect hand position, which for him was rather turned toward the thumb.

But to say that Ciampi was only concerned with technique, as some do, is completely false. My scores were full of his musical markings — at least as many musical markings as technical markings. We worked on a well-rounded repertoire of Bach, Beethoven, Liszt, Chopin, Schumann, Brahms — the Handel Variations, Paganini Variations, and Second Concerto — and of course Debussy and Ravel, but very little contemporary music. What I got most from him was respect for the text, respect for style, a particular manner of working, and a fascination with fingering. Ciampi had several assistants at that time, and I consider myself very lucky to have been able to work with Madame Bascourret de Guéraldi, who had been a student and later the right arm of Cortot. She was an extraordinary woman who complemented Ciampi's teaching very well. I felt a real communion of the spirit with her.

* * * *

CÉCILE OUSSET, who won a first prize in Ciampi's class at the Conservatoire in 1950, was a prize winner in numerous competitions, including the Geneva, Busoni, and Van Cliburn.

¶I first played for Ciampi when I was eleven, and he said that he wanted me to study privately with him for one year before I entered the Conservatoire, so that he could completely re-make my technique. At the time I was playing a bit in the Marguerite

Marcel Ciampi

Long way, with high fingers, a rather hard sound, and without much power. Ciampi's technique was that of Anton Rubinstein, which I believe he acquired through his contacts with Wanda Landowska [and especially with Marie Perez de Brambilla]. For six months I did nothing but exercises, three hours a day—at age twelve, mind you! I believe these exercises originated with Rubinstein, and they included drills for using the weight of the shoulders, much work on the wrists, and the development of various touches. I also did held-note exercises, and of course scales constantly, in thirds, sixths, and octaves, and arpeggios without turning the hand. Some of his exercises for the arm and shoulder were coordinated with breathing drills. These formed the basis of my technique.

The idea of strength radiating in a very natural way from the shoulder, not just from the arm or forearm, was the key to Ciampi's technique. Depth of sound was a special concern for him, with a solid finger-tip. His teaching was quite different from that of most Conservatoire teachers of his time. He stressed the need to listen critically to every sound we make, to get a deep, rich, warm tone—even when practising scales. All this was very different from the high wrists and shallow-keyed approach of Long, which completely lacked grandeur and was just fingers running along the keys.

● ● ● ●

JULES GENTIL

. . . was born in Annecy on 10 February 1898. He studied first with his mother, who had been a pupil of Georges Mathias, and then with Santiago Riera at the Paris Conservatoire, where he won a first prize in 1916. He later studied for a time with Lazare-Lévy. He often performed with his violinist-brother Victor, cellist Gérard Hekking, and soprano Claire Croiza, and in 1946 he played the Montréal première of Fauré's Ballade. During the 1920s he began his long association with the Ecole Normale de Musique, and in 1938 was asked by Cortot to share with him the executive position of musical director of that institution. Altogether, Gentil was

Cortot's assistant at the Ecole Normale for twenty-five years, and he continued teaching there until 1985. At the same time, he held appointments at the Schola Cantorum and the Conservatoire. At the latter institution he taught first as an assistant-professor (from 1922), then as professor of a preparatory class (from 1941), and subsequently as professor of an advanced class (from 1947 to 1975). He also taught master classes at Webster College and Washington University in St. Louis, Northwestern University, and the Ecole Vincent-d'Indy in Montréal. For many years he was an advisor for Fulbright scholars in France. He died on 25 May 1985 at La Verrière-en-Yvelines, near Paris.

Gentil's students included Steven Barwick, Karen Keys Bryan, Seth Carlin, Gail Delente, Pierre Froment, Marie-Catherine Girod, David Lively, Robert Lurie, Barbara English Maris, Jean Micault, and Shirley Seguin.

* * * *

The American pianist DAVID LIVELY, a prize winner in the 1972 Queen Elisabeth of Belgium Competition and the 1974 Tchaikovsky Competition, studied in St. Louis with Gail Delente, and then at the Ecole Normale with Gentil from 1969 to 1974.

¶Gentil was at his best teaching the romantic repertoire, and his approach was basically coloristic. He favored dramatic contrasts of dynamics and touch. Pedaling, fingering, and musical rhetoric were his major concerns, along with the need for constant physical relaxation at the piano. My scores are filled with his signs for musical breathing, weight, and hand releases. I didn't get any specific exercises from him, and he didn't have set theories about technique outside of the basic premise of ease. Rather, he would modify his technical approach to suit the student and the music at hand.

He was a very direct man who preferred music that made an immediate effect. He never tired of Beethoven's Sonata, Op. 53, for example, even if the students weren't so good! I remember that he also favored Beethoven's Op. 2, No. 3 and Op. 57, Bach's G Major Toccata, Brahms's Handel Variations and Paganini Variations,

Jules Gentil

Schumann's *Etudes symphoniques* and *Carnaval*, and the Liszt
Sonata. The Chopin études were real cornerstones for him. He
had no great attraction to contemporary music, yet he taught it
very effectively—for example, the sonatas of Barber, Dutilleux,
and Prokofiev.

Though he was musically intuitive, his technical ideas were
worked out quite analytically. He believed, like Chopin, that each
finger had its own "personality". He rather liked acrobatic fingerings, to liberate the hand, and he believed in playing on the pad
rather than the tip of the finger. He taught the feeling of dead
weight, dropping into the key, coaxing the deepest, richest sound
possible out of the instrument. Generally, the fingers were to work
less than the larger muscles. This was certainly not the stereotypi-
cal French approach.

His classes at the Ecole Normale were exciting because he was
always shouting directions while the student was playing. He knew
what he wanted, and didn't tolerate different opinions. You
learned to accept this, as Europeans do. He was not "philosophi-
cal". He was an efficient, pragmatic teacher who taught how to attain the most as quickly as possible.

* * * *

The American pianist BARBARA ENGLISH MARIS studied with
Rudolph Ganz and Soulima Stravinsky prior to working with Gentil at the
Ecole Normale in 1958 and 1959 on a Fulbright fellowship.

¶Gentil's class at the Ecole Normale included many international
students. As a teacher he was very supportive of his students and
very interested in them. Gentil rarely demonstrated a technical
concept or played portions of pieces that students were working
on. Most of the suggestions he made were specific ones, relating
to a particular passage, rather than generalities to transfer to
other repertoire. Some suggestions included pedaling for coloristic effects and using the thumb on single, deep bass notes for a
free-floating gesture that provided better control of resonance.

During my period of study with Gentil I had a weekly one-hour lesson at his home and a weekly performance class for several hours at the Ecole Normale. At the end of the year I presented myself for the exams for the *sixième degré*, which meant that I prepared a full recital program by May and, after the preliminary exam, learned an additional piece that was announced after the May hearing. My repertoire for the first stage included works by Bach (a toccata), Beethoven (a sonata), Chopin (a scherzo and two nocturnes), Debussy (the first book of *Images*), and Franck (the *Variations symphoniques*). This exam was heard by a committee of the school's piano faculty, and the students who passed it received permission to proceed to the final exam. That year the extra piece, to be learned in four weeks, was Liszt's *Don Juan* Fantasy.

The things I remember most from my lessons with Gentil were not any specific words of wisdom but more general aspects of what it meant to be a serious student. At the Ecole Normale there seemed to be a sense that people valued breadth of musicianship. It was explained to me that when Cortot founded the school his requirements, which included chamber music, theory, and music history, were considered revolutionary in contrast to the Conservatoire's total emphasis on performance exams. No, I never did scales, études, or other exercises with Gentil, so I don't know how he developed this aspect in a student. I would love to know that today![51]

• • • •

YVONNE LEFÉBURE

... was born in Ermont, near Paris, on 29 June 1898. After winning a first medal in Marguerite Long's preparatory class, she studied in Alfred Cortot's advanced class and received a first prize in 1912. In subsequent years she also won first prizes in harmony, accompanying, counterpoint, and fugue. Her early major performances included concertos with the Lamoureux and Colonne orchestras. These were followed by recitals and concerto performances throughout Europe and in the United States, in-

cluding with conductors such as Furtwängler, Sawallisch, Paray, Ansermet, Mitropoulos, and Walter. In 1950 Casals invited her to participate in
the first Prades Festival. Throughout her career she championed French
music, especially the works of Dukas, Fauré, Maurice Emmanuel, and
Ravel (she performed the Concerto in G nearly one hundred times). In
1964 she founded a summer festival, Juillet Musical de Saint-Germain-en-
Laye, where she also taught master classes that drew students from around
the world. She was professor of piano at the Ecole Normale, where she
was Cortot's assistant until 1939, and she taught an advanced class at the
Conservatoire from 1952 to 1967. She also taught at the Conservatoire
Européen from 1971 to 1985. She died in Paris on 23 January 1986. An international piano competition was established in her name in 1990.

Lefébure's refined musicianship, orchestral coloring, and probing intelligence made her an ideal interpreter of works by Bach, Beethoven, and
contemporary French composers. Her recordings include Beethoven's
Diabelli Variations and last three sonatas, Schubert's Sonata in B-flat,
Schumann's *Davidsbündlertänze,* and numerous works by Bach, Debussy,
Dukas, Emmanuel, and Ravel. Of her last recordings, made in her
eighties, the most memorable is perhaps that devoted to Fauré, which includes an especially fine account of the *Thème et variations.* Recordings
have also been issued of her live performances of Ravel's Concerto in G
with Ansermet, Mozart's Concerto in D Minor with Furtwängler, and
Schumann's Concerto with Dervaux.

Lefébure's students included Walid Akl, Randall Blatt, Hélène Bos-
chi, Catherine Collard, Imogen Cooper, Evelyne Crochet, Nadine
Desouches, Janina Fialkowska, Suzanne Fournier, Samson François,
Martin Hughes, Michaël Levinas, Dinu Lipatti, Ray Luck, Theodore
Paraskivesko, Pierre Reach, Sébastien Risler, Morey Ritt, Inger
Södergren, Michael Studer, and Françoise Thinat.

* * * *

EVELYNE CROCHET, who later studied with Edwin Fischer and
Rudolf Serkin, won a first prize in Lefébure's class at the Conservatoire
in 1954.

¶Before my study with Yvonne Lefébure, I was in the preparatory class of Rose-Aye Lejour, a wonderful teacher who made us aware of our responsibilities to the music and really taught us how to practice "from A to Z" on every single type of problem, musically and technically. Lejour had studied with Marguerite Long, but she had a natural, beautiful, and deep tone that most of the Long students did not have. Lejour taught how to play the piano in a natural way. She was very conscious of posture, hand position, and total control over each finger. Every gesture had to be correct. You were in her hands, and she was able to mould something out of almost nothing! Both she and Lefébure had that gift — to be able to bring out of students the best that they had.

I worked with Lefébure during my last year in the preparatory class and for one year in the advanced class. I wish it had been longer, for I could have benefited very much from another year or two with her; but I got my first prize after only one year. After graduation I was able to have some more lessons with her, but on a private basis.

Madame Lefébure's teaching was the perfect extension of my work with Lejour. She [Lefébure] taught music through the piano. Each weekly class lasted from 1:00 to 8:00 in the evening, with hardly any stop. Style and phrasing were among her great concerns, and the architectural aspects of a piece were always discussed. Her energy, endless enthusiasm, intensity, and devotion were incredible! I don't remember once being bored for a moment of those long classes, at which everyone had to play each week. Often she would give two hours to a student, and not always the most gifted one. She gave time when it was needed, without counting minutes.

She rarely talked of her study with Cortot. She had a very strong personality and was a born performer, so the contribution she gave was her own, not second-hand Cortot. But sometimes she would mention Cortot in reference to a particular work, especially by Chopin, Schumann, or Liszt. And she had us study from his editions.

She talked about sound a lot, and also about very precise pedaling and the need to find the right finger for the right sound —

Yvonne Lefébure

things that were very much Cortot's concern. And textures: how to play a chord and control each note of it, even if it has eight notes, to get a special quality. Absolutely nothing was haphazard with her. Everything was thought out and completely understood, with musicianship of the highest level. As a performer she always knew the answers. I remember her inspiring playing of the late

Beethoven sonatas, of which her intellectual and emotional command was remarkable.

Of course Lefébure advocated slow practice. My own students often think I am pulling their leg when I tell them exactly how slowly they should practice. They say they can hear when they play faster, but I say that they can't. You can't hear what you can't control.

Most teachers at the Conservatoire at that time were there just to put their stamp on their students. Initiative was often discouraged. Lefébure wasn't that way, and Perlemuter wasn't, and most likely Yves Nat wasn't. Many of the other teachers, however, were — and they could be tyrants. Their teaching was limited to giving you a trade. But if you had an intelligent teacher, as I was lucky to have with Lefébure, they were excited if you had a personality, *une nature*.

●   ●   ●   ●

ROBERT CASADESUS

... was born in Paris on 12 April 1899. After early studies with his aunt and with Marie Simon, a former student of Marmontel (*père*), he entered the Paris Conservatoire in the class of Louis Diémer and won a first prize in 1913. He won a first prize in the harmony class of Xavier Leroux in 1919, and the Prix Diémer in 1920. The following year he married the pianist Gabrielle L'Hote, with whom he frequently performed four-hand and duo-piano music. (Later they performed and recorded works for three pianos with their son Jean.)

In 1924 Casadesus became the first pianist to play an entire recital of works by Ravel, with whom he had studied. (A piano roll of the Toccata, made in London at about this time, was once ascribed to Ravel but is now known to have been made by Casadesus.) He made his American debut in 1935 with the New York Philharmonic, playing Mozart's Concerto in D (K. 537).

In 1935 he was appointed professor of piano at the American Conservatory at Fontainebleau. During his summers there, and during his residence in the United States during the war, he coached many American pianists. In 1941 he gave his first Carnegie Hall recital. After returning to France in 1946, Casadesus was made director of the American Conservatory, a position he held for the next six years.

Casadesus's international career was at its height after the war, when he performed recitals and concertos throughout the world. (In Rome in 1956 he played his 2000th concert.) In 1958 he was awarded the Brahms Medal by the city of Hamburg, a significant achievement for a Frenchman. Casadesus's legacy as a composer is substantial, including seven symphonies, five piano concertos, two violin sonatas, four piano sonatas, and numerous short piano pieces. His publications also include cadenzas for piano concertos by Haydn, Mozart, and Beethoven. Casadesus died in Paris on 19 September 1972.

His temperamentally restrained outlook and his famous transparent sound made him an ideal interpreter of Ravel, Mozart, and the *clavecinistes*. Of his many recordings, special mention should be made of his set of Ravel's complete solo works, of which *Miroirs* and *Le Tombeau de Couperin* are the still-competitive highlights. The best of his Mozart concerto recordings with George Szell and the Cleveland Orchestra include No. 15 in B-flat (K. 450), No. 26 in D (K. 537), and No. 27 in B-flat (K. 595). The fullest measure of Casadesus's elegant and fastidious pianism may be heard on his recordings of Saint-Saëns's Fourth Concerto, with Leonard Bernstein and the New York Philharmonic, Weber's *Konzertstück*, with Szell and the Cleveland Orchestra, and Chausson's *Concert*, with the Guilet Quartet and Zino Francescatti. A rare example of his Brahms playing—the three violin sonatas with Francescatti, recorded in concert at the Library of Congress in 1949 and 1952—reveals some vigorous, boldly contrasted, and uninhibited pianism.

Casadesus's students included Hans Balmer, Mary Louise Boehm, Jean Casadesus, Monique Haas, Claude Helffer, Grant Johannesen, François-Joël Thiollier, Margaret Tolson, Marie-Aimée Varro, and Larry Walz.

* * * *

Robert Casadesus

CLAUDE HELFFER, a specialist in twentieth-century music, studied privately with Casadesus and did theoretical studies with René Leibowitz.

¶My mother knew Casadesus, and arranged for me to study with his Aunt Rose, who had in fact been his own first teacher. The arrangement was that if I studied with her he would hear me from time to time also. So I worked regularly with them both for about six years, he seeing me once a month or so, depending on when he was in Paris between tours. I made rapid progress, so that by the time I was ten he asked that I bring not just one new piece to a lesson, but a whole new program every time – for example, a complete Bach partita, a complete Beethoven sonata, a romantic work, and perhaps some Ravel or Debussy. This was a great challenge for me, and I responded to it well.

During World War II, Casadesus was living in the United States and I earned a degree at the Ecole Polytechnique and took part in the Resistance. When Casadesus returned to France in 1946 I told him that I wanted to continue to study with him. He told me that I should come to Fontainebleau with a specified program to play for him: Bach's C Minor Partita, Mozart's C Minor Concerto, Beethoven's Sonata, Op. 101, and some Schumann. I worked hard, and after I played these works for him he told me that he wanted me to give my first Paris recital in a year's time. I continued to have lessons with him occasionally, and made my debut. Later I attended the interpretation classes of Marguerite Long and Jacques Février, the latter a wonderful musician who never sought to impose his ideas. So I did not get the "classic" French piano training at the Conservatoire.

Casadesus had a very articulated technique, but at the same time it was deep into the keys. This is what made his style different from Long's. But it was not the strong, driven-in technique of the Russian school, either. Perhaps it combined the best of the French and German schools. The old French school was aimed, above all, at guaranteeing perfect playing, with no wrong notes. This, I think, is different from the German school, in which fingering, pedaling, nuances, dynamics – everything that has to do with the music – is worked on simultaneously. For the French, maybe rapidity and security came first, and other things after that. Also, the French seem to practice with less pedal than other schools, and Casadesus was in favor of this. But there have been exceptions to these things in France. I remember hearing Lazare-Lévy when I was a child, and though his technique was very digital, he played with a very deep sound, almost like that of Backhaus or Schnabel.

Technically, Casadesus had me do a number of Czerny and Moskowski études, plus exercises by Philipp, Pischna, Stamaty, and Brahms. I remember that he gave me the Brahms Exercises at exactly the time when he himself was playing a lot of Brahms's music, beginning in about 1937. His aunt functioned as his assistant, watching over the details of my technical development, so that he was free to deal with matters of interpretation and sound. He was not interested in "methods." My lessons with him always were always inspiring, and I would leave them exhilarated, longing for the next one.[52]

●   ●   ●   ●

JACQUES FÉVRIER

... was born at Saint-Germain-en-Laye on 26 July 1900. He studied with Edouard Risler and Marguerite Long, winning a first prize in Long's class at the Paris Conservatoire in 1921. A champion of French music and a friend of "*Les Six*", Février made several recordings with Poulenc and Auric. In 1932 Février and Poulenc played the première of the latter's Two-Piano Concerto, dedicated to Février. In 1937 Ravel chose Février to be the first French pianist to perform his Concerto for the Left Hand, a work which Février later played frequently throughout Europe and the United States. From 1952 to 1957 Février was professor of chamber music at the Paris Conservatoire. He died in Epinal on 2 September 1979.

Février's musicianship was of a very high order, with unusual sensitivity to the colors, moods, and textures of the French works in which he specialized. His recordings include stylish accounts of Debussy's Preludes, Etudes, and Violin Sonata (with Yehudi Menuhin); two fine versions of

Jacques Février

Ravel's Concerto for the Left Hand (one from 1942 with Charles Munch, the other from 1958 with Georges Tzipine); and Ravel's *Sonatine* — to choose just one highlight from his set of that composer's complete solo works.

Février's students included Marylène Dosse, Christian Ivaldi, Alain Motard, Alain Planès, Bernard Ringeissen, Gabriel Tacchino, and Valerie Tryon.

****

CHRISTIAN IVALDI, presently professor of chamber music at the Conservatoire, won five first prizes there in the 1950s, studying piano with Aline van Barentzen and chamber music with Février.

¶I studied chamber music with Février for two years at the Conservatoire, and I think he was a more important influence on me than any of my real piano teachers. He was a marvelous musician, but not a great virtuoso. This meant that he always had to ask himself how to do things, and this helped to make him such a fine teacher. His main concerns were musical imagination, style, projection, phrasing, nuances, relaxation, and especially different qualities of sound. We did a lot of the chamber music of Schumann, Brahms, Mozart, Fauré, Franck, and so on. It took me some years to fully understand and appreciate what he gave me, what he was trying to say. Since you knew the text when you went to him, he could talk mostly about the music. In any case, technique and the music were the same for him. He made it clear that you can't solve musical problems without solving technical problems — and the reverse. "To know a piece" means that you have done both.

****

MARYLÈNE DOSSE, a prize winner in the 1965 Casella International Competition, won a first prize at the Conservatoire in 1960, in the class of Jeanne-Marie Darré.

¶I entered the Conservatoire in Jean Batalla's preparatory class. This was at the end of his career, and I wasn't getting much from him, so I started studying with Février on the side, as a number of students did. When Jeanne-Marie Darré took over Batalla's advanced class I studied with her for two years, but I continued studying privately with Février. Darré was such a wonderful, natural pianist that she taught mainly by demonstrating. If things didn't go well when you tried it, she'd tell you to repeat it indefinitely.

So Février was like a savior for me. I don't understand why he never had an advanced piano class. So many students came to him for a kind of teaching that they weren't getting elsewhere that he jokingly called himself "The Chiropracter". With him, technique was always related to the music, it was never just technique for its own sake. He invented exercises based on the problems of the music. He was especially good for French music, and had known and worked with Ravel and so many other composers. I remember especially working on Ravel's Concerto in G and some Schubert Impromptus. He was more a musician than a pianist. And I think his ideas were perhaps better than what he could do himself.

He talked more about the use of the arm than most teachers, and he wanted us to sense articulation coming from inside the hand — not from the outside, with high fingers, which was the way of Long and Darré. He preferred rather flat fingers, and would press on our hand while we continued to try to articulate.

In his chamber music class he could be abrupt, pushing you off the bench and sometimes being insulting, but in a nice way. He really was a warm, often outrageous person, a free spirit, and for many of us his teaching was really a breath of fresh air.

* * * *

GABRIEL TACCHINO won a first prize in Jean Batalla's class at the Conservatoire in 1953, and the following year won second prize in the Busoni International Competition.

¶Musically, Février transformed me after I graduated from the Conservatoire. I worked with him perhaps longer than any other pianist did, from about 1954 off and on until his death in 1979. It was interesting to me that he often taught best the repertoire that he wasn't closest to. I remember particularly the Gershwin Concerto and the *Rhapsody in Blue*. He had an instinct for what was musically important. Although he was less interested in technique than most teachers, he was definitely influenced by the Russian school. It was Février who helped change the entirely digital, old French style. He was very familiar with the different kinds of technical approaches to piano playing, and went out of his way to meet many foreign musicians. He talked with them and absorbed a lot — from Horowitz, Rubinstein, and many, many others. He was familiar with the whole concert milieu and was constantly going to hear other pianists. For this reason I believe he was thinking about things like weight and tone production before some other teachers in France were. Now, because of recordings, international competitions, radio, television, and many more concerts and master classes by foreign artists, the idea of different, isolated, foreign schools of playing doesn't really exist any more.

Février taught a wide repertoire, but especially French music, and especially Ravel and Poulenc. It was through Février that I got to know and work with Poulenc. I was privileged to make several recordings with Février, of Poulenc's two-piano and four-hand music, of some major works of Schubert, and of Ravel's *Ma Mère l'Oye*, *Sites auriculaires*, and *Frontispice*.

As a teacher, Février adapted himself to each student's needs. His enthusiasm was such that he often gave the impression of hearing a work for the first time. Sonority interested him very much. He used to say, "Play the piano with your ears, not your fingers!" Phrasing and color were his first concerns.

He was adored by his students, though he could use extremely harsh words and be very nasty if you didn't please him. But if you did please him, then he could be extravagant in his praise. When I started studying with him he was so hard on me, so difficult and demoralizing, that I never would have dreamed that one day I would play concerts and make recordings with him! He was probably the only professor that I would see night after night at concerts — every night! That's how he always had at least three solutions to suggest musically. Sometimes he'd say, "I do it this way, Rubinstein this way, and Horowitz this way." It is unfortunate that he never became a piano professor at the Conservatoire. One reason, undoubtedly, was that all the professors detested him because they knew their students were going to him on the sly for lessons. Also, he never tried to have a big career as a soloist. He was above all a musician and chamber music specialist.

I remember something quite moving about Février that I don't think I encountered in any other teacher. At lessons sometimes he would be so moved by the music that his eyes would get moist and tears might even run down his face. I'm told that this sometimes happened when he went to concerts, too, despite the fact that he'd heard more concerts than anyone we knew. He was a musician through and through, and he never became jaded.

● ● ● ●

LUCETTE DESCAVES

. . . was born in Paris on 1 April 1906. She studied from an early age with Marguerite Long, in whose class she won a first prize at the Conservatoire in 1923. A champion of modern music, she performed Prokofiev's Third Concerto in Paris in 1932 (after being coached by the composer) and played the premières of numerous works, including Jolivet's *Danses rituelles* and Piano Concerto. She was especially identified with the latter work, which she performed more than one hundred times. Her notable teaching career at the Conservatoire included appointments as the assistant of both Long and Nat prior to being awarded her own advanced class, which she taught from 1941 until her retirement in 1976. She currently resides in Boulogne, near Paris.

Her recording of Jolivet's Concerto is a tour-de-force that demonstrates her command of the widest variety of musical and technical problems. She was equally at home in less extroverted music, and her recordings of Ravel's *Jeux d'eau* and Debussy's *Feux d'artifice* are unusually evocative, well contrasted in texture, and perfectly paced. Roussel's

Lucette Descaves and Jean-Yves Thibaudet

Ronde is also played with great color and rhythmic acuity, two qualities for which her 1940s recording of Falla's *Nights in the Gardens of Spain*, conducted by Eugène Bigot, has been justly admired.

She is the author of a book on the piano repertoire (*Un nouvel art du piano* [1966]), a collection of technical exercises, and a revision of Le Couppey's *L'ABC du Piano* and *L'Alphabet* (published together as *Nouvelle Méthode de Le Couppey*).

Descaves's students included Brigitte Engerer, Frédérique Fontanarosa, Christian Ivaldi, Catherine Joly, Katia and Marielle Labèque, Jean-Claude Pennetier, Georges Pludermacher, Bruno Rigutto, Pascal Rogé, Jacques Taddei, and Jean-Yves Thibaudet.

* * * *

JEAN-YVES THIBAUDET, winner of the 1980 Tokyo Competition and the 1981 Young Artists International Auditions, received a first prize at the Conservatoire in 1977.

¶I first studied with Lucette Descaves when I was eleven, coming to Paris for lessons once a month from my native Lyon. I entered the Conservatoire at thirteen, and studied two years with her there, until her retirement. I then studied with Reine Gianoli for one year, getting my first prize when I was fifteen. I then did the *troisième cycle* for three years, at first with Gianoli, and then after her death with Aldo Ciccolini.

I had a wonderful relationship with Madame Descaves from the beginning. She was like a grandmother for me, someone very special, kind, and really likable. Some say that she was preoccupied with technique, but that wasn't really true. Of course she wanted students to play the right notes, and cleanly, and into the keys strongly. But when you could do these things, she would take you much further. She had a lot of tradition behind her: she knew Fauré, Ravel, Roussel, Jolivet, Prokofiev, and many others. She had these memories very clearly in her mind when she taught.

Because of her enormous experience, as Long's assistant for many years, then as Nat's assistant, and finally with a class of her own, she knew exactly the right pieces to assign a student at the right time. This instinctive talent was really uncanny and reflected wonderful pedagogy.

It was also remarkable that you could work with her at any level. She had — and still has — the amazing gift of being able to teach equally well a child or the most advanced pianist, and either would always feel comfortable with her. She has pedagogy in her blood, and can change her approach as the student changes. This I think is very important — and very unusual.

She was wonderful for giving a sound technical base. She had a recipe for everything technical, with very ingenious ideas about how to practice certain passages. Every week, no matter how many hours you practiced, she would have new musical and technical things to say about the same piece. It could go on forever.

Although she came out of the tradition of Marguerite Long, and got good, practical teaching advice from her, I know that Madame Descaves certainly had her own ideas, her own exercises, and her own point of view. For example, she did not at all like playing that was just fast and high-fingered. Clean, yes, but not superficial. She wanted the fingers to go deep into the keys — and she would often press her hand on mine to make this point. She also stressed the use of shoulder, the need for relaxation, and how to develop a big sound without banging. For many years she had one of the best classes at the Conservatoire — maybe the very best. It seems that almost everyone studied with her to some extent, at one point or another.

IV. INTERVIEWS

The interviews that constitute this chapter have been selected because they are of particular interest or because they concern subjects not dealt with in detail earlier. To preserve the sense of history established in the previous chapters, these interviews are presented in chronological order, according to the year of the interviewee's birth.

● ● ● ●

PAUL LOYONNET

... was born in Paris on 13 May 1889 and studied with Charles de Bériot, Isidor Philipp, and Martinus Sieveking. His Paris recital debut took place in 1906, and during a fourteen-year period after that he played nearly 2,000 concerts as recitalist, duo-artist with violinist Lucien Capet and others, and as soloist with virtually all the major orchestras of Europe. Following a stay in North Africa during World War II, he commenced a world tour in 1946 that included his American debut, of which a *New York Times* critic wrote: "A new, really big pianist is among us. Here is technique in the best meaning of that much abused word, and here is interpretation of such marked individuality and musicianship that it can only denote an artist of high caliber." He returned to New York in 1953 for three all-Beethoven recitals that elicited the highest praise. In 1954 he settled in Montréal, where he taught at the Ecole Vincent-d'Indy and at McGill University. His recordings include Schumann's *Humoreske*, Fauré's Seventh Nocturne and *Thème et variations*, four Beethoven sonatas, and works by Haydn, Ibert, and Couperin. His publications include an edition of Beethoven's ten sonatas for piano and violin (with Lucien Capet) and four books: *Beethoven, ce mal-connu; Les 32 Sonates pour piano: Journal intime de Beethoven; Paradoxes sur le pianiste;* and *Les gestes et la pensée du pianiste Paul Loyonnet.* He died in Montréal on 12 February 1988.

Loyonnet's students included Claire Grenon-Masella, Jean Leduc, and Boris Roubakine.

Paul Loyonnet

May we begin with your recollections of your first important teacher, Charles de Bériot? Did you study with him at the Conservatoire or privately?

PL: At first privately, beginning when I was ten. Before that I had been studying with one of his former students, a young organist, and I had been practicing only an hour a day. So my audition with Bériot went horribly! He told me to work all summer for three or four hours a day and then come back. I worked hard on scales, arpeggios, and exercises from his book *Mécanisme et style*, and at the end of the summer I played Mozart's Sonata in G for him, and also the fifteenth study from Czerny's *School of Velocity*. He smiled and told my father, "This young man is *amusant*. I'll take him." Eight days later I had my first lesson, and immediately he dwelled on how to make a perfect legato and, in the slow movement of Mozart's Sonata in C Minor, how to bring out the top notes in a series of chords. He had me buy a little book he had written called *La Sonorité du piano*, which explained what he cared about as a teacher.

So from the start he emphasized slow practice and critical listening. . . .

PL: Oh yes. His main interest was clarity and a singing tone. He had studied with Thalberg and with [Hubert-Ferdinand] Kufferath, one of Mendelssohn's preferred students, and a singing line was especially important to those musicians. I remember that he often said, "If a singer did what you are doing, one would laugh at him!" He was sixty-five when I went to him, and he was easily annoyed by his students! Instead of Czerny's *Velocity* he put me on etudes by Cramer, which he considered more musical. Romantic that he was, he rarely made me study Bach. Instead we did pieces by Field, Dussek, Hummel, and so on, to develop expression and velocity.

Did he often demonstrate at lessons?

PL: Yes, he often showed exactly what he wanted. But aside from working on nuance, he gave little attention to technique *per se*, thinking, like some other professors, that technique will develop itself through the pieces studied. This in itself is all right if one has good work habits and preliminary formation of muscles. Unfortunately, he never told me how to organize my practice, and often if I played poorly he would say,"Play it again" — sometimes writing in a fingering.

What were some of the more positive aspects of his teaching?

PL: Certainly the use of the pedal, which began just a few weeks after my first lessons. Since my legs were still too short, he put a thick book on the pedals and we worked this way on Field's Fourth Nocturne. He was meticulous about the pedal, and because I was so young I think the rapport between the ear and the foot was lodged instinctively in me starting from those days. Another important and positive aspect of his teaching was his having us maintain a certain amount of old repertoire at all times. We had to devote one day a week entirely to old repertoire, and I think this was very good advice.

When did you prepare for your entrance to the Conservatoire?

PL: In 1903, when Bériot had me audit his class there. My entrance exam reflected his taste: the Chopin Polonaise, Op. 3 (with cello), the Beethoven Concerto in C Minor (exposition of the first movement), and Delioux's transcription of part of a Mozart string quintet! What a selection!

Can you recall the highlights of your first year?

PL: I remember that I worked on Chopin's first and third Ballades, Schumann's *Carnaval,* and Beethoven's "Waldstein" Sonata. In addition to our weekly class, we also met on Fridays, which were devoted solely to Bach and Chopin — we each had to learn a new Bach prelude and fugue each week *and* a new Chopin étude, *plus* a "transcendental" étude by Bériot himself! The Friday classes worked all right for the first month, and he was tolerant of our slow and often imperfect Chopin etudes. Gradually students stopped coming on Fridays, and he didn't mind, since it was his last year on the faculty and he was pretty detached already. I was one of the few who stayed in these Friday technique classes.

Did you hear his star former student, Ricardo Viñes?

PL: Oh yes, rather often. Bériot held monthly public classes in which we each had to play. Usually each session concluded with a performance by one of his former students, and it was often Viñes. Always he played the so-called "ultra-moderns," Debussy and Ravel, and I remember how Bériot would listen to this music with the same indulgent smile that one would show when a child misbehaved! He didn't really understand this music, and never under him did we play a single really modern work.

What other important pianists do you recall from that period?

PL: I remember being absolutely stupefied when we heard Moritz Rosenthal, then at his height. What an enormous technique and brio he had, with hands thrown high and wide with such liberty! Among the French, I heard Planté, Risler, Selva — really an endless stream . . . .

Who impressed you the most?

PL: Planté was unforgettable, really the most perfect of the French pianists then. His playing was marvelously articulated, and singing, too, when that was called for, and people have told me that it much resembled Liszt's. It had power without hardness, and at the same time I can say that no one in our time has surpassed him for sheer speed! Risler and Selva were a bit less exciting. Risler's playing was very accurate and faithful to the text, but for me it lacked real lyricism. I admired him more than I was moved by him. Selva was much the same, but with a drier touch, as I remember. Because of her enthusiasm for Breithaupt's ideas she became so relaxed that she seemed to drop weight on each note! The sound was very nice, but she seemed to avoid fast pieces.

I have recordings by Diémer, made exactly when you were at the Conservatoire in 1904.

PL: Diémer was a Parisian concert celebrity who was known as the "king of the scale and the trill." He married a rich woman, played free concerts, and never gave a private lesson. The competition held in his name was a very important one at the Conservatoire. It was held every three years and was open only to male first-prize winners of the preceding ten years. I remember hearing the Diémer Competition in 1903, when the jury consisted of Paderewski, Rosenthal, Pugno, Philipp, Saint-Saëns, and others. Imagine such names today! Only the best young pianists had the nerve to enter, with a jury like that! And two of the best were students of Bériot: Joaquin Malats and Fernand Lemaire. Malats was the best interpreter of Albeniz's *Iberia*. His *"Appassionata"* on this occasion was brilliant, though he seemed nervous and sat quite high with his body curved over the keyboard, as I still remember. Lemaire showed qualities that Viñes lacked: sober expression, real brilliance, and admirable touch. Then came two Diémer students, of whom Lazare-Lévy was the best example: his playing was extremely clear and "pearled," faithful to the text, strong, and he played the Saint-Saëns *Etude en forme de valse* in a way that was impossible to top! After much applause the jury deliberated, and Saint-Saëns wanted Lazare-Lévy to win. But more eminent members wanted Malats. Finally it was decided: Malats won the Prix Diémer, Lazare-Lévy won Honorable Mention. Diémer said that he had never heard *La Campanella* played better than Malats had then. Malats came to Bériot's class the next day and I played the Chopin *Berceuse* for him. What a loss that Malats died a few years later, barely forty!

May we return for a moment to Bériot's teaching? Can you remember any specifics about his technical or interpretive advice during that last year of his teaching?

PL: With him it was always "interpretation, interpretation, interpretation!" Slow practice and the quality of one's sound were his main concerns. He never suggested *how* we might practice in order to play as he wanted or as he illustrated. I remember that a student brought in Mendelssohn's *Variations sérieuses*, and Bériot stopped him after the first variation and played up to that point himself, to demonstrate that the top line must be brought out, and then he closed the book and let it be known that the student's twenty minutes were done. For four more weeks the scene was the same for the student! And if another student couldn't get the right sonority for the opening of Weber's Sonata in A-flat, he never got further than that page at a class lesson. To do him justice, though, I must say that all his students developed a taste for good musical "diction," a sense of good pedaling, contrasting touches, and clarity in fast tempos. My own longevity allows me to understand his value now.

Did he talk about Thalberg and Kufferath, his teachers?

PL: He mentioned Thalberg only once that I remember, regarding repeated notes. In a Liszt Hungarian Rhapsody, when a student was having trouble with repeated notes, he recommended Thalberg's Etude in A Minor. He said: "Each time that Thalberg played this etude, one wanted to go home and practice it immediately!" He also recommended that we buy Kufferath's etudes, which were more salon pieces than technical studies.

Did he have an assistant who taught technique?

PL: Not really. His main technical idea, and it was a big one, was that the fingers should always be close to the keys, to make an *impression* on them rather than to strike them. Though he didn't have an assistant, he did have a woman who gave me a few lessons. She in fact had quite a decisive influence on me. Her name was Madame Zeiger de Saint-Marc, and she had studied with Anton Rubinstein. She devoted her whole life to writing a series of three volumes of exercises that unfortunately weren't as useful as she thought they would be. But she was nonetheless a woman of genius. Her exercises had to do with finger independence of a frightening extreme, with different rhythms in the same hand simultaneously with opposing rhythms in the other hand: for example, three against four in the right hand while four against three in the left hand—four voices at once! She was a fervent follower of d'-Indy and she was the first to really reveal polyphony to me. She gave me unforgettable lessons on Beethoven's "*Appassionata*" and Chopin's *Berceuse*. Also Beethoven's Sonata, Op. 111. She would have been a wonderful teacher of the preparatory class at the Conservatoire, but d'Indyism and her infamous exercises prevented her being nominated.[53]

After your study with Philipp [discussed earlier in this book], you then worked with Martinus Sieveking, a principal disciple of Leschetizky. For a French pianist, that must have been an unusual decision.

PL: Philipp never forgave me for it. Many years later when I asked for a reconciliation with him, he refused.

In what principal ways did their teaching differ?

PL: The system of Sieveking, derived from Leschetizky, is based on the fact that the different muscular groups are able to be independent. Thus the fingers, the hand, and the forearm are each energized while the upper arm is relaxed. The fingers become pillars of weight. A relaxed arm and a strong hand were crucial, as with Breithaupt. But unlike Breithaupt, the Sieveking method called for strong, very articulated fingers. Only in that respect was it related to Philipp's concerns.

Did it also place more emphasis on color?

PL: In general, the Leschetizky school was more romantic, with a freer approach to tempo, as you can hear in Leschetizky's piano roll of

Chopin's Nocturne in D-flat. And I think that it was more concerned with the complete education of the fingers and the different kinds of attacks—so in that sense, yes, you can talk about color. On the other hand, the French notion of "the atmosphere of a dream"—in which the music can nearly approach silence, pianississimo—was contrary to Leschetizky's ideal that everything always had to "*sing*", to have a round sound even when it was quiet.

From my study and conversations with elder French pianists, I am under the impression that—except for Cortot, Selva, Nat, Lazare-Lévy, and Ciampi—the notions of piano playing in France were pretty much an extension of the ideals and means of the clavecin *school.*

PL: The use of weight and arm was not much cultivated in France, that is true. Today of course, the picture has changed. But the Russians and Germans have always used more, and the reason is that their music demands it. It is a fact that composers engender the education of interpreters. For the French, there can be grandeur without heaviness and passion without violence. The dreamlike aura of Fauré is rarely appreciated in full outside France, and even there it is not meant to act directly on a crowd, like Tchaikovsky can.

Did you hear some Russian pianists before the Revolution?

PL: Yes, especially Lhevinne and Gabrilowitsch. Lhevinne was closer to the French style, in that he played quite strictly in tempo, cleanly, and fast. Gabrilowitsch was quite the opposite, very free, and with a technique that was frankly quite feeble. Among Russian composers, I think that Prokofiev in his *Visions fugitives* is the least different from the French aesthetic.

In your youth did you know or play for Debussy and Ravel and their contemporaries?

PL: Oh yes – for many of them, beginning when I was in my teens. At some of Philipp's monthly public classes he had all his students play works by a single composer. I remember that Fauré and Widor attended, and they gave us their ideas on interpretation. Later I became friends with both of them. As for Debussy, I don't know why, but never during my [more than six] years with Philipp did a single Debussy work get played!

But did you play for Debussy eventually?

PL: Yes, I went to his house and played some of his preludes for him. He wasn't always in agreement with me in some matters of tempo and sonority. In one of the pieces he said my tempo was too fast, so I said, "Give me your tempo," and when I played it again in his tempo, he said, "No, it's decidedly too slow!" And then I remember that when I played *La cathédrale engloutie*, Debussy said, "Well, it's too *engloutie!*"

Was Ravel more helpful?

PL: Not really. I played *Gaspard de la nuit* and *Le Tombeau de Couperin* for him, but he didn't have much to say. For *Ondine* he commented that "If you don't count the exact number of rhythms in the opening figure, it doesn't matter!" Oddly enough, he never spoke to me about details of pedaling, color, or interpretation. I remember only that he liked to hear certain notes vibrate longer than they were written, usually at cadences.

● ● ● ●

GABY CASADESUS

... (née Gabrielle L'Hote) was born in Marseille in 1901 and won a first medal at the Paris Conservatoire in the preparatory class of Marguerite Long in 1915, followed by a first prize three years later in the class of Louis Diémer. She went on to win the highest pianistic award for women in

France at the time, the Prix Pagès. Soon thereafter, she interpreted the music of Moszkowski, Fauré, Florent Schmitt, and Ravel under their personal guidance. She has performed throughout the world, both as soloist and as duo-pianist with her late husband Robert, and has also appeared as chamber musician with Zino Francescatti and the Juilliard and Guarnieri quartets. Her recordings include many works of the French repertoire and several Mozart concertos. She has taught at the summer school of the Mozarteum, the American Conservatory at Fontainebleau, the Schola Cantorum, and the Ravel Academy at St-Jean-de-Luz. In 1975 she was instrumental in founding the Robert Casadesus International Piano Competition. She has prepared editions of Ravel's solo piano works based on her husband's personal copies of the scores, and these — as well as her own editions of Ravel's *Jeux d'eau* and Debussy's *Pour le piano* — are published by G. Schirmer. Her memoires, *Mes noces musicales*, were published in France in 1989. She presently resides in Paris.

In your rich career you have known many great musicians, and achieved so much in your own right, that you may think it odd that I'd like to ask you most about your recollections of Diémer. But he was at the heart of the old French school, and I believe that you are his sole surviving student . . . .

GC: I think so. It's amusing that I got to study with Diémer completely by accident. I wanted Cortot, but he was too busy to hear me, and recommended Marguerite Long. So I entered her preparatory class at the Conservatoire and got my first medal two years later. I was able to sit in on Cortot's interpretation course at the Salle Pleyel for a year, and then I went into Diémer's class. As you know, classes were segregated by sex in those days, and Diémer had always taught the men's class. But because of the war there weren't enough men to fill it, so he had to accept women for the first time ever!

Diémer taught so many great pianists — your husband, Alfred Cortot, Yves Nat, Edouard Risler, Robert Lortat . . . and it's curious that they all played quite differently.

GC: Yes, but he certainly gave a technical base that was rooted in the fingers. The best thing that I remember about his teaching was his regimen. He demanded that we bring to class, every five days, an etude by Chopin, or one by Liszt, or something by Bach. For him, Bach was the essential thing, and his style at the piano was really just an extension of the French harpsichord technique. Also, we went through all the Beethoven sonatas, in order. I remember doing some Saint-Saëns with him, and Ravel's *Jeux d'eau*. In my last year I won the Prix Pagès, and my repertoire then included Schumann's *Carnaval*, Beethoven's Op. 110, Chopin's Ballade in F Minor, and Balakirev's *Islamey*.

Can you recall any specifics about his teaching?

GC: He was preoccupied with our playing the notes. He didn't talk about pedaling, the arms, or using dotted rhythms in practicing. Although he could be very demanding, he could also fall asleep in class! The best recollection I have of him is the systematic way he made us work on etudes and Bach. For young pianists a regimen is important, to give them a good strong base. It was different with Cortot, who might give the Schumann Fantasy to a talented fifteen-year-old. Cortot would sit at the piano and play the Schumann Fantasy so wonderfully, and after you got home you had only one aim in life: to play it like him! Later I realized that that is not really good pedagogy. That kind of wonderful inspiration works best after you are mature enough to understand, not when you are fourteen or fifteen.

I believe you also worked with Risler for a time?

GC: Yes, I had the great fortune to work with him for nearly a year. He was a wonderful pedagogue, and at that time he was as great a pianist as Cortot. He was a methodical, intelligent and interesting person, and as a teacher he was careful to advise us to work realistically for tempo and detail, always to build up gradually from what we could do. In a way, I think I never had a better teacher than Risler ... unless, for technique, Moszkowski.

Gaby Casadesus

Did he put you through his famous School of Double-Notes?

GC: Yes, indeed. That was his specialty, and something that people in
France didn't really work on too much at that time. And I remember
that I also had lessons with him on the Schumann Toccata and some
Chopin. Moszkowski was wonderful for technique — though very few
people had him as a teacher. I know that Vlado Perlemuter was working with him at the time I was.

May we talk a bit about the old French school?

GC: Most people associate it with Madame Long and Isidor Philipp. But
there were other ways of playing here — think of Cortot, Risler, Lazare-
Lévy. And Blanche Selva. She used much more arm and had more suppleness than Long. Selva specialized in Franck, d'Indy, Séverac, and,
especially, Bach. Her technique was a bit like Lazare-Lévy's, which was
good and complete — though some of his students seemed to use so
much wrist that they lost finger control. Another great French pianist
who was different from Long and Philipp was Francis Planté, a really
wonderful Chopin player. My husband and I spent a memorable day
with him when he was in his early nineties, and I remember that he
played the Chopin Barcarolle in an incredible way even then. He knew
some Chopin students, including Georges Mathias, who is remembered most for having taught Raoul Pugno and Philipp. It's interesting
that Philipp used the same diminished-seventh chord as the basis for
his exercises as Chopin used for some of his.

Do you use the Philipp exercises for extension?

GC: Sometimes, if a student needs some stretching. Philipp gave my husband some extension exercises when he was twelve or so, and he found
these and other Philipp exercises good for certain things, but in
moderation. I tend to favor the Brahms Exercises.

Your classes at Fontainebleau and St-Jean-de-Luz have attracted many fine young pianists, and I know that you were the principal teacher of Philippe Bianconi, the second-prize winner of the 1985 Van Cliburn Competition. Can you describe your approach?

GC: Well, I don't have a particular regimen, if that is what you mean. For technique, of course, you must have good scales, arpeggios, and octaves. For scales, I stress doing double-notes in thirds and sixths, in parallel and contrary motion and, of course, chromatically. But every pianist is different and needs different things. Chamber music can teach you a lot, too. Two of my husband's uncles were members of the Capet Quartet, which played Beethoven wonderfully. Hearing them rehearse and talk did a lot to form him musically, even before he was in his teens. You know, my husband was not my teacher, in a literal sense, but he was always such an inspiration for me, especially when we played on two pianos or four-hands. It was a challenge to feel the same way he did, to phrase the same, to be so instinctively musical. He never said, "Now I am going to make a crescendo" — or whatever. He just played naturally, and that's the approach I try to bring out in my students.

●   ●   ●   ●

PIERRE SANCAN

. . . was born in Mazamet, in southern France, on 24 October 1916. His early piano studies were in Morocco and Toulouse. In 1934 he entered the Paris Conservatoire and won a first prize in Yves Nat's class in 1937. Subsequent first prizes were in harmony, fugue, accompaniment, and composition. He also studied conducting with Charles Munch and Roger Désormière. In 1943 he won the Grand Prix de Rome, and his compositions since then have included an opera (*Ondine*), several ballets, a symphony, a piano concerto, and numerous works for piano solo. Sancan has performed regularly as a soloist and as partner with various artists, including cellist André Navarra, with whom he recorded Beethoven's five sonatas. His other recordings include Schumann's *Papillons*, Ravel's *Sonatine*, a group of Debussy's preludes, and Mozart's concertos for two and three pianos (with Jean-Bernard Pommier and Catherine Silie). In 1956 he was appointed Nat's successor at the Conservatoire, from which position he retired in 1985.

Sancan's students included: Jean-Efflam Bavouzet, Michel Béroff, Mélisande Chauveau, Jean-Philippe Collard, Cecilia Dunoyer, Abdel Rahman El Bacha, Olivier Gardon, Marc Laforêt, Jacqueline Méfano, Emile Naoumoff, Jean-Bernard Pommier, Jacques Rouvier, Catherine Silie, and Daniel Varsano.

Your great success as a teacher seems to have been based on your ability to combine the best of the French and Russian schools. May we begin with this?

PS: Well, I don't like to put a name on what I've done. I was rather young when I was appointed professor at the Conservatoire. I was lucky to have some gifted students, and I knew that if they didn't get a really good technique they would not be able to continue in the professional world. I realized that there were some things that we didn't know in France, or else had forgotten — for example, *la chute libre* (free fall), which may have interested writers perhaps more than teachers in recent years. In France, pianists used mostly their fingers, like the students of Marguerite Long. She was a good professor, with some good students, but they did not all play the same, so it is difficult to generalize about them.

In France, then, the idea of weight and forearm came mainly from Cortot?

PS: Yes, and his students played differently from the students of Long. Cortot's students were artists, immense artists sometimes. They learned the feeling of weight, which many gifted students today don't have. So I asked myself why certain students, good musicians, couldn't do what some others were able to do so easily. I talked with doctors, and with my wife, who is a doctor. I did experiments, I looked at X-rays, I studied muscles, and yes, I talked with some Russians. One of my basic conclusions was that if the shoulder is well-positioned, the arm will be lighter and freer. Certainly it is bad to play something like the opening of the Schumann Fantasy only with the fingers! But that is what some good pianists were trying to do. So maybe a teacher would tell them to relax more. But how? Hunched over, with floppy movements of the arms — the way pretty young girls used to play Chopin's *Fantaisie-Impromptu?!* No, the sound has to have weight behind it. So I thought about these things, and I also learned from some of my better students.

What is your feeling about rhythmic displacement exercises, for difficult passages?

PS: I think they are mostly useless. The fingers, when playing fast, are always in motion — like a runner doing the 400-meter dash. Does a runner train his body by doing three quick steps and then stopping? And then, after a pause, three more quick steps? [Sancan proceeded to do a parody of this, running a few steps at a time and pausing to wipe his brow at each stop.] No! Does the professional runner practice by first accenting the *left* foot for ten meters?! Of course not. He simply learns to get efficient, *natural* movements at a slow pace, and then he gradually builds up speed. So, while I have fantastic admiration for Cortot, both as a pianist and as a teacher, I must say that I think his rhythmic exercises — in his editions and in his book — are mostly a waste of time. Maybe it is good to practice in *one* new rhythm sometimes, but not in every possible rhythm. Of course, the notion of rhythmic practice was not unique to Cortot.

What you say is very persuasive, and it seems to be based on good common sense. But don't you think there is a value in drilling the reflexes to respond more quickly than a passage requires — which these rhythmic exercises would seem to guarantee?

PS: Yes, but let us back-track a step. All technique can be reduced to simply finding the correct, most efficient positioning. When the correct

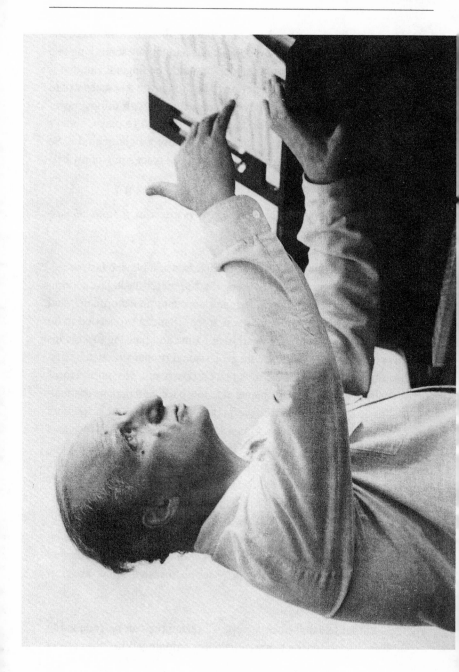

Pierre Sancan

musical and technical gestures have been learned – especially their preparations – you will play well. To return to the idea of the runner, he makes continuous and smooth movements, rising a bit on his toes no matter how fast he is running. An athlete learns first to walk, then to run, and then, if he is so inclined, to pole-vault. Pianists must condition themselves in the same way. At a certain stage, Pischna, Hanon, and Czerny are necessary, and so is very slow practice. But after that, if a student can "pole-vault," he must think about every gesture that he makes.

How, specifically, do you train a gifted pianist to accomplish that?

PS: Constantly we must search for the most efficient movements, working slowly and with smooth motions. With scales and arpeggios we must analyze the slowest motion of each finger and of the wrist. (The wrist, for me, is usually rather stationary and not high.) After that, you have understood all the basic problems of piano playing. No ungifted student will ever become significantly better just by practicing Czerny and Pischna blindly, without analyzing every motion of every finger for maximum efficiency. But slow motions are not the same as fast ones, so one must build up, again like the runner. Even amateur runners do not run flat-footed. Instinctively they know better. And so should pianists instinctively do the right things. Unlike runners, we pianists must use our brains – and at every step of the way. I constantly tell my students, "The brain is the boss." The potential for the greatest artistry resides there and there alone. An American, George Kochevitsky, has written along these same lines. Another fairly recent book of value is the one by Heinrich Neuhaus [*The Art of Piano Playing*].

In your classes I was interested to find you constantly watching the students' bodies rather than their fingers.

PS: Absolutely! Nine times out of ten, when there is a wrong note the *body* is doing something wrong – especially the arm or shoulder. Naturally we are talking about advanced pianists who can already play the notes up to tempo. Always I try to pinpoint the problem in anatomical terms, to discover the motion that uses the least effort. Then the motion itself must be practiced slowly, for freedom and security, perhaps with no particular notes in mind. Later, aiming for the written notes, one can work faster and faster for accuracy, gradually minimizing the motions. Another thing is posture. As I'm sure you know, many pianists cause problems for themselves by a hunched-over position. I'm convinced that one must sit back, letting the arms hang down in a natural, free way. A hunched shoulder is death, producing an uninteresting sound as well as stiffness and inaccuracy.

What about sonority? Do you have some special approaches?

PS: Well, first you must be intelligent enough to decide on the kind of sound you want and from where it can best originate. You don't want the same sound for Chopin's "Ocean" Etude [Op. 25, No. 12] and his "Thirds" Etude! Maybe you want total flexibility in each joint of your shoulder, arm, and wrist — or maybe you want it just in the wrist. It depends on the piece or the passage. But I must repeat what I said earlier about the forearm's importance. Piano playing is not just fingers, as we used to think in France.

I'd like to return to that idea for a moment. How do you get a "finger-pianist" to learn the use of forearms?

PS: I can tell you a most amusing story about that! A few years ago a young American pianist came to me, with his mother. He was preparing to play a major New York recital, and he wanted my advice. Since he came all the way from America, I saw him. He played Chopin's Ballade in G Minor for me quite well, but at the E-flat passage in double notes [bars 170-173] he missed many notes, flopping his wrist about in different positions. I suggested that he keep *one* hand position and move the wrist up and down with the arm. He tried it, and then jumped up and cried, "Mother! Mother! Now I can play it!" Then he and his mother flew home, happy with this fabulous "insight!"

So there is no mystique about your teaching? Is it so completely pragmatic?

PS: I try to make my students think intelligently about technique as well
as about music. Technically, I am merely a teacher of positions. Just
find the best one for each passage and then practice it ten, fifty, maybe
a hundred times.

*If that is your secret, you are very modest. May we return for a moment to
your ideas about sonority? Do orchestral colors stimulate your teaching and
playing?*

PS: Oh, absolutely. As you may know, I am also a composer, and I won
the Prix de Rome for that. So naturally I want to "orchestrate" all piano
music. I insist that my best students study orchestration and conducting, and that they learn to play an orchestral instrument, however feeb-
ly. The piano must be viewed as a small orchestra, with the potential of
strings, winds, brass, and percussion. This is why I love Debussy's piano
works so much—they are perfectly conceived for the piano, but the
possible orchestrations are unlimited. Never is it simply trombones versus flutes. Maybe you know the account written by a student of
Chopin's, who had a lesson with him on the Nocturne in C Minor (if I
remember correctly, though it doesn't really matter). Chopin devoted
a very long time to the opening few bars, how they should be colored
and inflected, and the student had to repeat these few measures over
and over and over again. Maybe that student was trying to do everything with curved fingers, when Chopin wanted flatter ones, a looser
arm, and maybe a better ear for nuances. Sonority, not fingers, was his
interest, at least in that nocturne. The sound that you want must dic-
tate your physical gestures, whether the speed is fast or slow or somewhere in between. To get the right sound by the most efficient movements has been at the heart of my teaching for many years.

Did this approach stem from your years of study with Yves Nat

PS: Only indirectly. Nat was a formidable pianist, a really great player of Beethoven and Schumann. His playing was always an inspiration, and very aristocratic—not just the fast, digital approach. As a teacher, he was interested only in the best students. But as advanced as we may have been, he gave us his fingering for every piece that we studied— sometimes literally for every note of a piece! He had very broad fingers, and the fingering he chose fit his hand—but not always the hands of his students. He was a great pianist who mostly wanted to practice and compose. Although he taught at the Conservatoire, he never really threw himself into it—and certainly he didn't go out of his way to do some of the things that teachers must sometimes do in order to get and keep a long line of fine students. That route, which detracts from a performer's energies, simply didn't interest him. He took himself very seriously as a composer, and I vividly remember one day when I came for a lesson on Schumann's Fantasy. After I played the first page or so, he stopped me and said that it was very good. Then he pulled out his new orchestral work, *L'Enfer*, and he played it for me for twenty minutes. Then we returned to my Schumann, but when I got to the fourth or fifth page he said, "You really play it very well, but let me play the rest of *L'Enfer* for you." It was a three-hour lesson, but I never got to play all of the Schumann Fantasy! He was not always like that, of course. It depended on his mood. And my technique was pretty well formed by then. So I must say that most of what we have been talking about today I did not get from Nat. But he was a great pianist and a great teacher of musicianship.

● ● ● ●

JEAN-JOËL BARBIER

. . . was born in Belfort, in eastern France, on 25 March 1920. In addition to his private musical education, he received a degree from the Sorbonne in Greek and Latin studies. After the war he divided his time between performing and writing fiction, criticism, and poetry. His books include *Ishtar* (1946), *Les Eaux fourrées* (1951), *Irradiante* (1954), *Dictionnaire des musiciens français* (1961), and *Au piano avec Erik Satie* (1986). As a pianist, he has been praised for his refined and poetic performances of the music of Séverac, Chabrier, Debussy, Ibert, and Satie. His recording of the complete piano works of Satie won a Grand Prix du Disque. In 1974 he was appointed director of the Conservatoire de Charenton. He presently resides in Paris.

I know that you were influenced by the teaching of Blanche Selva, whose ideas about piano playing were quite contrary to the traditional ones in France. Also I seem to hear a reflection of her approach in your excellent recording of Séverac's Cerdaña suite, which she premiered. At what point in your training were you exposed to her ideas?

J-JB: Right from the beginning. When I was six I started piano study in Belfort with Louise Terrier, a woman who was greatly influenced by Selva's teaching. She had attended Selva's summer courses for years. I worked with Terrier for eleven years, and then from 1937 to 1939 I studied with Selva's main assistant, Libussé Novak. Novak had heard Selva's classes in Prague around 1920 and had been so impressed that she followed Selva to France and became her assistant. She played a great deal of French music wonderfully. She was a very dynamic teacher — more so than Selva, who could be quite discouraging to students. Although I never actually studied with Selva, I heard her perform often, went to her courses, and, as I say, studied with these two women who were so influenced by her. I was preparing to enter the Conservatoire when the war broke out and I was mobilized. So I was not able to come back to music until after the war.

How would you summarize Selva's approach?

J-JB: Selva's three or four most important ideas were developed at great length in her teaching and writing. The most fundamental was the concept of muscular decontraction, in which the arm was to fall on the

Jean-Joël Barbier

keyboard with dead weight but with firm fingertips; then the arm was to be raised while the fingers still clung to the keys. In various exercises the weight of the arm was used in conjunction with finger and hand movements. Firm fingertips were very important in these drills, in order to avoid the sense of complete floppiness. (I might add parenthetically that arm weight was natural for Selva, because she was such an immense woman!)

Secondly, she had her students develop what might be called a "scratch" technique, in which the finger pulled toward the edge of the key as it went down. Each movement had to be practiced over and over very slowly while counting a certain number of beats. For beginners, she had exercises to be done away from the piano, in which the fingers of the closed hand, resting on a flat surface, had to spread open to the maximum in ten graduated steps, each held for four slow beats. Then the contrary, with the fingers gradually closing again into a rounded position in another ten slow steps. Also she had exercises for snapping the wrist, and these too were to be practiced on a table or desk.

Finally, like Rudolf Breithaupt, whose writings I think influenced her very much, she never tired of emphasizing arm rotation. But she went further than that. For beginners, she advocated the euryhthmic drills of Emile Jaques-Dalcroze, and I remember that at one time she brought in a woman from Basel who specialized in them. This teacher would have children walk or run to music played in various tempos and meters, and have them wave one arm in two beats while the other waved in four. This of course encouraged participation of the whole body, an approach that was at the heart of Selva's playing and teaching.

Because of this preoccupation with large muscles, do you think Selva put less emphasis on finger articulation than other French teachers at that time?

J-JB: Possibly a bit less. But she was very preoccupied with finding different timbres for different moods and different notations. She experimented a great deal with various degrees of attack and with the speed of key descent, and her books are full of explanations of different kinds of touch. So I would say that articulation was definitely one of her concerns.

You also studied with Lazare-Lévy. Did you find his ideas compatible with Selva's and Novak's?

J-JB: I studied with Lazare-Lévy for two years, at about the same time that I was studying with Novak, and their teaching of technique only differed in one main respect. While he always wanted the fingers to push the keys down, and often wanted the fingers to be rather flat, Selva and Novak often wanted the fingers to pull inward while playing, and thus to be more curved at each joint. But I don't think that Lazare-Lévy was necessarily against Selva's approach. Cortot, on the other hand, didn't care for her ideas at all. He told one of her students who came to study with him that it would be necessary for her to start studying technique all over again, from zero.

What purely musical advice do you recall from Selva's courses?

J-JB: I remember that she mentioned the value of breathing a phrase as you played it. She herself phrased in such a natural way, with long, long lines, never stopping halfway through a phrase to emphasize a particular note or harmony. Perhaps this was better for Baroque and contemporary music than for romantic works. For example, in Chopin's Ballade in G Minor, when in the middle of the second theme you have a B-flat in the right hand against a C in the left hand [bar 80], she would never have stopped to make the expressive effect that so many pianists try to do there.

Selva never played from memory, though she always knew the music well. She was part of a school that was against virtuosity for its own sake. Viñes also often played with the music, even with orchestra in Falla's *Nights in the Gardens of Spain*. Of course, both Selva and Viñes were often playing premières, and sometimes they would perform the same new work just a week or two apart from one another.

Was Selva a popular teacher? I have found it difficult to trace any of her students.

J-JB: She was greatly respected by musicians, especially those aligned with the Schola Cantorum, where she taught from an early age. Also she taught master classes in Strasbourg, Brive, Prague, and Barcelona, and they were well-attended.

But I know that she was an extremely critical and impatient teacher, and it is possible that students didn't stay with her too long. Her concepts were very intellectual, and they couldn't be learned quickly. Certainly she taught the necessity of having good ears – but also that it is the brain that initiates the search for the means to get what you want at the piano. It seems obvious to us now, but it wasn't always back then.

● ● ● ●

GRANT JOHANNESEN

... was born on 30 July 1921 in Salt Lake City, Utah, where he began piano studies at age six. He worked privately with Robert Casadesus in Princeton from 1941 to 1946, and subsequently with Egon Petri at Cornell University. He also studied composition with Roger Sessions and Nadia Boulanger. In 1944 he made his New York debut, and since then has performed throughout the world, including as the only soloist on two tours each with the New York Philharmonic and the Cleveland Orchestra. Johannesen was president of the Cleveland Institute of Music, where he taught for many years, and is presently on the faculty of the Mannes College of Music in New York City. His many recordings include the complete solo works of Fauré, Saint-Saëns's Fourth Concerto, Fauré's Ballade and Fantasy, the Grieg Concerto, and numerous works by Bach, Chopin, Copland, Schumann, and twentieth-century French composers. He currently resides in New York City.

I can't think of an American pianist who has performed more French music for a longer time than you have. I am interested to know about your early identification with this repertoire.

GJ: I had very early exposure to French music through my first teacher in Salt Lake City, Mabel Borg-Jenkins. She was a woman of rather remarkable intellectual breadth who had studied with Sigismund Stojowski [who had studied with Diémer]. She was a great promoter of new music and of new French music, and she was one of the assistants of the French pianist, E. Robert Schmitz. As you know, Schmitz had studied with Diémer and been in Debussy's circle, and he wrote a book on interpreting Debussy. He came to the United States in the 1920s, founded a cross-cultural association known as Pro Musica, and premiered many French works here. He had a network of assistants around the country, so I was able to play for him numerous times.

I know his books. What was he like as a teacher?

GJ: Schmitz's approach was very intellectual, and he was very preoc- cupied with the physiology of piano playing. In this respect he was somewhat like Abby Whiteside, though more detailed in his explana- tions. He published some interesting editions of Chopin's etudes, Bach's inventions, and Ravel's *Alborada del gracioso*. He developed a system of abbreviations that clearly identified which muscles should be used for which passages, how the arm or wrist should move, and so on. His whole approach is clearly laid out in his book, *The Capture of In- spiration*, and his ideas about tone – which I teach in part today – are based on sound physiological principles.

They would not seem to be related to his study with Diémer.

GJ: Oh, Schmitz was much more modern in his thinking. In fact, his method has nothing to do with the so-called French school. His basic concept was that the long fingers should always be on black notes. He

Grant Johannesen

devised new fingerings for all the scales, and these are explained in *The Capture of Inspiration*. Schmitz was a very interesting man, though a rather quirky performer.

I know that your main studies were with Casadesus, who also was not exactly in line with Diémer, Long and Philipp.

GJ: Yes, Casadesus was different. If you want to talk about the old French school, I would say that Jeanne-Marie Darré has been the best example of what it was all about. She had a certain reserve about her playing, and a wonderful *petite technique* of fingers and wrists. But she was also drawn to the big literature, and was not arty and precious, as some French pianists have been. Novaes, too, was a good example of the best of the French school. I think it is perhaps easier to define the Russian school than the French school. To me, Casadesus was not what you would call a French pianist. He played Brahms when most French pianists didn't, his thinking was in line with George Szell and a number of non-French conductors, and he was more popular in the United States than in France. His own music, like his personality, was poised and classical. He loved the music of Scarlatti, Rameau, Mozart, Bach, Milhaud, and Roussel.

Can you describe some specific aspects of his teaching?

GJ: I studied with him in Princeton off and on for five years. I remember lessons on Mozart's Concerto in C Minor, Ravel's Concerto in G and *Gaspard de la nuit*, the Liszt Sonata, the Schumann Fantasy, and many other pieces. His advice for the Schumann really stuck with me. He wanted the architecture of it to be clearly projected and to seem continuous. This meant thinking about where to take time — and especially where not to — and whether pauses after the climaxes were necessary. Generally he was against pausing after lifting the pedal, which of course introduces silence and tends to make the piece sound even more sectional. Naturally, it is fine to make pauses when the pedal is sustaining sound. He didn't like to spend time on technical problems. He would send students to his wife Gaby if they needed help. He didn't talk about weight, or putting your elbow out, or similar physical aspects about playing. I was already formed, technically, and I think I was in line with him in that respect. He was simple and direct in his demands, and his main aim was to give you the idea of what the piece was all about, and how to make it sound interesting from the beginning to the end. He was a composer, after all, and he could make a recital seem short because of his marvelous concentration, which would draw you into the music with such simple means. He was very generous, and his master classes weren't full of talk. They were never at all academic. You played, and he demonstrated, and if you had eyes and ears you could pick up things that might take years to learn otherwise.

I regret never having heard him in concert. You must have many vivid memories . . . .

GJ: His playing was so natural that you couldn't believe there was any other way to do it. His sound was unique. He hunched over the piano, embracing it rather like Gieseking did, and his range of colors was near-ly as great as Gieseking's. Though he wasn't known as a Liszt player, I remember a performance he gave in New York of the Sonata that bowled me over! The piece really had an audible form and a natural-ness about it that was unique in my experience. He played it so that one section followed another so naturally, and the fermatas didn't make the music stand still. Rather, they held the music in a kind of grip for a mo-ment, and then they let it move forward.

Did Casadesus talk much about pedaling?

GJ: No, not much. In general, he liked clean textures and didn't pedal too much. But speaking of pedaling, Poulenc once gave me some ex-cellent and unusual advice when I played for him. He told me to use more pedal, but at the same time to play more cleanly. It worked — and

I think the sound you get from this approach works very well not just in Poulenc but in other French piano music. Poulenc said that most Americans played his music too dryly, "as though they were on a diet. I tell them to put the *butter* in the sauce!"

I know that you also studied with Busoni's great disciple, Egon Petri. Did his approach have much in common with that of Casadesus?

GJ: Casadesus was more international in outlook, Petri more Central European, but Casadesus admired Petri's playing very much and seemed in agreement with some things that Petri taught me. My study with Petri was most valuable for what he had to say about Beethoven's sonatas and concertos. I also worked on some Bach with him — the partitas and the Fantasy and Fugue in A Minor. Unlike Casadesus, Petri had a condescending attitude toward Mozart's concertos. He told me not to bother memorizing them — "just have fun with them!" Petri made a really great recording of Liszt's Concerto in A . . . and so did Casadesus.

● ● ● ●

PIERRE BARBIZET

. . . was born in Arica, Chile, on 20 September 1922. After early piano studies in Santiago, he moved to Paris and entered the Conservatoire, where he received a first prize in 1944 in the class of Armand Ferté. He won first prize in the International Competition at Scheveningen in 1948, and the following year was a prize winner in the Marguerite Long — Jacques Thibaud Competition. He performed frequently as a soloist and chamber musician, especially with violinist Christian Ferras. Their recordings include the complete sonatas by Beethoven and Brahms, and sonatas by Debussy, Franck, Lekeu, and Enesco. Barbizet's other recordings include Beethoven Sonatas, Opp. 57, 81a, and 101, Chabrier's complete piano works, Chausson's *Concert* (with Ferras and the Parrenin

Quartet), Schumann's Piano Quartet (with the Parrenin Quartet), and Chopin's Rondo for Two Pianos, Op. 73 (with Samson François). Barbizet taught for a time at the Paris Conservatoire, and in 1963 was appointed director of the Conservatoire de Marseille, where he was also professor of piano. His students included Bernard d'Ascoli, Edouard Exerjean, Jacques Gauthier, and Hélène Grimaud. He died in Marseille on 19 January 1990.

I know that your early study was in Santiago. Was there a Chilean school of playing?

PB: There were some great Chilean pianists, Arrau and Rosita Renard above all. But the Chilean, Argentine, and Brazilian schools were not as different as the different national schools in Europe. They were mostly influenced by German musicians. I began my piano studies in Santiago with a Swiss-German teacher, Margareth Boetsch. She and my mother had founded a Bach choral society in Santiago, together with a great Chilean musician, Domingo Santa Cruz. He had me begin music study as a singer, but I was quickly converted to the piano. I practiced lots of exercises and got into the Conservatory of Santiago, which, as I say, was a German-type school. I learned a very practical technique, with the hand very calm, with no turning, always in front of and near the keys. Only later, but not from the older French pianists, did I learn about the use of the upper arm.

Was Armand Ferté a major influence on you?

PB: No, not really. He was a very cultivated man, but I didn't get much from him pianistically. Those who influenced me the most pianistically were Arrau, Renard, Manuel Infante, Iturbi, Nat, Cortot, and Philipp. From each of them I learned things that were important, essential, and sometimes very simple. Ferté was best for the Beethoven style, but not for the piano. He was very strict about note values in Beethoven — an eighth is an eighth, a quarter is a quarter, and nothing in between. That I remember. I also learned from him to look for the real text. In France at that time we had bad editions, and Ferté was one of the first to talk about good, authentic editions. His own Beethoven edition isn't an *Urtext*, but it is close to the sources and in that same scholarly spirit. The same applies to his edition of the *Well-Tempered Clavier*. Although one might disagree with details of interpretation, the musical text he presented was a good one.

I know that you also had lessons with Nat, Casadesus, Philipp, Long....

PB: Yes. Why don't I give you a mini-history of French pianism as I see it? The French school descends from the clavecinists through Saint-Saëns to Diémer and his students. Saint-Saëns was a fantastic pianist. Just imagine what a school of playing you'd have if you combined the approaches of Busoni and Saint-Saëns! The playing would be *into* the keys but with a horizontal technique. Aldo Ciccolini plays a bit like that. Although Diémer was a modern pioneer for harpsichord recitals, he also had a great piano technique, but with a fixed position. There's a generation of pianists between Saint-Saëns and Debussy who had that harpsichord-like approach which worked fine even for the music of Chabrier. Lots of important — and differing — pianists studied with Diémer, especially Cortot, Nat, and Casadesus. Cortot had a technique that combined the best of Diémer with aspects of the Liszt school, and he discovered how to make the French piano sing. Then there was Marguerite Long, who had a horizontal technique but made attacks with a high forearm. That's dangerous. I asked Sviatoslav Richter what he thought of that kind of flamboyant playing, and he said, "It's hard enough to play when you're *near* the keys!" Long came from the school of high fingers. Cortot also could play that way, and we must not forget what a great finger technique he had. But he coupled that with arm rotation. I worked some with Casadesus, who liked the clavecinists, Chabrier, Mozart — everything that involved finger technique, equality, and elegance. From my generation there was Samson François, the greatest pianist in the world! He was a very strange player, stupefying sometimes. He got some of that from Cortot. Of Long he didn't say much except that she gave him discipline. She would hit him if he hadn't practiced enough, and rightly, because was a very rebellious youngster! What made François a genius at the piano came from Cortot. Isidor Philipp had a post-Brahmsian viewpoint. He showed me how to do some of his exercises, and I played Schumann's *Etudes symphoniques* for him. He told me that when you practice difficult chordal passages, like in this work or, for example, in the coda of the finale of Beethoven's Op. 57, you should practice them heavy and loud, close to the keys and *into* the keys. Not staccato, but as legato as you can. After that kind of work you will then be able to play them as light and staccato as you want.

Long recommended practicing in dotted, long-short rhythms, and I think that's good for chordal practice. But I don't recommend it for practicing scales or arpeggios. It will kill legato. But for Chopin's Etude, Op. 25, No. 1, she gave me good advice for practicing the groups of six little notes in three groups of two notes and then in two groups of three notes.

I played several times for Yves Nat, who had a wonderful explanation for using arm weight: "You must *close* the suitcase!" He wanted you to imagine a suitcase that is stuffed full of clothes, and in order to close it you have to press down with your arms, your shoulders, whatever—your testicles, too, maybe! But *not* just with your wrists! "*Close* the suitcase!" I've never forgotten that.

How would you contrast the playing of Long and Cortot?

PB: Long's playing was rather small-scaled and it often exemplified the *jeu perlé* style. But that way of playing isn't unique to France. Beethoven, in a letter to Czerny, used the word "pearly," and I must say that that technique seems appropriate even in some of his late works. Think of the opening page of the Sonata, Op. 110. Yes, the main theme is super-legato, but the fast notes in the right hand at the bottom of the page must be "pearled"—not legato, not staccato, but fast and even.

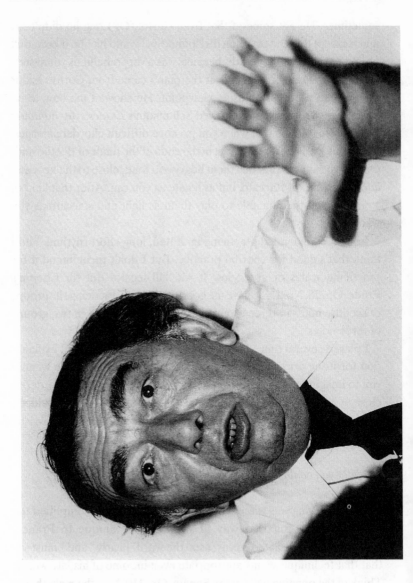

Pierre Barbizet

Madame Long specialized in playing pearly works, including Ravel's Concerto in G, *Le Tombeau de Couperin*, Mozart, and many of Fauré's pieces. The "pearls" of Long had to do with timbre. I associate the filigree in Debussy's *Bruyères* with her — very clean and clear. Cortot got a different, more shadowy sound in that piece. He was more romantic in every way, playing the hands not quite together, and so on. His legato playing was as marvelous as her "pearled" playing. But they both could play the opposite way too. There's a Latin proverb: "Truth lies in the middle." The last movement of Schumann's Concerto has to be played *perlé*, as do many of Chopin's études.

What about the use of flat versus curved fingers?

PB: Curved, curved, curved, and *CURVED!* Once a student learns to play well with a curved position, then it will be easy for him to use a flat one when necessary. But to do the reverse is difficult and maybe even dangerous. In most French music, clarity is important, and this is perhaps why our teaching has been a bit different from the German school, where using a flatter hand and pressing deep into the keys is often related to the heavier emotional content of their music. Naturally the approach depends on the music. You can't play the legato opening of Chopin's Ballade in A-flat with curved fingers. Also, think of the opening of the slow movement of Mozart's Concerto in A (K. 488). If you want clarity for every note of this pure and beautiful melody, you will sometimes have to lift your fingers off the keys sooner than you would if you were playing a perfect legato.

I assume that your own teaching is a melange of these many ideas, and that you are really outside any "school."

PB: Exactly. I was lucky to work with some wonderful musicians. But Long didn't say the opposite of Cortot; Cortot didn't say the opposite of Nat; Iturbi didn't say the opposite of Arrau; Arrau didn't say the opposite of Philipp. They were complementary to one another. We must take what we need from each teacher. I doubt that every student I teach takes exactly the same thing from me.

I haven't mentioned Georges Enesco, who was probably the most important of all influences on me, because he himself was a synthesis. He didn't speak specifically about piano playing, but one day Christian Ferras and I played for him Fauré's Sonata in A. After hearing a bit of the first movement, he stopped us and said, "Monsieur Barbizet, don't play the piano like a Remington!" That kind of "typing" style was Long's, and he didn't much like it. He added, "Monsieur Barbizet, flat fingers, please — for a better sound. You need a sense of freedom and peace here." Also I remember him saying things like, "I don't hear the second horn there," or "Just *one* trumpet here!" He always thought in terms of orchestral colors. Also I remember him suggesting that the sound of octaves should be lightened up by bringing out the upper notes in both hands. Especially in Brahms. Enesco imparted a sense of liberty that was very important in my development. He was a great musician and an inspiring influence on Menuhin, Haskil, Lipatti, Grumiaux, Ferras, and many others. I knew him until the end of his life. I remember the last time I saw him I pestered him about the correct tempo of the slow movement of Bach's "Italian" Concerto. He was very sick then, and he looked up and said, "The right tempo for any piece is the one that allows the shortest note-values to remain expressive." That advice, and "*Close* the suitcase!" have become my constant by-words . . . .

●   ●   ●   ●

JEAN-PHILIPPE COLLARD

. . . was born at Mareuil-sur-Ay, near Epernay, on 27 January 1948, and received a first prize in the class of Aline van Barentzen at the Paris Conservatoire in 1964. Thereafter he studied privately with Pierre Sancan and soon won prizes in a number of important competitions, including the national competition of the *Guilde française des artistes solistes*, the Marguerite Long — Jacques Thibaud Competition (1969), the Fauré Prize, the

Cziffra International Competition, and the Albert Roussel Award. Since his brilliant Paris and American debuts, both in 1973, he has performed with all the world's major orchestras and recorded a vast repertoire, including the complete solo works of Ravel and Fauré, Rachmaninov's *Etudes-Tableaux* and Second Sonata, Chopin's Second and Third Sonatas, concertos by Mozart, Ravel, and Rachmaninov, chamber music with Augustin Dumay (violin) and Fréderic Lodéon (cello), and four-hand piano works with Michel Béroff. He presently resides in Paris.

You are probably the best-known French pianist of your generation. Could we begin by discussing your early training. Was it unusualy good and comprehensive?

J-PC: Not at all. I first studied with a local teacher near Epernay. Then, completely by chance when I was ten years old, Aline van Barentzen heard me play and suggested that I study with her at the Paris Conservatoire. I ended up working with her for a total of five years. She had been a pupil of Marguerite Long. As a former child-prodigy she was an instinctive player with a natural technique. She had never had to ask herself the "hows" and "whys" of technique, so of course she didn't have the patience to teach it. She never explained why the third finger might be better here rather than there, or why the arm might be stiff. No details. Instead, whenever a student played a wrong note she would take a big red pencil and circle the note and say, "Fix that for next week." You can't go far with advice like that!

I know her recordings. It doesn't seem that as a performer she was a good representative of Long's approach.

J-PC: Not exactly, because in addition to Long she studied with Leschetizky. The old French school hasn't really existed since Long died in the mid-1960s. And happily so, for it was a very poor school! It was just finger technique, Saint-Saëns, Philipp, and so on. It was only suitable for a tiny bit of the vast panorama of piano literature. Sixty or seventy years ago, yes, there was a particular way of playing the piano that was "French". But now it's useless to think of playing like that. Today all the so-called schools have combined — the Russian, the French, the German, the Japanese, or what have you. The school of Long was wonderful for digital playing — "diggy-diggy-diggy-dee" — but it had nothing to do with participation of the arm, shoulder, or body. Pierre Sancan was undoubtedly the person most responsible for killing off the old French school!

What types of exercises did he have you do?

J-PC: Oh, many, many things for shoulder, upper arm, forearm, and fingers, each of those elements in turn. He always analyzed the functions of the muscles. He demanded that I know exactly what muscles in my arm and shoulder were activated when I raised, for example, my fourth finger. So he had me buy medical books and study diagrams of muscles.

Would you say, then, that Sancan's own technique was not as natural as van Barentzen's?

J-PC: Well, like her he never had anyone who told him "do this, do that, raise your wrist, put out your elbow." His main teacher had been Yves Nat, a very inspiring interpreter who spoke very little about technique. So Sancan had to fabricate a personal technique by going to anatomy books to understand how the muscles work. "Whys" and "hows" mattered to him.

What were some of his principles, specifically?

J-PC: When he first heard me — and bear in mind that I had already won the highest of all the first prizes given in my graduation year at the Conservatoire — he said that I had a natural flexibility, but that my technique was really pretty weak. So he began by teaching me exercises that

Jean-Philippe Collard

are normally given to children, such as *tenues*, trills for the fourth and fifth fingers, thumb-under drills, and so on, all of which I had to do for hours and hours. He corrected my hand position because, since I have very long fingers, I had been turning my hand unnaturally, to compensate. Also he gave me some Russian-type exercises for the forearm, using much less wrist than I had before, in order to gain a lighter, better-controlled technique. He had me practicing octaves for hours, using the arm, not the wrist. For eight months I practiced technique for two or three hours every morning: octaves, thirds, sixths, everything. He explained so many things to me for the first time: how to relax — which begins with a relaxed attitude, without visible muscular tension; the need to locate the exact places where the greatest relaxation is possible in each piece you play; and to always question everything: the position of the hands and elbows, the degree of power that is needed at a particular point and from where it should originate, what motions are needed to get a full but not percussive sound, and so on. To get a student to think about these sorts of things is real teaching!

Were these exercises devised by him, or did he use traditional ones?

J-PC: I would say that about half the exercises he gave me were original with him. In a few minutes' time he would write out exercises for me that were meant to solve a specific problem. His exercises were always adapted to the individual student's hand or technique. But he also used traditional exercises by Hanon, Philipp, Brahms, Ferté, and others. He loved his students, and they loved him. He was very generous with his time, and he might work with you until three in the morning if he thought you needed it before a competition. To my knowledge, in France there isn't anybody who teaches like him. In fact, teachers all over the world seem concerned mostly with how to get their students to play faster and louder. As a result, the playing is usually forced and percussive, and though all these young pianists can play virtually anything, they don't have the simple aptitude for relaxing and making a pleasant sound.

Sancan explained to me why he doesn't agree with Cortot and others about the value of dotted-rhythm practice for difficult passages. Do you agree?

J-PC: Oh yes, Sancan is right about that. The problem with practicing in a dotted rhythm is that there is an unnecessary contraction of the muscles just prior to playing the shorter note. Sancan always wanted suppleness, no matter how difficult the passage was, and his advice was always to practice with uniform note values and smooth, efficient motions.

So the things that Sancan passed on had little to do with his own teacher, Nat?

J-PC: Occasionally he talked about Nat's interpretations, his natural phrasing, his musicality. But Sancan's main technical ideas stemmed, I think, from his later visits to Russia, when he was on competition juries and got to talk with pianists and teachers there about the arm and body. But even before then he got to know all the great pianists who visited Paris. For years he haunted the Salle Pleyel, where he talked with virtually every pianist who rehearsed there. Especially Michelangeli and de Larrocha. He would often come to a lesson and say, "Well, Michelangeli practices this passage this way," or "This is how de Larrocha gets her special sound in this passage." He was open to everything, as a great teacher must be. Everything he learned he used in his teaching, to one degree or another. He was the furthest thing from a pedant. At lessons he rarely looked at a student's fingers or hands. Instead he watched their arms or shoulders. Often he could tell what was wrong physically simply by listening. It was almost as though he was clairvoyant!

I sense that you don't have too good memories of your Conservatoire years, before Sancan.

J-PC: No, because the Conservatoire is no longer a selective school. Each year they award twenty to twenty-five first prizes in piano, and each year the level gets lower and lower. The professors are sometimes not active performers, so they don't have a real idea of the artistic life of today. Also, a student can't change teachers unless he withdraws completely and takes the entrance examination again — and because the teachers can be jealous of one another, the outcome of the exam can be uncertain. I think it was also very wrong to admit students at age ten or eleven and allow them to graduate at sixteen under the delusion that they would have a grand career just because they won a first prize. At that age one lacks experience, repertoire, technique, everything. It's a totally artificial, delusory system. If you want some statistics, I can tell you that since I graduated in 1964 the Conservatoire has awarded some 500 first prizes in piano, but there are only five or six of us who have been able to make a living entirely from giving concerts and making recordings. The diploma isn't sufficiently prestigious to make a career.

In the United States it isn't either, but it certainly opens up some avenues . . . .

J-PC: Yes, maybe for international competitions it helps if you can put down that you graduated with a first prize. But that's all it's good for. I think the Conservatoire recognized this when they started offering the "third cycle." It's a post-graduate course for "perfection" in performance. The idea was to bring in well-known outside teachers like Magaloff, Badura-Skoda, and others, and also to give the students a chance to perform with good orchestras and to give major recitals. But in reality, there isn't enough money for the course, there aren't many foreign teachers involved, and if you get to play with an orchestra it is often a very bad one. So you see, there are many things that need changing in the famous Conservatoire de Paris!

From all you say, I think you'd make a wonderful teacher. Have you thought about it?

J-PC: Yes, I'd like to teach someday, for a few years. But I know that if I started now, I could not maintain my concert career. Also there is the danger that each year a teacher may care less and less about his students, listen less, and just become bored or boring. But if I were to become a teacher, I would consider it part of my duty to give students insight into the realities of concertizing—always having to play better than the last time, always traveling, always trying to balance old and new repertoire—so that they understand the real challenges and difficulties of the profession today.

● ● ● ●

BRIGITTE ENGERER

. . . was born on 27 October 1952 in Tunis. She studied with Lucette Descaves from an early age, and performed Mozart's Concerto in A (K. 488) at the Théâtre des Champs-Elysées when she was ten. At the Paris Conservatoire she won a first prize in chamber music in the class of Jean Hubeau in 1967 and a first prize in piano in the class of Descaves in 1968. After winning a prize in the Marguerite Long—Jacques Thibaud Competition the following year, she studied with Stanislav Neuhaus at the Moscow Conservatory for five years.

In 1974 she was a prizewinner in the Tchaikovsky Competition, and in 1978 won third prize in the Queen Elisabeth of Belgium Competition. Her international career began in earnest in 1980, when Herbert von Karajan invited her to perform with the Berlin Philharmonic. Since then she has performed throughout the world as recitalist and with major orchestras, including the New York Philharmonic, London Symphony Orchestra, Vienna Symphony, Orchestre de Paris, Los Angeles Philharmonic, Montréal Symphony, and many others. Her recordings for Philips, Melodia, Le Chant du Monde, and Harmonia Mundi include works by

Chopin, Liszt, Schubert, Beethoven, Rachmaninov, and Schumann's *Carnaval* and *Faschingsschwank aus Wien* (Grand Prix du Disque, 1984).

I know that you studied in Moscow for quite a few years, so I am anxious for you to elucidate some of the differences between the French and Russian schools of playing. Could we begin with your studies in France?

BE: My parents had read an article about a Parisian teacher named Lucette Descaves, so when I was five I began studying with her. I entered her class at the Conservatoire when I was ten, and remained there until I was sixteen. I won a prize in the Long–Thibaud Competition in 1969, and then I decided that I should study outside France. I had some lessons with Kurt Neumüller in Salzburg, and it was he who told me of the great Russian pianist and teacher Stanislav Neuhaus, the son of Heinrich Neuhaus [teacher of Richter, Gilels, Malinin, Lupu, and others]. So I studied with Neuhaus for five years, and I must say that I can no longer consider myself a good representative of the French school.

Certainly the French school has some very good characteristics: clarity, transparency, a natural lightness of the fingers — these are excellent for certain music, above all for Debussy and Ravel. Lucette Descaves had been a student of Marguerite Long, so she transmitted that approach. But her assistant had been a student of Lazare-Lévy, who had a very different approach. So sometimes Madame Descaves and her assistant would tell me to do opposite things in the same piece during the same week. The assistant drilled Czerny and Hanon, and advised us to practice each difficult measure in four or five different rhythms, as Cortot advises in his editions. I found this a poor way to spend practice time, numbing the sensations that a musician should have when he sits at the piano. Madame Descaves, I must say, was more flexible, and she never forced me to do things that went against my nature.

Did Neuhaus change your technique when you first went to him?

BE: No, he never said it was necessary to change my technique or to start again at zero. But right from the beginning he started talking often about the importance of the shoulders, because I was playing only with some forearm, not with the shoulder, or back, or lower back. If you play from your back, the arms will be freer. He would illustrate this at one piano and I would observe and copy his movements, and the result was a natural and progressive change in my approach to playing. I remember the first day I went to him, and he said, "Well, what do you want to study?" I showed him a list of works that I wanted to learn, and he said, "All right, come in ten days with two of Liszt's Transcendental Etudes and also the Brahms First Concerto, memorized, to play at two pianos." So I worked liked a crazy woman! Then for the following week he asked me to bring Schubert's "Wanderer" Fantasy, also memorized, of course. Working this way was a bit of a shock for me. Later I learned that he was testing the limits of possibility with me, so that he could understand how I was working at the time I came to him.

As in Paris, the lessons were class lessons, but they were conducted differently. Madame Descaves used to sit next to us and talk with us, but in Moscow the teacher sat at one piano while the student sat far away at another one. Also, Neuhaus's classes were usually open to the public, and other teachers' students would often come to play in them. Can you imagine that happening at Juilliard or at Paris, with the students of Descaves, for example, coming to play in the classes of Sancan or Lefébure? I must say that these open classes were a fantastic experience for the students.

Even at the first lesson on a work, Neuhaus expected an interpretation, a full vision of the work — even when he asked me to bring the Prokofiev Seventh Sonata after I had been practicing it for only eight days. So I had to change my work habits — otherwise I would have had to practice nine hours a day, which might have been physically damaging and certainly would have worked against the flexibility of the muscles.

Brigitte Engerer

How would you describe his approach to teaching?

BE: It was really comprehensive. He thought that technique alone was nothing, that the really important thing was to understand a work completely and profoundly, to really love it and not just be able to explain it. He wanted you to study a major work for a very long time, six months or more, to really penetrate it to the core – not just to be able to play it. I remember that a student once told him that he didn't like Chopin's Ballade in F Minor, and Neuhaus said, "Maybe it's the Ballade that doesn't like *you*!" And he was right. It's not possible to love something that you don't understand.

Technically, as I said earlier, there was a real emphasis on the use of the upper torso. Articulation in the the Russian school is not done just with the fingers and wrists, but also very much with the arm. Even in arpeggios, a single arm movement, in effect, does the playing. But for him there was not just one technique. You had to be able to change your technique, sometimes radically, depending on whether you were playing Beethoven, or Chopin, Prokofiev, or whatever. The same muscles can't be used in the same ways for different types of works and composers. He made it clear that a pianist needs to develop many, many kinds of attacks. You need two or three hours to think about these things just to be able to play well the first page of Chopin's Sonata in B Minor. What he urged on us was a kind of "global vision" of all the possibilities of sound.

In fact, I would say that the primary lesson of Neuhaus had to do with sound. To take a very simple, almost idiotic, example: in romantic music, when you see *forte* it is necessary that you play *less* than that with the left hand, otherwise the balance will be off. The left hand will just be noisy if it equals the right hand. The idea seems so simple and obvious, yet Neuhaus had to tell this to each new pianist who came to him, whether from Czechoslovakia, Poland, Italy, Germany, or wherever. He would often petrify students because he would do imitations of their playing, exaggerating the bad aspects, and then he'd say, "Now I would prefer to hear it like *this*," and it would be wonderful. I think teaching by imitation is valid. Certainly, throughout history painters have learned technique by copying their masters until they found their own style.

I remember seeing Richter play often with raised shoulders. Was this a Neuhaus trait?

BE: Yes, Stanislav Neuhaus sometimes would lift up his right shoulder to vibrate a sound, and I do it too at times. It is typically Neuhaus. It's like putting pressure on the string of a violin. The idea is to get to the "bottom" of the sound that way, to make it vibrate more. I think it does more visually or psychologically than physically. But Richter always remains relaxed and supple when he plays — otherwise he couldn't practice hours and hours every day like he does. I think that when you understand what you want to do musically, and then think about what the right gestures should be, then most of the problems get solved rather quickly. Often it is a question of liberating the forearm. I remember getting quite stiff in the forearm when I first worked on Ravel's *Ondine*, years ago, and I almost had to stop playing for two months. I later had to learn what was physically right for me to do in that piece.

What other aspects of Neuhaus's teaching were important for you?

BE: He had enormous respect for the text. Although he talked a lot about what he wanted, he rarely marked the music much, just a little breath mark here, or a little stress there, or a little added dynamic sign. Basically he felt that the text should tell you everything you need to know, and his task was simply to make you perceive what the composer wanted. But that opens up an interesting subject. I think that at the time I was studying you might ask a Russian pianist and a French pianist to play the same work with an exact observance of the nuances, and you would get two very different interpretations. They would have started from different understandings of the nuances, because a certain point of view had already been acquired. Maybe today the differences would be less.

From what you say, it seems that Neuhaus did not advocate the kind of dotted-rhythm exercises that one finds in editions by Cortot and others.

BE: No, I don't think that Russian pianists do much of that kind of work. Certainly neither Neuhaus nor his father did. Instead, I think that when you have a difficult passage you must work it with all your head, all your heart, all your intensity, to find why it is difficult, if your fingering is good, if your movements are right for that particular passage, and so on. And when you find the answers to these questions, then you practice slowly and progessively faster, thirty, forty times. There is a story that a neighbor once heard Richter practicing a particular passage from the finale of Prokofiev's Seventh Sonata fifty times a day for three consecutive days. Finally the neighbor said, "I can't stand it any more! Hasn't he gotten beyond the problem by now?" Obviously we must *always* go beyond the problem. It's not enough to practice a passage five or six times, each time faster, and then think that you have it for life.

Heinrich Neuhaus makes a nice analogy in his book [on page 3] between how to work and how to boil water. You must put the kettle on the stove and *leave* it there until the water boils. If you take it off before then, to go do something else, then the water will cool down and you will have to start all over again. I think of this analogy often when I am practicing.

I have heard some of Heinrich Neuhaus's recordings of Bach and Beethoven . . . .

BE: His recording of the Sonata, Op. 27, No. 2 is really wonderful. He had a sense of sonority that was rare.

Also I have Stanislav's recording of the two Chopin Sonatas, which I think was done live ....

BE: Yes, that was issued after his death. He never liked the microphone, and he would play differently at a concert if he knew a microphone was there.

Did you study with Neuhaus some of the works that you've recorded?

BE: Yes, the "Wanderer" Fantasy, but not *Faschingsschwank aus Wien*, which I learned on my own, as well as the Schubert-Liszt transcriptions. Do you know Vladimir Sofronitzky's recording of them? He was a fantastic pianist who really made the piano speak. Some pianists make the piano play, but Sofronitzky was one who could make it speak. This was also Stanislav Neuhaus's ability. Neuhaus wasn't just a "professor of piano." He felt that it was necessary to know all instruments in order to teach one, and to be able to understand orchestral colors. He also talked a lot about architecture, painting, literature, poetry, and the theatre. He thought that interpretation of a musical work should be like directing a play, with a moment of silence here, a quicker movement there, and so on. And in romantic works he asked us to look for moments that were equivalent to crying, laughing, or whatever emotions seemed appropriate. We needed to be able to identify both the most dramatic moment and the calmest moment in a work, so that the drama would be complete.

Rachmaninov said the same thing, that one should always make clear where the big moment is in each work — *the emotional or structural highpoint.*

BE: Yes, and that is especially difficult to do in Rachmaninov's own music! Think of the Third Concerto. Maybe it is easier to find *the* big moment in a piece by Chopin or Brahms .... Structure, sound, and the character of the music were very important to Neuhaus. Among French pianists, I think that maybe only Cortot and Samson François put such a strong emphasis on sound. François was a fantastic pianist — on most days. A real romantic. He had a magical presence when he played in public. From the moment he sat down, you were enveloped by the richness of his sound, and its gentleness. Hardly any of that is captured on his recordings. But when you heard him in a concert, he could make you forget where you were, what day it was, who you were sitting with . . . . I remember being so mesmerized after one of his recitals that a friend ran up to me in horror and said, "Oh, my dear, you look terrible! What has happened?!" *That* was the effect of Samson François on a good night . . . .

V. CODA: THE FRENCH SCHOOL, PAST AND PRESENT

A national school of playing can develop when a country's leading composers, performers, teachers, and instrument makers hold common aesthetics and are able to influence one another. We have seen that in France these circumstances allowed a distinctive pianistic style to develop during the 150-year period from the time of Louis Adam and his students, circa 1810, to that of Marguerite Long and her students, circa 1960. Some of the attributes of that style — clarity, precision, restraint, and technical finish — have been discussed earlier. Here we might reach a fuller understanding of the nature of this style by quoting some French musicians on the subjects of French music and the characteristics of the French people.

Marguerite Long has described the French school in this way:

> In spite of the diverse temperaments of our great virtuosos, one can observe certain common features among them. Pianists as different as Planté, Diémer, Pugno, Risler, Saint-Saëns, and Delaborde were united by an innate kinship of technique and style made up of clarity, ease, moderation, elegance, and tact. French playing is lucid, precise, and slender. If it concentrates above all on grace rather than force, preserving especially its equilibrium and sense of proportion, it does not bow to any other in its power, profundity, and inner emotion.[54]

Claude Debussy found a model in Rameau:

> We have . . . a purely French tradition in the [operatic] works of Rameau. They combine delicate and charming tenderness, exact tones, and strict declamation of the recitatives, without any affected German profundity, over-emphasis, or exhausting explanation . . . . For too long French music has been following paths that

led away from the clarity of expression and conciseness and precision of form that are the very particular qualities of French genius.[55]

The critic Romain Rolland wrote of *Pelléas et Melisande*:

One understands only too well the revolt of the French mind, in the name of naturalness and good taste, against exaggerations and extremes of passion. . . . [Debussy's orchestration] is as sober and polished as a fine classic phrase of the latter part of the seventeenth century. . . . Like the impressionist painters of today, he paints with primary colors, but with a delicate moderation that rejects anything harsh as if it were something unseemly.[56]

The noted baritone Pierre Bernac wrote:

In the French *mélodie* the singer and pianist must succeed in combining precision with lyricism. But it must be controlled lyricism, for just as the French composer never gives way to sentimentality or emphasis and abominates overstatement, so in the same way his interpreters must have a sense of moderation of expression, a critical capacity, which after all is no more than one of the most vigorous forms of intelligence. There can be no doubt that it is easier for performers to give themselves up to the sentimental outpourings of German music and poetry than to re-create the subtle poetic climate, the intellectual refinement and the controlled profundity of French music and poetry.[57]

The pianist E. Robert Schmitz stated:

I suppose [my method] can be called a "French Method" because I am French and have born within me every Frenchman's natural admiration for clarity of design, precision, and logical exactness. . . .I may say that the French love for exactness differs from the German, in that it is less massively concrete, and more logical, clearer, and easier to understand. I may say, further, that these are the qualities which distinguish the "French School" of piano playing, of singing, of composition, of art – of anything at all that has its roots in a French mind and heart.[58]

French musicians have sometimes been accused of having more skill than original artistic talent. The British pianist Harold Bauer, who for a number of years was invited to judge the Conservatoire's competitions, attributed this to the "insistence on technical proficiency that stems from French academic tradition."[59] We might go further and point out that the French conservatory system is unique in requiring a student to work with two different teachers each week. One, the assistant, primarily teaches technique; the other, the main teacher, primarily teaches interpretation. The French system, more than any other, seems to have been built on the supposition that technique and interpretation can be separated.

We have observed earlier how closed and rigorous the French system of musical education has been. The fact that the teaching of Liszt, Anton Rubinstein, and Leschetizky had remarkably little impact in France is accounted for by the Conservatoire's ingrown system, which guaranteed adherence to its own methods of teaching. By and large, the approaches of these foreign masters – based mainly on the German and Russian repertoire and on the advances made by German piano manufacturers – were seen as irrelevant to French music-making. This self-satisfied attitude carried over into piano manufacturing. Even after 1900 French piano makers continued to produce weak-toned, salon-style instruments that failed to reflect the changes in performance style, composition, and teaching that were taking place in the rest of the world. Thus, at the time of his 1904 Paris debut, Arthur Rubinstein failed to find an Erard, Pleyel, or Gaveau piano that was not "tinny" or "weak" compared with his favored Bechstein.[60]

By the 1920s, however, some of the ideals and methods of the old French school were modified or rejected by such major pianists as Risler, Cortot, Lazare-Lévy, Selva, Nat, and Ciampi, who all favored a greater use of arm weight and a more serious – and more Germanic – repertoire than did many French pianists of the time. Nevertheless, it was still an isolated event when a French pianist played one of the virtuosic concertos of Brahms, Tchaikovsky, or Rachmaninov. One can single out Roger-Miclos's performances of the Tchaikovsky First Concerto in 1898, Pugno's of the Rachmaninov Second in 1906, and Cortot's of the Rachmaninov Third in 1920. The Brahms Second did not have an outstanding French champion until Robert Casadesus in the 1930s. (The first French pianist to record concertos by Tchaikovsky, Rachmaninov, and Brahms was Monique de la Bruchollerie, in the 1950s. These discs reveal an always efficient and sometimes coloristic artist, but one lacking in sufficient personality, large sonority, and architectural projection for these works.)

The decline of the old French school dates from the postwar period, when new horizons were opened up through recordings, television, radio broadcasts, international competitions, and the increased ease and speed of travel. During the 1950s and 60s many of the top prizewinners in the Marguerite Long—Jacques Thibaud Competition were Soviet artists, including Eugeny Malinin, Dmitri Bashkirov, Igor Zhukov, Victor Eresco, Elisabeth Leonskaya, and Dmitri Alexeev. Their styles naturally affected the thinking of young French musicians. Also during these same decades numerous French pianists sought instruction with foreign artists after completing their studies at the Conservatoire: Gérard Frémy in Moscow with Heinrich Neuhaus, André Krust in France with the Russian émigré Pierre Kostanoff, Evelyne Crochet in Switzerland with Edwin Fischer, Eric Heidsieck and Michèle Boegner in Italy with Wilhelm Kempff, Marie-Françoise Bucquet in Austria with Edward Steuermann, Marylène Dosse in Austria with Alfred Brendel and Paul Badura-Skoda, Dominique Merlet in Switzerland with Louis Hiltbrand, Thérèse Dussaut in Germany with the Russian émigré Vladimir Horbowski, Pascal Rogé in Paris with the American pianist Julius Katchen, Brigitte Engerer in Moscow with Stanislav Neuhaus, and so on.

Two of the most influential postwar Conservatoire teachers have been Pierre Sancan and Dominique Merlet. As we have seen, Sancan devised a very successful personal approach that was based on a close study of musculature, Russian pedagogy, and the writings of Marie Jaëll. Merlet, who has taught at the Conservatoire longer than any other current teacher and whose students are among the most impressive of the younger generation, summed up his approach in an interview with the author:

> My study at the Conservatoire was with Jean Doyen, who placed a
> great emphasis on articulation. This was good training, but I then
> decided I should study in Switzerland with Louis Hiltbrand – and
> in three months he changed my playing in amazing ways.
> Hiltbrand viewed the fingers as an extension of the arms, and em-
> phasized three important things: relaxation and elasticity in the
> hand, a perfect legato, and the cultivation of a beautiful, warm
> sound. This was a different approach from the old French one, in
> which the fingers were often conditioned like automatons.
> Hiltbrand's approach was related to some Russian ideas that I
> later picked up from a colleague who studied with Kostanoff, who
> talked a great deal about weight, arm technique, and prona-
> tion/supination.[61] I try to include all these facets in my teaching.
> Arms, wrists, and shoulders are just as important as fingers. I find
> that too much emphasis on fingers often leads to locked
> shoulders. I advocate practicing a sliding finger technique, in
> which the muscles pull the finger from the middle of the
> depressed key out toward the edge – and also from the middle of
> the key in toward the fall-board. This technique [also used by
> Kalkbrenner, Selva, Debussy, and many Russian pianists] is the op-
> posite of the fast, high, straight-into-the-key approach. For dif-
> ficult passages, I think that practicing with rhythmic variants is
> beneficial, but always rather slowly and melodically, not with ac-
> cents and over-dotting. I am also cautious about using too many
> exercises with held notes. I believe in both slow and fast practice.
> Working slowly allows you to perfectly control the sound and to
> test your memory; working at a fast tempo teaches you which mo-
> tions are or are not useful.

Another influential French pedagogue is Jeannine Vieuxtemps, who studied with Nat and Sancan and has taught at the Conservatoire as the assistant of Bruchollerie, Lefébure, Barbizet, and Merlet. In her recent book[62] Vieuxtemps gives a series of detailed exercises designed to replace those of Czerny, Hanon, and Philipp, which she regards as stylistically and pedagogically antiquated, needlessly lengthy, and possibly leading to stiff muscles (due to much repetition) or locked wrists (due to held notes). Her exercises include: the movement of the fingers in relation to a stable hand; a combined hand and finger movement; a combined hand and forearm movement; the movement of the hand in relation to a fixed forearm; sliding each finger in and out on the keys; a sliding motion of the entire forearm into the key; rotation of the forearm and hand; and lateral movement of the hand and forearm. These are followed by finger exercises using various intervals and double-notes, and arm exercises using octaves and chords. Vieuxtemps's thorough discussion of the necessary involvement of the upper torso represents a remarkable departure from traditional French teaching and again illustrates the current influence of foreign, and especially Russian, pedagogy.

Since the early nineteenth century the Conservatoire has drawn its professors from among its most brilliant former students. During the postwar years, however, several noted teachers were appointed who had not received their principal training at the Conservatoire: Reine Gianoli, who studied with Cortot at the Ecole Normale and with Nat and Edwin Fischer privately; Aldo Ciccolini, who graduated from the Naples Conservatory under Busoni's pupil Paolo Denza; and Ventsislav Yankoff, who studied mainly in Berlin under Carl Adolf Martienssen and Wilhelm Kempff. Some postwar professors who studied outside France after graduating from the Conservatoire were: Aline van Barentzen, who studied in Vienna with Leschetizky; Raymond Trouard, who studied in Vienna with Emil von Sauer; and Monique Haas, who studied in Switzerland with Rudolf Serkin.

The current (1991) piano professors at the Conservatoire are: Michel Béroff, Gérard Frémy, Jean-François Heisser, Dominique Merlet, Theodore Paraskivesco, Jean-Claude Pennetier, Bruno Rigutto, Jacques Rouvier, Gabriel Tacchino, and Ventsislav Yankoff. The background of this unusually young faculty is more diverse than that of any group of piano professors at the Conservatoire before 1945. It reflects not only the teaching of the old French school but also the pedagogy of Ciampi, Descaves, Lefébure, Perlemuter, and Sancan—as well as the foreign influences of Neuhaus and Hiltbrand.[63]

Today, one of the most tradition-bound conservatories in the world has moved to a new "Corbusier-style" complex in a remote part of Paris, away from the mainstream of musical activity. Its new director (since December 1991) is the organist and composer Xavier Darasse, who has a number of changes in mind, including a greater emphasis on music history, contemporary music, and master classes. In an interview after his appointment, Darasse responded to the question of whether or not the French orchestra had died: "The death of the French orchestra is its wish to imitate the sound of foreign orchestras. We have our own character, our own sound, or own personality. We must guard them and defend them."[64]

This statement is curious in light of the fact that French orchestras have been losing their "national" sound, character, and personality ever since the late 1960s, with the creation of the Orchestre de Paris and its succession of foreign music directors: Herbert von Karajan, Sir Georg Solti, Daniel Barenboim, and Semyon Bychkov. That a similar process of "homogenization" has affected French pianism is evident from the fact that Jean-Yves Thibaudet, a thirty-year-old pianist trained entirely in France, was recently chosen to record the complete concertos of Rachmaninov with the Cleveland Orchestra conducted by Vladimir Ashkenazy. Thibaudet is the first French pianist to have been invited to record this cycle with a Russian-born and Russian-trained conductor.

Another young French-trained pianist, Cyprien Katsaris, summed up his generation's outlook in an interview with the author:

> The Russian school of playing sometimes produces a hard sound, with emphasis on arm-weight and not enough refinement of the fingers, while the old French school had a lot of refinement, but sometimes too much emphasis on the fingers. The current combination of the French and Russian schools is a very important trend here in France. Although the old French school doesn't exist anymore, I think that France today has the highest rate of excellent pianists in Europe, in proportion to the population.

It is certainly true that in the leading international competitions held between 1955 and 1985, pianists from France won more top prizes than pianists from any country except the Soviet Union and the United States. This is a remarkable achievement, given the relatively small size of France's population, and it is a sure indication that the Conservatoire has not been as dormant during the postwar period as some of its critics have maintained. Of the French pianists born since 1950, particularly interesting and distinctive playing has been heard from Philippe Bianconi, Laurent Cabasso, Michel Dalberto, Pascal Devoyon, François-René Duchâble, Brigitte Engerer, Hélène Grimaud, Cyprien Katsaris, Katia and Marielle Labèque, Jean-Marc Luisada, Pascal Rogé, and Jean-Yves Thibaudet. It is almost certain that in the years to come some of these performers will have changed our ideas of French pianism just as Risler, Cortot, Lazare-Lévy, Selva, Nat, and Ciampi did during the first decades of this century.

APPENDIX I
BIOGRAPHIES OF INTERVIEWEES

*(Note: Only the biographies of interviewees
quoted in the text are given below.)*

JEAN-JOËL BARBIER: see Chapter IV.

PIERRE BARBIZET: see Chapter IV.

JACQUELINE BLANCARD, born in Paris in 1909, received a first medal
at the Conservatoire in 1923 in Joseph Morpain's preparatory class.
She then studied with Isidor Philipp, winning a first prize in his class
in 1926. She has performed throughout the world as soloist and with
numerous orchestras and chamber musicians. She was the first pianist
to record Ravel's Concerto for the Left Hand (1938, with Charles
Munch conducting). In 1948 she made an acclaimed debut in the
United States, playing three Mozart concertos in New York's Town
Hall. She currently resides in Geneva.

GABY CASADESUS: see Chapter IV.

FRANCE CLIDAT, born in Nantes in 1932, studied at the Conservatoire
with Lazare-Lévy from 1948 to 1950, in which year she won a first prize.
A specialist in the works of Liszt, she made a prize-winning series of
24 LPs of his music for Véga Records. Her recorded repertoire also
includes the complete works of Satie and the Rachmaninov Third Concerto. She lives in Paris, where she teaches at the Ecole Normale de
Musique.

JEAN-PHILIPPE COLLARD: see Chapter IV.

EVELYNE CROCHET, born in 1934, won a first prize in Yvonne Lefébure's class at the Conservatoire in 1954. She later studied with Edwin Fischer and Rudolf Serkin. Her American debut was as partner to Francis Poulenc in the American première of his Two-Piano Concerto, with the Boston Symphony Orchestra under Charles Munch. Among her recordings are the complete solo works of Fauré. She has taught at Brandeis University, New England Conservatory, and Rutgers University. She makes her home in New York City.

JEANNE-MARIE DARRÉ, born in Givet in 1905, won a first medal in Marguerite Long's preparatory class at the Conservatoire in 1917 and a first prize in Isidor Philipp's class in 1919. She later continued her study with Philipp privately. In 1926 she performed all five concertos by Saint-Saëns in one evening, with Paul Paray conducting the Lamoureux Orchestra. This event launched a distinguished international career. In 1958 she was appointed professor at the Conservatoire, and in 1962 she made an acclaimed New York recital debut. Her students have included Chantal de Buchy, Marylène Dosse, Jacques Gauthier, Raymond Jackson, Maria de la Pau, Françoise Regnat, and Ilana Vered. She currently lives in Paris.

MARYLÈNE DOSSE, born in 1939, won a first prize at the Paris Conservatoire in 1960 in the class of Jeanne-Marie Darré. She also studied piano and chamber music with Jacques Février. After winning prizes in competitions in Salzburg and Naples, she came to the United States as assistant to Paul Badura-Skoda. She has toured extensively and made a number of recordings, including the complete solo works of Saint-Saëns for Vox. She is the pianist of the Castalia Trio and presently resides in State College, Pennsylvania, where she is a professor of piano at Pennsylvania State University.

THÉRÈSE DUSSAUT, born in Versailles in 1939, studied with Rose-Aye Lejour and Marguerite Long for five years and won a first prize at the Conservatoire in the class of Jean Doyen in 1952. She then studied in Stuttgart with Vladimir Horbowski and in Geneva with Louis Hiltbrand. In 1956 she won first prize in the Munich Competition. Subsequently she studied with Pierre Sancan and Eugeny Malinen. She has performed on several world tours and recorded the complete keyboard works of Rameau and major works by Debussy, Ravel, and Schumann. She presently lives in Paris and teaches a *classe de perfectionnement* at the Toulouse Conservatory.

BRIGITTE ENGERER: see Chapter IV.

PHILIPPE ENTREMONT, born in Reims in 1934, studied with Marguerite Long and her assistant Rose-Aye Lejour from 1944 to 1946, and privately with Long in 1949, the year he won a first prize at the Conservatoire in the class of Jean Doyen. In 1953 he received the highest prize in the Marguerite Long—Jacques Thibaud Competition, and in 1954 made his debut in the United States. He has made dozens of recordings, both as pianist and conductor. He currently lives in Vienna, where he is conductor of the Vienna Chamber Orchestra.

DANIEL ERICOURT, born in Jossigny in 1903, received a first medal in the preparatory class of Georges Falkenberg in 1915 and a first prize in the class of Santiago Riera in 1919. Additional studies were with Jean-Jules Roger-Ducasse and Nadia Boulanger. In 1924 he won the Prix Diémer. His orchestral debut was at the Concerts Colonne, with Gabriel Pierné conducting. He settled in the United States, and from 1957 to 1963 taught at the Peabody Conservatory. He currently resides and teaches in Greensboro, North Carolina.

LÉLIA GOUSSEAU, born in Paris in 1909, studied with Madame Giraud-Latarse before entering the Conservatoire, where she won a first prize in the class of Lazare-Lévy in 1925. Subsequently she won the Prix Pagès, the Prix Roussel, and a prize in the 1937 Chopin Competition in Warsaw. Her international career began after the war and included performances in 1952 with the Boston Symphony, New York Philharmonic, and Philadelphia Orchestra. She was a professor of piano at the Conservatoire from 1961 to 1978. Her students have included Haakon Austbö, Pascal Devoyon, Anne Queffélec, and Alain Raës. She lives in Paris.

MONIQUE HAAS, born in Paris in 1909, won a first medal at the Conservatoire in the preparatory class of Joseph Morpain in 1922 and a first prize in the class of Lazare-Lévy in 1927. She also studied in Switzerland with Rudolf Serkin and in Paris with Robert Casadesus. During an illustrious career she performed and recorded with such leading musicians as Georges Enesco, Paul Hindemith, Igor Stravinsky, Paul Paray, Ferenc Fricsay, Eugen Jochum, and Pierre Fournier. Her recording of Debussy's *Douze Etudes* won the *Grand Prix du Disque* in 1954. She made her New York debut in 1960 with Charles Munch and the Boston Symphony Orchestra, playing Ravel's Concerto for the Left Hand and Mozart's Concerto in D Minor. She taught at the Conservatoire from 1968 to 1970. She was the dedicatee of Milhaud's Second Sonata and works by Florent Schmitt and Marcel Mihalovici. She died in Paris on 9 June 1987.

ERIC HEIDSIECK, born in Reims in 1936, studied at the Ecole Normale with Alfred Cortot and his assistant Blanche Bascourret de Guéraldi from 1944 to 1952. After winning a first prize at the Conservatoire in the class of Marcel Ciampi in 1954, he studied privately with Cortot and Wilhelm Kempff. In 1969 he recorded Beethoven's thirty-two sonatas for EMI and also performed the complete cycle in Paris. His Mozart and Fauré recordings have won the *Grand Prix du Disque*. He resides in Paris and is professor of piano at the Conservatoire National Supérieur de Lyon.

CLAUDE HELFFER, born in Paris in 1922, studied privately with Robert Casadesus and did theoretical work with René Leibowitz. A specialist in twentieth-century music, he has premiered major works by Amy, Boucourechliev, Jolas, Xenakis, and others. His recordings include works by Barraqué, Bartók, Debussy, Prokofiev, Ravel, and Schoenberg. During his 1966 tour of the United States he played four concertos with the Chicago Symphony under Jean Martinon. He has given courses in interpretation in Paris and Aspen, and his students have included Suzanne Fournier and Louis-Philippe Pelletier. He lives in Paris.

NICOLE HENRIOT-SCHWEITZER, born in Paris in 1923, won a first prize in Marguerite Long's class at the Conservatoire in 1938. Since the war she has performed throughout Europe and North and South America. She made her debut in the United States in 1948, with Charles Munch and the New York Philharmonic. She taught at the Liège Conservatory from 1970 to 1973, and more recently at the Brussels Conservatory. She presently resides in Louveciennes, near Paris.

JEAN HUBEAU, born in Paris in 1917, studied composition with Paul Dukas and received a first prize in piano at the Conservatoire in the class of Lazare-Lévy in 1930. He also studied conducting with Felix Wiengartner in Vienna, and for a time was director of the Versailles Conservatory. In 1957 he was appointed professor of chamber music at the Paris Conservatoire. He has performed and recorded with numerous artists, including Pierre Fournier, André Navarra, Paul Tortelier, and the Via Nova Quartet. He lives in Paris.

CHRISTIAN IVALDI, born in Paris in 1938, began his piano studies with Lucette Descaves and won a first prize at the Conservatoire in the class of Aline van Barentzen. Today he is one of the most active accompanists and chamber musicians in France, and has performed and recorded with numerous artists, including Salvatore Accardo, Boris Christoff, Régine Crespin, Michel Debost, Hughes Cuénod, Geneviève Joy, Gérard Souzay, and Rita Streich. He lives in Paris, where has taught at the Conservatoire since 1969, first as professor of sight reading and currently as professor of chamber music.

GRANT JOHANNESEN: see Chapter IV.

ROY JOHNSON, born in Beckley, West Virginia, in 1929, studied privately with Walter Bright and received the Artist Diploma and Doctor of Musical Arts degree from the Eastman School of Music, where he studied with Sandor Vas. In 1952 and 1953 he studied in Paris on a Fulbright fellowship with Yves Nat. His recordings include John Powell's *Sonate psychologique* and *Sonata Teutonica* and works by Balakirev, Scriabin, and John Pozdro. He taught at the University of Kansas from 1954 to 1965, and at the University of Maryland from 1965 to 1991. He presently resides and teaches privately in College Park, Maryland.

GENEVIÈVE JOY, born in Bernaville in 1919, studied at the Paris Conservatoire with Yves Nat, receiving a first prize in 1941. In 1944 she was appointed choral conductor for the Orchestre National, and in the same year she formed with Jacqueline Robin a very active piano duo. From 1962 to 1966 she taught chamber music at the Ecole Normale in Paris, after which she succeeded Jacques Février as professor of chamber music at the Conservatoire. She has premiered a number of important works, including the *Sonate* by her husband, Henri Dutilleux. She makes her home in Paris.

CYPRIEN KATSARIS, born in Marseille in 1951, studied at the Paris Conservatoire with Aline van Barentzen and Monique de la Bruchollerie, winning a first prize in 1969. He won the Prix Roussel in 1970, and prizes in the 1972 Queen Elisabeth of Belgium Competition and the 1974 Cziffra Competition. He has performed with leading orchestras throughout the world and recorded a large repertoire, including Liszt's transcriptions of the nine Beethoven symphonies. He resides in Paris.

ANDRÉ KRUST, born in Belfort in 1926, studied at the Paris Conservatoire with Jean Doyen, winning a second prize in 1950. He then worked with Yves Nat and Pierre Kostanoff, and won a prize in the Franz Liszt Competition in Budapest in 1956. He has taught at the conservatories of Amiens and Montreuil, at the University of Ottawa, and at the Luxembourg Conservatory. He presently lives in Aulnay-sous-Bois, near Paris.

FERNANDO LAIRES, born in Lisbon in 1925, received a diploma from the National Conservatory (Portugal) after study with Lucio Mendes and Winfried Wolf. In 1944 he performed Beethoven's thirty-two sonatas in Lisbon. He then worked privately in New York with Ernest Hutcheson and James Friskin, but primarily with Philipp from 1947 to 1949. He has performed throughout the world since 1950, and is the recipient of the Harriet Cohen Award. A co-founder of the American Liszt Society, he has taught at the University of Texas at Austin, Peabody Conservatory, and The Catholic University of America. He presently resides in Rochester, New York.

MONIQUE LEDUC, born in Asnières in 1927, studied in the preparatory and advanced classes of Armand Ferté, receiving her first prize in 1946. She took up permanent residence in the United States after the war, and has performed regularly since, notably with the pianist Charles Engel, with whom she formed a duo in 1969. She has taught at the Philadelphia Settlement School and at Temple University. She now makes her home in Tijeras, New Mexico.

YVONNE LEFÉBURE: see Chapter III.

DAVID LIVELY, born in Ironto, Ohio, in 1953, studied in St. Louis with Gail Delente and at the Ecole Normale in Paris with Jules Gentil. He was a prize-winner in a number of important competitions, including the 1971 Marguerite Long—Jacques Thibaud, the 1971 Geneva, the 1972 Queen Elisabeth of Belgium, the 1974 Tchaikovsky, and the 1977 Dino Ciani. His recordings include the major works of Copland, the Busoni Concerto, Fauré's thirteen nocturnes, and works by Prokofiev, Ravel, and Stravinsky. He lives in Paris and directs the Festival de Saint-Lizier.

YVONNE LORIOD, born in Houilles in 1928, worked first with her god-mother, Madame Sivade, who had been Lazare-Lévy's assistant. She then studied at the Conservatoire with Lazare-Lévy for two years, but his tenure there was interrupted during the war, causing her to complete her training with Marcel Ciampi, in whose class she won a first prize in 1942. She has championed much modern music, especially the works of Boulez, Jolivet, Barraqué, Schoenberg, and all the piano works of her husband, the late Olivier Messiaen. From 1967 to 1989 she taught at the Paris Conservatoire, where her students included Pierre-Laurent Aimard, Hortense Cartier-Bresson, Michaël Levinas, Roger Murano, and Pierre Reach. She resides in Paris.

PAUL LOYONNET: see Chapter IV.

GUTHRIE LUKE, born in New York City in 1932, studied at the Halifax Conservatory and at Oberlin Conservatory before becoming a regular performer in Alfred Cortot's master classes in Paris, Lausanne, and Siena beginning in 1953. He studied privately with Cortot from 1957 to 1962. Since then he has performed widely in Europe as a soloist and chamber musician. He has taught at the Royal College of Music in London, where he presently resides.

NIKITA MAGALOFF, born in St. Petersburg, Russia, in 1912, began lessons with a pupil of Leopold Godowsky. When his family moved to Paris, he studied with Isidor Philipp's assistant, Hélène Chaumont, before entering Philipp's class at the Conservatoire, where he won a first prize in 1929. He has performed throughout the world, including cycles of the complete works of Chopin, and has recorded a vast repertoire. He has taught regular summer master classes at the Geneva Conservatory, the Accademia Chigiana in Siena, and at Taormina. He lives in Switzerland, near Vevey.

BARBARA ENGLISH MARIS, born in Granite City, Illinois, c. 1937, studied with Rudolph Ganz, Joseph Battista, and Soulima Stravinsky prior to working with Jules Gentil at the Ecole Normale in Paris in 1958 and 1959, on a Fulbright fellowship. She later received her Doctor of Musical Arts degree from Peabody Conservatory, where she studied with Walter Hautzig. She has performed widely, and is professor of piano and piano pedagogy at The Catholic University of America, in Washington, D.C. She resides in Hyattsville, Maryland.

DOMINIQUE MERLET, born in Bordeaux in 1938, studied first in his native city and then with Jean Doyen at the Paris Conservatoire, where he won a first prize in 1956. In 1957 he studied in Switzerland with Louis Hiltbrand and won first prize in the Geneva Competition. Since then he has performed throughout the world. His Schumann recordings have won two Grands Prix du Disque. He has also been active as the organist at Nôtre-Dame-des-Blancs-Manteaux in Paris since 1956. He was appointed professor at the Paris Conservatoire in 1974, and his students have included Frédéric Aguessy, Philippe Cassard, Cyril Huvé, and Jean-Marc Luisada. He lives in Paris.

MARTHE MORHANGE-MOTCHANE, born in Paris in 1897, studied first with Eva Duménil and then with Alfred Cortot at the Conservatoire, where she won a first prize in 1919. She performed throughout Europe in the 1920s and 30s, and taught at the Ecole Normale from 1921 to 1940, becoming director of the children's department. In 1940 she settled in the United States, where she has since been an active teacher. She has edited works by Rameau, Couperin, Scarlatti, Albeniz, and Ravel, and has published a popular method for beginners, *Le petit clavier*. She presently resides in Montclair, New Jersey.

CÉCILE OUSSET, born in Tarbes in 1936, studied with Marcel Ciampi at the Conservatoire, where she won a first prize in 1950 and the Prix Pagès in 1953. She also won prizes in numerous international competitions, including the Marguerite Long–Jacques Thibaud (1953), the Geneva (1954), the Queen Elisabeth of Belgium (1956), the Busoni (1959), and the Van Cliburn (1962). She has performed throughout the world and recorded a vast repertoire, including concertos of Brahms, Grieg, Liszt, Mendelssohn, Poulenc, Prokofiev, Rachmaninov, Ravel, Schumann, and Tchaikovsky. She lives in Paris.

VLADO PERLEMUTER, born in Kowno, Lithuania (now Kaunas, Poland) in 1904, studied in Paris with Moszkowski and won a first prize in Alfred Cortot's class in 1919. He also studied with Robert Lortat, and privately with Cortot and Ravel, whose complete works he was among the first to perform in public. He has appeared throughout the world as soloist and chamber musician, and his recordings, especially of Ravel and Chopin, have received special recognition. He is the co-author, with Hélène Jourdan-Morhange, of *Ravel According to Ravel*. From 1951 to 1977 he was a leading teacher at the Conservatoire. His students have included Michèle Boegner, Michel Dalberto, Jean-François Heisser, Danielle Laval, Jacques Rouvier, Ilana Vered, and Christian Zacharias. He makes his home in Paris.

JEAN-BERNARD POMMIER, born in Béziers in 1944, studied first with the Russian pedagogue Mina Kosloff, then with Yves Nat, and finally with Pierre Sancan at the Paris Conservatoire, where he received a first prize in 1961. He has had an active international career both as pianist and as conductor, and has given master classes in Tokyo, London, Chicago, and Washington. His recordings include the complete Mozart sonatas and a complete Beethoven cycle (in progress). He currently lives in Switzerland, near Vevey.

PIERRE SANCAN: see Chapter IV.

JEAN-PAUL SEVILLA, born in Algeria in 1934, received a first prize at the Paris Conservatoire in the class of Marcel Ciampi in 1952. He won first prize in the Geneva Competition in 1959 and has toured throughout Europe, Asia, and South America since then, making his debuts in Canada and the United States in 1962. His recordings include works of Roussel and d'Indy. Since 1970 he has been a professor of piano at the University of Ottawa, in which city he resides.

GABRIEL TACCHINO, born in Cannes in 1934, began his studies in Nice and won a first prize at the Paris Conservatoire in the class of Jean Batalla in 1953. He then attended master classes at Marguerite Long's school and worked with her periodically during the late 1950s. He won prizes in the 1953 Viotti Competition, the 1954 Busoni Competition, the 1955 Geneva Competition, and the 1956 Casella Competition. His debut in the United States was with the Boston Symphony Orchestra in 1962. His recordings include the five Saint-Saëns concertos and the complete piano works of Poulenc. He has taught at the Conservatoire since 1975, and presently lives in Sèvres, near Paris.

MAGDA TAGLIAFERRO, born of French parents in 1893 in Petropolis, Brazil, studied at the Paris Conservatoire with Antonin Marmontel, winning a first prize in 1907. She then performed in Alfred Cortot's master classes and often worked privately with him. A brilliant career followed, with appearances throughout the world and recordings that received three *Grands Prix du Disque*. She taught at the Conservatoire from 1937 to 1939. After spending the war years in Brazil, she returned to Paris in 1947 and revived her European career. At the age of ninety she performed acclaimed recitals in Paris, London, New York, and South America. Her students included Vladislav Kedra, Daisy de Luca, Germaine Mounier, Cristina Ortiz, James Tocco, Flavio Varani, and Daniel Varsano. She died in Rio de Janeiro on 9 September 1986.

JEAN-YVES THIBAUDET, born in Lyon in 1961, studied first with Marcelle Herrenschmidt and Suzy Bossard, and then with Lucette Descaves at the Paris Conservatoire, where he won a first prize in 1977. Subsequently he was admitted to the Conservatoire's *cycle de perfectionnement* and studied with Reine Gianoli and Aldo Ciccolini. In 1981 he won the Young Concert Artists Auditions in New York City, as well as first prize in the Tokyo International Competition. He has performed with most of the major orchestras in Europe and the United States, and has recorded solo works by Ravel, Liszt's Concertos in E-flat and A, Messiaen's *Turangalîla-Symphonie,* and numerous chamber works. He currently lives in New York City.

DANIEL WAYENBERG, born in Paris in 1929, studied in The Hague with Ary Verhaar, and then worked privately in Paris with Marguerite

Long periodically from 1947 to 1966. He won second prize in the Marguerite Long—Jacques Thibaud Competition in 1949, and has performed widely since then, including appearances with Dimitri Mitropoulos and the New York Philharmonic in 1953. He has recorded works by Brahms, Gershwin, Jolivet, Rachmaninov, and Ravel. He lives in Mandres-les-Roses, near Paris.

BEVERIDGE WEBSTER, born in Pittsburgh, Pennsylvania in 1908, began lessons with his father, the founder of the Pittsburgh Conservatory. In 1921 his family moved to Paris, where he studied privately with Isidor Philipp until 1924. He then studied in Philipp's class at the Conservatoire, winning a first prize in 1926. He performed widely in Europe before returning to the United States in 1934, in which year he was soloist with the New York Philharmonic and played two recitals at Carnegie Hall. From 1946 to 1990 he was a leading teacher at the Juilliard School, where his students have included William Black, Michel Bloch, Raymond Jackson, Paul Jacobs, Thomas Mastroianni, Thomas Schumacher, and Jeffrey Swann. He resides in Hanover, New Hampshire.

APPENDIX II
SELECTED DISCOGRAPHY

This list is intended to give an overview of recordings by French-trained pianists. Occasionally the most available reissue of a 78 rpm recording is cited, rather than the original issue. For complete discographies of pianists born before 1873, see James Methuen-Campbell, *Catalogue of Recordings by Classical Pianists,* Volume I (Chipping Norton: Disco Epsom, 1984).

All recordings are 33-1/3 rpm, except those for which the following symbols are used:

      *   after the record number signifies: cassette tape
      #   after the record number signifies: 78 rpm recording
  (CD)   after the record number signifies: compact disc

AIMARD, Pierre-Laurent
   Ligeti: *6 Etudes,* Book I; *Trio* (w/ Deleplancque, Le Dizès-Richard). Erato 2292-45366-2 (CD)
   Messiaen: *Quartet for the End of Time* (w/ Le Dizès, Damiens, Strauch). Adda CD-581929 (CD)
D'ARCO, Annie
   Chabrier: Piano works. Calliope 1828/9
   Franck: *Prelude, Chorale & Fugue; Prelude, Aria & Finale.* Calliope CAL 1804
   Mendelssohn: *6 Preludes & Fugues,* Op. 35. Musical Heritage Society MHS 1172
BARBIER, Jean-Joël
   Albeniz: Recital. Accord 200332 (CD)
   Chabrier: Recital. Accord 200312 (CD)
   Satie: Complete piano works. BAM CALB 64/68
   Séverac: Recital. Accord 200322 (CD)

BARBIZET, Pierre
  Beethoven: *Sonatas,* Opp. 10/3, 31/2, 57. Lyrinx CD 106 (CD)
  Brahms: *Violin Sonata,* Op. 100 (w/ Ferras). DGG 415615-4 *
  Chopin: *Rondo* for Two Pianos, Op. 73 (w/ François). EMI 2C 269-10603 *
  Mozart: *Concertos,* K. 467 & 482 (cond. Rampal). BAM LD 078
  Recital (Chabrier, Couperin, Daquin, Debussy, Fauré, Rameau, Ravel Lyrinx). 7907-018/19

BARENTZEN, Aline van
  Beethoven: *Sonatas,* Opp. 53 & 57. Gramophone FALP 199
  Brahms: *Paganini Variations.* Gramophone DB 5181/2 #
  Falla: *Nights in the Gardens of Spain* (cond. Coppola). Victor 9703/5 #
  Mozart: *Sonata,* K. 330. Pathé DTX 197

BENVENUTI, Joseph
  Liszt: *Concerto 1* (cond. Munch). Pathé PDT 49/50 #
  Mozart: *Sonata,* K. 332. Pathé DTX 197
  Ravel: *Trio* (w/ Benedetti, Navarra). Pathé PGT 37/9 #

BÉROFF, Michel
  Debussy: *Preludes & Etudes* (complete). EMI 167-14171/2
  Messiaen: *Vingt Regards sur l'Enfant-Jésus.* Connoisseur Society CS2-2133
  Prokofiev: *5 Concertos* (cond. Masur). EMI C 069-02795 & 02764
  Schumann: *Kreisleriana; Waldszenen.* Connoisseur Society CS 2138
  Stravinsky: *Concerto; Mouvements; Capriccio* (cond. Ozawa). Angel S-36875

BIRET, Idil
  Berlioz-Liszt: *Symphonie fantastique.* Finnadar 9023
  Brahms: *Sonatas 1 & 2.* Naxos 8 550351 (CD)
  Ravel: *Gaspard de la nuit; Miroirs; La Valse.* Price-Less D 13442 (CD)

BLANCARD, Jacqueline
  Debussy: *Etudes 1, 3, 4, 8, 10, 11.* Polydor 27297/9 #
  Mozart: *Sonatas,* K. 281, 570, 283, 545. Decca LXT 2666
  Ravel: *2 Concertos* (cond. Ansermet). London LL 797

Schumann: *8 Novelettes,* Op. 21. London LL 1266

BOEGNER, Michèle

Bach: *Concertos 1, 4, 5* (cond. Hartemann). Calliope 1615 *

Haydn: *Sonatas 38, 42, 48, 50, 53, 54, 58, 60, 62.* Erato 2292-45705-2
(2 CDs)

BOSCHI, Hélène

Mozart: *Concerto,* K. 482 (cond. Klima). Supraphon LPV 205

Schubert: *Sonata* in B-flat (+ Haydn: Sonata in E-flat, Hob.
XVI/49). Artia ALP-708

Schumann, C.: Piano solo works; *Trio* (w/ Jodry, Péclard). Calliope
121112

BOSKOFF, Georges

Liszt: *Transcendental Etude 11.* Gramophone DB 5090 #

Mozart: *Concerto,* K. 459 (cond. Cloez). Columbia G-60025/7 #

BOUKOFF, Yuri

Bach Recital. Bourg BG 3016

Beethoven: *Sonatas,* Opp. 13, 27/2, 57. Philips 412497-4 PB *

Liszt: *2 Concertos* (cond. Somogyi). Cassette 412292-4 *

BOYNET, Emma

Fauré: *6 Nocturnes.* Vox PL 7520

Fauré: *Quintet 1* (w/ Gordon Qt.). Schirmer set 9 #

Weber: *Rondo,* Op. 62. Pathé PAT 2 #

Recital (Albeniz, Falla, Granados). Vox VIP 45.500

BRUCHOLLERIE, Monique de la

Brahms: *Concerto 2* (cond. Reinhardt). Vox PL-7950

Mozart: *Concertos,* K. 466 & 488 (cond. Paumgartner). Nonesuch H
71072

Rachmaninov: *Rhapsody on a Theme by Paganini* (+ Franck: *Symphonic Variations,* cond. Perlea). Vox 9750

Saint-Saëns: *Toccata.* Gramophone DA 1888 #

Tchaikovsky: *Concerto 1* (cond. Moralt). Vox H-4954V

BRUNHOFF, Thierry de

Chopin: *20 Nocturnes.* 2-Pantheon D-22727 (CD)

Chopin: *Preludes,* Op. 28. Price-Less D 12160 (CD)

Schumann: *Humoreske; Davidsbundlertänze.* Pathé DTX 338

Weber Recital. Angel EAC-70030

CASADESUS, Gaby

R. Casadesus: *Sonata 4; Etudes,* Op. 28. Columbia M 33505

Debussy: *Pour le Piano* (+ Fauré: *Fantasy,* cond. Bigot). Vox PL 1780

Fauré: *Dolly* (+ Debussy: *Petite Suite;* Chabrier: *Trois Valses romantiques;* Satie: *Trois morceaux en forme de poire,* w/ R. Casadesus). Columbia ML 5723

Fauré: *Ballade* (cond. Rosenthal). Vox PL 6450

Fauré: *Violin Sonata 2* (w/ Guilet); *Quartet 1* (w/ Guilet Qt). Concerteum CPL-197

Mozart: *Sonata* for Two Pianos, K. 448; *Variations,* K. 501 (+ Schubert: *Fantasy; Andantino Varié,* w/ R. Casadesus). Columbia ML 5046

Saint-Saëns: *Carnival of the Animals; Variations on a Theme by Beethoven,* Op. 35; *Polonaise,* Op. 77 (w/ Entremont). CBS 76735

CASADESUS, Jean

Bach: *Concertos 1 & 5* (cond. Vandernoot); *Toccata* in C Minor. Columbia FCX 548

Chabrier: *Bourrée fantasque; Pièces pittoresques; Cinq morceaux pour piano; Impromptu.* Sony MPK 46729 (CD)

Debussy: *Preludes,* Book I. RCA Victor LSC 2415

CASADESUS, Robert

Beethoven: *Concertos 1 & 4* (cond. Van Beinum). Columbia MS 6111

Beethoven: *Sonatas,* Opp. 27/2, 57, 78, 81a. Columbia ML 5233

Chopin: *Sonata,* Op. 58 (+ Mozart: *Sonata,* K. 332; Haydn: *Sonata* in A-flat). CBS 72386

Brahms: 3 *Violin Sonatas* (rec. live w/ Francescatti). CLC-3 (CD)

Debussy: *Estampes, 6 Images, Masques, L'Isle joyeuse.* CBS 1500

Mozart: *Concertos,* K. 537 and 595 (cond. Szell). Columbia MS 6403

Mozart: *Concerto* for Two Pianos (w/ G. Casadesus); *Concerto* for Three Pianos (w/ G. and J. Casadesus, cond. Ormandy). Sony MPK 46736 (CD)

Rameau: 4 Pieces (+ Scarlatti: 6 *Sonatas*). Columbia ML 4695

Ravel: Complete solo works; works for four-hands (w/ G.
Casadesus), Columbia ML 4518/20

Saint-Saëns: *Concerto 4* (+ Fauré: *Ballade,* cond. Bernstein). Columbia ML 5777

Schumann: *Papillons, Waldszenen, Etudes Symphoniques.* Columbia
ML 5642

CASELLA, Alfredo

Beethoven: *Trio,* Op. 70/1 (+ Harris: *Trio;* Schubert: *Sonata* [Trio],
D. 28; Casella: *Concerto* for Violin, Cello & Piano, w/ Poltronieri
& Bonucci, cond. Koussevitzky). 2-Tima Club EC-1

CHAILLEY-RICHEZ, Céliny

Bach: *Brandenburg Concerto 5* (w/ Rampal & Ferras, cond. Enesco).
Decca FAT 173.530

Beethoven: *Violin Sonata,* Op. 47 (w/ Enesco). Columbia FC 1058

Enesco: *Violin Sonata 3* (w/ Enesco). Remington 149-42

Schumann: *Piano Concerto* (cond. Heger). Masque M 10.010

CHAMINADE, Cécile

Chaminade: *Danse Créole,* Op. 94/2. Gramophone and Typewriter
GC 5555 #

Chaminade: *Pierrette,* Op. 41. Gramophone and Typewriter GC
5556 #

CIAMPI, Marcel

Chopin: *Scherzo 2.* Columbia D. 15225 #

Chopin: *Nocturne* in C Minor. Columbia D. 15226 #

Debussy: *Preludes,* Book I, 5 & 9 (Book I). Columbia D. 13075 #

Franck: *Quintet* (w/ Capet Qt.). Columbia D 15102/6 #

Liszt: *St. Francis Walking on the Waves.* Columbia LFX 186 #

Mozart: *Sonata* in A. Pathé DTX 197

CIANI, Dino

Beethoven: *Sonatas* Opp. 7, 31/2, 79, 110. Italia ITL 70025

Debussy: *Preludes,* Book II. DGG 2535261

Schumann: *Sonata 1* (+ Beethoven: *Eroica Variations;* Balakirev: *Islamey;* Liszt: *Chasse-neige;* Chopin: *Etude,* Op. 10/1, *Nocturne,*
Op. 62/1; Scriabin: *Etude,* Op. 8/11). Dynamic CDS-55 (CD)

Weber: *Sonatas 2 & 3.* DGG 2530026

CLIDAT, France

Grieg: *Concerto* (+ Franck: *Symphonic Variations,* cond. Macal). Forlane UM 3536

Liszt: Complete solo works. Véga 8.009/012; 8.013/016; 8.017/020; 8.021/024; 8.025/28; 8.029/32 (24 discs)

Liszt: *Concertos 1 & 2* (cond. Norrington). Peters International PLE 082

Rachmaninov: *Concerto 3* (cond. Macal). Forlane UM 3535

COLLARD, Catherine

Schumann: *Davidsbündlertänze; Fantasy.* Erato STU 70.814

Schumann: *Sonata 1; Papillons; Arabesque; Kinderszenen.* Lyrinx CD 083 (CD)

Schumann: *Papillons; Arabesque; Sonata 2; Romances.* Erato STU 71.145

COLLARD, Jean-Philippe

Chopin: *4 Ballades; Sonata 3.* EMI CDC 7 54006 2 (CD)

Debussy: *Images, I & II; Estampes; L'Isle joyeuse; Masques.* EMI 2C 069-14139

Fauré: *13 Nocturnes; Theme & Variations.* Connoisseur Society CS 2072

Fauré: *13 Barcarolles.* Angel CDC 47358 (CD)

Rachmaninov: *Concertos 1 & 3* (cond. Plasson). Angel CDM-69115 (CD)

Ravel: Complete solo works; works for four hands & two pianos (w/ Béroff). EMI 2C 167-73025/7

Schumann: *Sonata 3; Impromptus,* Op. 5. Connoisseur Society CS 2081

COOPER, Imogen

Mozart: *Concerto* for 3 Pianos (arr. for 2 pianos by Mozart); *Concerto* for 2 Pianos (w/ Brendel, cond. Marriner). Philips 416364-2PH (CD)

Schubert: *Sonata* in A Minor, D. 845. Ottavo OTR C88817 (CD)

CORTOT, Alfred

Beethoven: *Trio,* Op. 97 (w/ Casals, Thibaud). Seraphim 60242

Chopin: *24 Preludes; 4 Ballades; Berceuse.* Music & Arts CD-317 (CD)

Chopin: *Fantasy.* Gramophone DB 2308/10 #

Chopin: *Concerto 2* (w/ Barbirolli). Gramophone DB 2612/5 #

Chopin: *Etudes,* Op. 10. Gramophone DB 2027/9 #

Chopin: *Etudes,* Op. 25. Gramophone DB 2308/10 #

Debussy: *Preludes,* Book I. Gramophone DB 8578/82

Franck: *Symphonic Variations* (cond. Ronald); *Prelude, Chorale & Fugue; Prelude, Aria & Finale.* EMI 2C 061-01354

Saint-Saëns: *Concerto 4* (cond. Munch). Gramophone DB 2577/9 #

Schumann: *Carnaval.* Gramophone DB 1252/2 #

Schumann: *Concerto* (cond. Ronald). Gramophone DB 2181/4 #

Schumann: *Kreisleriana; Davidsbündlertänze.* Pathé COLH 86

CROCHET, Evelyne

Bach: Transcriptions. Mercury SR 90519

Fauré: Complete piano solo works. Vox SVBX 5423/4

Schubert: *Grand Duo; Lebensstürme* (w/ Brendel). Turnabout TV-S 34516

DALBERTO, Michel

Brahms: Piano Pieces, Opp. 10, 117, 118. Erato ECD-75097 (CD)

Mozart: *Concertos,* K. 456 & 503 (cond. Jordan). Musical Heritage Society 4738L

Schubert: *Sonatas,* D. 279 & 894; *Waltzes.* Denon 81757 6865-2 (CD)

Schumann: *Kreisleriana; Fantasy; Blumenstück.* Erato ECD-75353 (CD)

DAMASE, Jean-Michel

Debussy: 6 *Images.* Decca FS-123.606

Fauré: 13 *Barcarolles.* Decca F-163.868

DARRÉ, Jeanne-Marie

Chopin: *24 Preludes; Fantasy; Berceuse.* Vanguard VSD-71151

Chopin: *4 Scherzi; Nocturne,* Op. 27/2. Vanguard VSD-71162

Chopin: *14 Waltzes.* Vanguard VCS-10115

Franck: *Piano Quintet* (w/ Pascal Qt.). Pathé. DTX 123

Liszt: *Sonata; 3 Etudes; Valse oubliée; Sonetto 123.* Vangaurd VSD-71150

Saint-Saëns: *Toccata*. Gramophone C 2336 #

Saint-Saëns: 5 *Concertos* (cond. Fourestier). EMI Trianon 33.317/9

DELFORGE, Lucienne

Franck: *Prelude, Chorale & Fugue*. Gramophone DB 5195/6 #

Liszt: *Les jeux d'eau à la Villa d'Este*. Gramophone DB 5102 #

DESCAVES, Lucette

Debussy: *Feux d'artifice*. Gramophone DB. 5192 #

Falla: *Nights in the Gardens of Spain* (cond. Bigot). Gramophone
 DB 5095/7 #

Franck: *Quintet* (w/ Bouillon Qt.). Gramophone DB 5123/6 #

Jolivet: *Concerto* (cond. Bour). Ducretet-Thomson WL 5239

Mozart: *Sonatas 10 & 11*. Pathé DTX 197

Pierné: *Concert Etude* (+ Roussel: *Ronde*). Gramophone DB
 11138 #

Ravel: *Le Tombeau de Couperin*. Decca FA 133031

DEVOYON, Pascal

Ravel: *Gaspard de la nuit; Sonatine; Jeux d'eau; Pavane*. Erato STU
 71385

Saint-Saëns: *Concertos 2 & 4* (cond. Petitgirard). ADDA 590077
 (CD)

Tchaikovsky: *Concerto 1* (cond. Dutoit). RCA 60010-2-RG (CD)

DIÉMER, Louis

Chopin: *Nocturne,* Op. 27/2. Gramophone and Typewriter 35544 #

Diémer: *Grande Valse de Concert,* Op. 37. Gramophone and
 Typewriter 35543 #

Mendelssohn: *Spinning Song.* Gramophone and Typewriter 35545 #

DORFMANN, Ania

Beethoven: *Concerto 1* (cond. Toscanini). Victor LM 1039

Mendelssohn: *Concerto 1* (+ Grieg: *Concerto,* cond. Leinsdorf).
 RCA A-630263

Mendelssohn: *Andante & Rondo Capriccioso; Songs Without Words,*
 Opp. 62/1 & 67/4 (+ Chopin: *Ecossaises*). RCA 95.253

DOSSE, Marylène

Debussy: *Fantasy* (cond. Froment). Candide CE 31069

Granados: Complete solo works. Vox SVBX 5484/5

Saint-Saëns: Complete solo works; works for four hands (w/ Annie Petit). Vox SVBX 5476/7

DOYEN, Ginette

Chopin: *4 Ballades*. Véga C-30-A-10

Mendelssohn: 15 *Songs Without Words*. Westminster WL 5192

Saint-Saëns: *Toccata; Allegro appassionato; Thème Varié; Etude en forme de Valse* (+ Chabrier: 7 Pieces). Westminster WL 5294

DOYEN, Jean

Chopin: 14 *Waltzes*. Philips A-77.405

Fauré: *Ballade* (+ Franck: *Variations symphoniques,* cond. Fournet). Philips N-00704

Mozart: *Variations,* K. 353. Pathé DTX 196

Ravel: 2 *Concertos* (cond. Fournet). Epic LC 3123

Saint-Saëns: *Concerto 2* (+ d'Indy: *Symphony on a French Mountain Air,* cond. Fournet). Epic LC 3096

DUCHÂBLE, François-René

Brahms: *Paganini Variations,* Opp. 79 & 117. Erato 2292-45477-2 (CD)

Chopin: *Sonatas 2 & 3.* Erato ECD 88083 (CD)

Chopin: *Etudes,* Opp. 10 & 25. Erato ECD 88001 (CD)

Liszt: *Sonata; 2 Legendes; Bénédiction de Dieu dans la solitude.* Erato ECD 88091 (CD)

DUPONT, Jacques

Chopin: *Etudes,* Op. 25/3, 4, 6, 11. Pathé PAT X 9902

Chopin: *Scherzo 2.* Pathé PAT X 9978

DUSSAUT, Thérèse

Debussy: *Preludes,* Book I. FY 097

Rameau: *Suites* in G and A. FY 062

Ravel: *Miroirs; Valses nobles et sentimentales; La Valse; Pavane.* Pierre Verany 787022 (CD)

Schumann: *Kreisleriana; Kinderszenen; Arabesque; Blumenstück.* FY 084

ENGERER, Brigitte

Beethoven: *Sonata,* Op. 110; *Variations,* Op.76; *Rondos,* Op.51. Harmonia Mundi France 401346 *

Chopin: *Sonata 3;* Posthumous works. Chant du Monde K 270 *
Mussorgsky: *Pictures at an Exhibition; Night on Bald Mountain;*
Hopak; Une Larme; Scherzo; Nyanya. Harmonia Mundi France.
HMC-90.1266 (CD)
Rachmaninov: Works for 2 Pianos (w/ Maisenberg). Harmonia
Mundi France. HMC-901301/2 (CD)
Schumann: *Carnaval; Faschingsschwank aus Wien.* Philips 411 147-1
ENTREMONT, Philippe
Franck: *Symphonic Variations* (+ d'Indy: S*ymphony on a French*
Mountain Air; Fauré: *Ballade,* cond. Ormandy). CBS M 37269
Jolivet: *Concerto* (cond. Jolivet) (+ Milhaud: *Concerto 1* (cond. Mil-
haud; La Création du Monde). Columbia MS 7432
Mozart: *Concertos,* K. 414 & 449 (cond. Entremont). Schwann
Musica Mundi CD-11001 (CD)
Saint-Saëns: 5 *Concertos* (cond. Plasson). Odyssey MB2K 45624
(CD)
Schumann: *Quintet* (w/ Berg Qt.). Angel CDC-47439 (CD)
Tchaikovsky: *Concerto 1* (+ Rachmaninov: *Rhapsody on a Theme of*
Paganini, cond. Ormandy). Odyssey YT-39779
ERICOURT, Daniel
Debussy: Complete solo works. Kapp 9061-S; 9065-S; 9067/8-S;
KDX-6501-S
Liszt: *Mephisto Waltz 1* (+ Ravel: *Valses nobles et sentimentales;*
Chopin: *Waltzes*). Kapp 9021-S
EYMAR, Jacqueline
Brahms: *Handel Variations.* Chant du Monde LDS-8198
Franck: *Prelude, Chorale & Fugue; Prelude, Aria & Finale.* Philips N-
00597
Migot: *Le Zodiaque.* Cybelia CY 665/6
FAURE, Henriette
Ravel: *Miroirs.* Decca AF 209/10 & AF2 8/9 #
Ravel: *Gaspard de la nuit; Jeux d'eau; Prélude.* Decca FS 123639
FÉVRIER, Jacques
Debussy: Complete piano works. Véga 19.195/9

Debussy: *Cello Sonata* (w/ Gendron); *Violin Sonata* (w/ Menuhin).
EMI C 069-14.038

Poulenc: *Two-Piano Concerto* (w/ Poulenc, cond. Prêtre). Angel S-
35993

Poulenc: *Soirées de Nazelles, Napoli,* and other solo works. EMI
VSM C 063-10.739

Ravel: *Left-Hand Concerto* (cond. Munch), EMI VSM 2912163

Ravel: Complete solo works; works for four-hands (w/ Tacchino).
Adès 7.041

Schubert: Four-hand music (w/ Tacchino), Seraphim S-60317

FOURNEAU, Marie-Thérèse

Chopin: *Polonaise-Fantasy; Mazurka,* Op. 50/3. Columbia LFX 1012

Debussy: *Etude 11; Jardins sous la pluie.* Columbia LFX 693

FRANÇOIS, Samson

Chopin: *Concerto 2* (cond. Fremaux) (+ *Rondo*, Op. 73 w/ Barbizet).
EMI 2C 269-10603 *

Chopin: *Sonatas 2 & 3.* EMI 2 C 069-12525

Chopin: Recital. EMI 2 C 059-78046

Debussy: *Preludes,* Book I; 6 *Images.* EMI Jap. EAC-55073

Liszt: *Concertos 1 & 2* (cond. Silvestri). EMI 1103501

Prokofiev: *Concertos 3 & 5* (cond. Rowicki). Angel 36193

Ravel: 2 *Concertos* (cond. Cluytens). Angel S-35874

Ravel: Complete solo works. Seraphim SIC-6046

FRÉMY, Gérard

Berio: *Tempi Concertati* (w/ Debost, Jarry, Lavilléon, Eda-Pierre,
cond. Amy). Adès 12.001

Cage: *Sonatas and Interludes* for Prepared Piano. Etcetera KTC-
2001 (CD)

GAILLARD, Marius François

Debussy: *Reflets dans l'eau.* Odéon 171071

Debussy: *Jardins sous la pluie.* Odéon 171057

Debussy: *Masques.* Odéon 166317

GIANOLI, Reine

Bach: *English Suites* (complete). Westminster XWN 18382/3

Chopin: 19 *Waltzes.* Adès 10.001

Debussy: *Preludes,* Books I & II; *Estampes.* Westminster XWN
18512/3

Ravel: *Gaspard de la nuit; Miroirs; Jeux d'eau; Pavane.* Westminster
XWN 18008

Schumann: Complete solo works. 13 Adès 14075-2, 13242-2/13253-2
(CD)

GIROD, Marie-Catherine

Dutilleux: *Sonata* (+ Jolivet: *Sonata 1).* Solstice SOL 18

Emmanuel: 6 *Sonatines; Sonata* for Clarinet, Flute & Piano (w/
Vieille & Marion). Accord 149175 (CD)

Weber: *Sonatas 2, 3, and 4.* FYCD 924 (CD)

GOROG, André

Brahms: *Handel Variations;* 10 *Hungarian Dances.* Calliope CAL
1626

Schumann: *Carnaval; Papillons; 8 Pieces from Album for the Young.*
MAG 2007

Stravinsky: *Concerto* for Two Solo Pianos; *3 Easy Pieces* for Piano
Four-Hands (w/ Ringeissen). Adès 14090-2 (CD)

GOUSSEAU, Lélia

Chopin: *Ballade 2; Etude,* Op. 25/1; *Impromptu,* Op. 51. Pléiade P.
45149

Chopin: *Scherzo 3; Nocturne,* Op. 27/2. Pléiade P.45150

Falla: *Nights in the Gardens of Spain* (cond. André). Telefunken
TC5 18008

Roussel: *Concerto* (cond. Sacher). Philips A-00251

Roussel: Piano works, Opp. 14, 16, 49. Pléiade P. 3072

Schumann: *Papillons* (+ Brahms: *Rhapsodies,* Op. 79). Pléiade P.
3069

GRIMAUD, Hélène

Rachmaninov: *Sonata 2; Etudes-Tableaux,* Op. 33; *Preludes,* Op. 32/2
& 12. Denon CO-1054 (CD)

Schumann: *Kreisleriana* (+ Brahms: *Sonata 2).* Denon CO-73336
(CD)

Schumann: *Sonata 1* (+ Chopin: *Ballade 1;* Liszt: *Dante Sonata).*
Denon CD 1786 (CD)

GUILBERT, Carmen
   Debussy: *Toccata.* Pathé X 98136 #
   Fauré: *Theme & Variations; Nocturne 3.* Pathé PAT 113/14 #
   Ravel: *Alborada del gracioso.* Pathé PAT 23 #
GULLER, Youra
   Beethoven: *Sonatas,* Opp. 110 & 111. Nimbus NI 5061 (CD)
   The Art of Youra Guller (Bach/Liszt; Chopin; Scarlatti; Couperin;
      etc.). Nimbus NI 5030 (CD)
HAAS, Monique
   Bartók: *Concerto 3* (cond. Fricsay). Decca DL 9774
   Chopin: 24 *Etudes,* Opp. 10 & 25. Erato STU 70941
   Debussy: Complete solo works. Musical Heritage Society 1536/41
   Hindemith: *Concert Music* for Piano, Brass, and Two Harps, Op. 49
      (cond. Hindemith). Decca DL 9969
   Mihalovici: *Sonata,* Op. 90; *Etude in Two Parts,* for Piano, Winds,
      Brass, Celeste, and Percussion, Op. 64 (cond. Constant). Erato
      STU 70634
   Prokofiev: *Violin Sonata 2* (+ Milhaud: *Violin Sonata 2;* Debussy:
      Violin Sonata, w/ Voicou). Decca STS 15175
   Ravel: Complete solo works; *Ma Mère l'Oye* (w/ Marika). Musical
      Heritage Society 1084/6
   Ravel: 2 *Concertos* (cond. Paray). DGG 2535 312-10
   Schumann: *Concerto* (cond. Jochum) (+ Mozart: *Concerto,* K. 488,
      cond. Leitner). Decca DL 9868
   Stravinsky: *Capriccio* (cond. Fricsay) (+ Ravel: *Concerto* in G, cond.
      Schmidt-Isserstedt). Decca DL 9515
HASKIL, Clara
   Beethoven: *Sonatas,* Opp. 31/2 & 31/3. Philips 420088 2PH (CD)
   Beethoven: Complete *Violin Sonatas* (w/ Grumiaux). Philips
      6733.001
   Chopin: *Concerto 2* (+ Falla: *Nights in the Gardens of Spain,* cond.
      Markevitch). Philips 416443-2PH (CD)
   Mozart: *Concertos,* K. 466 & 491. Philips 412254-2PH (CD)
   Mozart: *Violin Sonatas,* K. 301, 304, 376, & 378 (w/ Grumiaux).
      Philips 412253-2PH (CD)

Schubert: *Sonata* in B-flat (+ Mozart: K. 330). Philips PHC 9076
Schumann: *Concerto* (cond. Van Otterloo); *Kinderszenen;*
Waldszenen; Abegg Variations. Philips 420851-2 PH (CD)
HEIDSIECK, Eric
Beethoven: *Sonatas,* Opp. 2/3 & 7. EMI 2C 065-12168
Beethoven: *Sonata,* Op. 106. EMI 2C 063-11269
Beethoven: Complete *Cello Sonatas* (w/ Tortelier). EMI SLS 836
Chopin: *Sonata 2; Nocturne* in C Minor; *Barcarolle; Polonaise-Fantasy.* Metropole 2599 021
Fauré: 13 *Nocturnes; Theme & Variations.* EMI 2C181-12038/9
Handel: *Suites,* Nos. 9, 11, 12, 14. Cassiopée 969 209 (CD)
Liszt: *Sonata; Ballade 2.* Charlin SLC-29
Mozart: *Concertos,* K. 466 & 488 (cond. Vandernoot). Capitol SG 7240
Ravel: *Le Tombeau de Couperin; La Valse* (w/ T. Heidsieck). Cassiopée 369 204
HEISSER, Jean-François
Brahms: *Clarinet Sonatas 1 & 2* (w/ Dangain). Calliope CAL 9695 (CD)
Brahms: *Sonata,* Op. 5; *Variations,* Op. 9. Erato 2292-45633-2 (CD)
Falla: Complete solo works. Erato 2292-45481-2 (CD)
HELFFER, Claude
Barraqué: *Sonata.* Astrée AS 36
Bartók: *Concerto 3* (+ Prokofiev: *Concerto 3,* cond. Maderna). Festival Classique FC 438
Boulez: 3 *Sonatas.* Astréé Auvidis E 7716 (CD)
Debussy: 12 *Etudes.* GMS 8910 (CD)
Jolas: *Stances* (cond. Constant). Adès 14.013
Ravel: Complete solo works. Harmonia Mundi France HM 922/24
Schoenberg: Complete solo works. Harmonia Mundi France HMA 55752
HENRIOT-SCHWEITZER, Nicole
Fauré: *Ballade* (rec. live, w/ Munch). Music & Arts CD-236(2) (CD)
d'Indy: *Symphony on a French Mountain Air* (cond. Munch). RCA 6805-2-RG (CD)

Ravel: *Concerto* in G (+ Prokofiev: *Concerto 2*, cond. Munch). RCA
Victrola VIC-1071

HUBEAU, Jean

Dukas: Piano works. Erato 2292-45421-1 (CD)

Fauré: *Piano Quartets 1 & 2* (w/ Gallois-Montbrun Qt.). Erato ECD-
71564 (CD)

Fauré: *Piano Quintets 1 & 2* (w/ Via Nova Qt.). Erato ECD-71563

Saint-Saëns: *Violin Sonatas,* Opp. 75 and 102; *Berceuse; Elégies;
Romance* (w/ Charlier). Erato 245017-2 (CD)

ITURBI, José

Beethoven: *Concerto 3* (cond. Iturbi). Victor M 801 #

Chopin: Recital. Seraphim 4XG-60186 *

Debussy: 2 *Arabesques.* Victor 18237 #

Mozart: *Concerto,* K. 466 (cond. Iturbi). Victor M 794 #

Mozart: *Sonata,* K. 331. Victor 11593/4 #

IVALDI, Christian

Britten: *Cello Sonata* (+ Debussy: *Cello Sonata;* Malipiero: *Cello
Sonatina,* w/ Meunier). Arion ARN-90411

Mendelssohn: *Sonatas,* Opp. 6, 105, 106. Arion ARN-38405

Milhaud: Piano works (w/ Lee, Béroff, Collard). EMI C 065-12076

Schubert: Works for four hands (w/ Lee). 2-Arion ARN-268038
(CD)

Stravinsky: *Le Sacre du Printemps; Petrouchka* (w/ Lee). Arion ARN-
68041 (CD)

JACQUINOT, Fabienne

Saint-Saëns: *Concerto 5* (+ d'Indy: *Symphony on a French Mountain
Air,* cond. Fistoulari). MGM E 3068

Schumann: *Davidsbündlertänze.* Ducretet-Thomson 255. C-031

Strauss: *Burleske* (cond. Fistoulari). MGM E 3004

JOHANNESEN, Grant

Casadesus: *Sonata 2* (+ Milhaud: *Album de Madame Bovary*). Gold-
en Crest S-4060

Chopin: *Polonaises, 1-4, 6, 8, 9, 10.* Allegretto ACD-8043 (CD)

Dukas: *Variations, Interlude & Finale on a Theme by Rameau* (+
Roussel: *3 Pieces,* Op. 49; Séverac: *Sous les Lauriers Roses; Pipper-
mint-Get*). Candide CE 31059

Fauré: Complete solo works. 6-Golden Crest CR 40308

Fauré: *Ballade; Fantasy* (w/ Froment)(+ Chausson: *Quelques dances;* Saint-Saëns: *Concerto 4,* cond. B. Kontarsky). Vox PVT 7201
(CD)

Grieg: *Concerto* (cond. Abravanel). Turnabout CT-2121 *

JOHNSON, Roy Hamlin

Powell: *Sonate pyschologique,* Op. 15; *Variations and Double Fugue
on a Theme by F. C. Hahr,* Op. 20. CRI SD 505

Powell: *Sonata Teutonica,* Op. 24. CRI SD 368

Scriabin: *Sonata 5* (+ Balakirev: *Islamey;* Pozdro: *Sonatas 2 & 3*).
EDUL ED-022

JOY, Geneviève

Dutilleux: *Sonata* (+ Ohana: *Caprichos; Sonate monodique*). BAM
LD 020

Mozart: *Sonata* for Two Pianos (+ Clementi, Couperin, W.F. Bach,
J.C. Bach, w/ Robin-Bonneau). Musidisc RC 664

Poulenc: *Sonata* for Two Pianos (w/ Robin-Bonneau) (+ Milhaud:
Concerto 2 for Two Pianos and Percussion, w/ Robin-Bonneau, J.-
C. Casadesus, Drouet, Masson, Fran,çois). Erato STU 70.224

Milhaud: *Concerto* for Two Pianos (w/ Marika, cond. Milhaud).
Westminster XWN 19101

Stravinsky: *Les Noces* (cond. Boulez). Nonesuch H-71133

KAHN, Claude

Beethoven: *Concerto 3* (cond. Rössler). Epidaure 10033

Ravel: *Gaspard de la nuit* (+ Fauré: *Theme & Variations; Nocturne
6*). Epidaure EPI 1940

Schumann: *Carnaval* (+ Liszt: *Funérailles, La Campanella, Hungarian Rhapsody 6*). Epidaure EPI 110 001

KARS, Jean-Rodolphe

Debussy: *Fantasy* (cond. Gibson). London STS 15503

Messiaen: *Le merle noir; Regard de l'esprit de joie; Regard du silence*
(+ Liszt: *Wilde Jagd; St. Francis of Paul Walking on the Waves;*
Nuages gris; La lugubre gondola 1). London CS 6604
Schoenberg: Complete solo works. EMI VSM C 065-12.278
KARTUN, Léon
Chopin: *Ballade 1.* Parlophone L 10960 #
Mendelssohn: *Spinning Song.* Odéon 177.242 #
Ravel: *Toccata.* Odéon 171.069 #
Ravel: *Le Gibet; Oiseaux tristes.* Gramophone DB 11175 #
KATSARIS, Cyprien
Beethoven/Liszt: *Symphony 3.* Teldec 6.43201
Brahms: *Sonata 3; Rhapsodies,* Op. 79; *Theme & Variations* in D
Minor. Teldec 44255 ZK (CD)
Chopin: *4 Ballades; 4 Scherzi.* Teldec CDT 43053 (CD)
Rachmaninov: *Chopin Variations* (+ Liszt: "*Weinen, Klagen, Sorgen,*
Zagen" Variations; Schumann: *Exercices*). Teldec 6.42787
KRUST, André
Schubert: *Sonata* in A, D. 664; *Sonata* in A, D. 959. Harmonia
Mundi HMO 30.546
Schumann: *Carnaval; Faschingsschwank aus Wien.* Musical Heritage
Society 1009S
KYRIAKOU, Rena
Chabrier: Complete piano works. Vox SVBX 5400
Haydn: Complete Sonatas, Vol. II. Vox SVBX 574
Mendelssohn: Complete solo works. Vox SVBX 5411, 5412, 5413,
VBX 414
LABÈQUE, Katia and Marielle
Bartók: *Sonata* for Two Pianos and Percussion (w/ Gualda, Drouet).
Erato STU 70.642
Gershwin: *An American in Paris* (+ Grainger: *Fantasy on Gershwin's*
"Porgy and Bess"). EMI 4DS-38130 *
Rachmaninov: *Suites 1 & 2.* Erato STU 70.761
LAIRES, Fernando
Beethoven: *Sonata,* Op. 53 (+ Liszt: *Mephisto Waltz; Spanish Rhap-*
sody). PMP-EMB-2000

LAUSNAY, Georges de
Chopin: *Etude*, Op. 25/1. Pathé PAT X 5437 #
Chopin: *Nocturne*, Op. 9/2. Pathé PAT X 5438 #
LAVAL, Danielle
Mozart: *Variations* (complete). Accord CD 201442 (4 CDs)
Roussel: *Concerto* (cond. Jacquillat). EMI VSM C 063 10.546
LAZARE-LÉVY
Chabrier: *Pièce pittoresque 4*. Voix de son maître DB 5049 #
Chopin: *Mazurkas*, Opp. 6/2 & 50/2 (+ Schumann: *Des Abends*, Op. 12/1). Jap. Victor SD 55 #
Debussy: *Masques*. Gramophone W. 1059 #
Mozart: *Fantasy* in C Minor, K. 475. Gramophone DB 4808 #
Mozart: *Sonata 8*. Pathé DTX 196
Mozart: *Sonatas 10 & 11*. Ducretet-Thomson LP 8518 #
Roussel: *Sicilienne*. Gramophone L 909 #
Schumann: *Kreisleriana*. Rococo 2054
LeDUC, Monique
Poulenc: *Sonata* for Two Pianos; *L'Embarquement pour Cythère* (+ Ravel: *La Valse;* Debussy-Ravel: *Fêtes;* Lutoslawski: *Paganini Variations*, w/ Engel). Orion 76238
LEFÉBURE, Yvonne
Bach: *Partita 1; Toccata* in D; *Chromatic Fantasy & Fugue; Prelude & Fugue* in E-flat Minor (*Well-Tempered Clavier*, I); *3 Chorale Preludes; Sicilienne* (+ Bach-Liszt: *Prelude and Fugue* in A Minor). Solstice SOCD 65 (CD)
Beethoven: *Diabelli Variations; 6 Bagatelles*, Op. 126. FY 022
Debussy: *Preludes*, Book I (+ Dukas: *Variations, Interlude & Finale on a Theme by Rameau; La Plainte au loin du faune; Prélude élégiaque;* Roussel: *3 Pieces*, Op. 49). Vogue 671. 672004 (CD)
Fauré: *Theme & Variations; Nocturnes, 1, 6, 7, 12, 13; Impromptus 2 & 5*. FY 088
Mozart: *Concerto*, K. 466 (cond. Furtwängler). Fonit Cetra FE 18
Ravel: *Le Tombeau de Couperin; Valses nobles et sentimentales; Jeax d'eau; Ma Mère l'Oye* (w/ Sabran). FY 018

Schumann: *Kinderszenen; Concerto* (+ Ravel: *Concerto* in G, cond.
   Paray). Solstice SOCD 55 (CD)

LEROUX, Germaine
   Debussy: *Preludes,* Book II. Supraphon 16407/13 #
   Ravel: *Le Tombeau de Couperin.* Ultraphone H.15203/5 #
   Ravel: *Sonatine.* Mercury MG 15006

LEVINAS, Michaël
   Beethoven: *Sonatas,* Opp. 27/1 & 106. Adès 941402 (CD)
   Chopin: *4 Ballades; Fantasy; Berceuse.* Adès 14.076-2 (CD)
   Schumann: *Kreisleriana; Fantasy.* Adès 14.044

LIPATTI, Dinu
   Bach: *Concerto 1* (cond. Van Beinum)(+ Chopin: *Nocturne,* Op.
      27/2; *Etudes,* Opp. 10/5 and 25/5). Turnabout TV 34832
   Bach: *Partita 1; 3 Chorale Preludes; Sicilienne* (+ Mozart: *Sonata 8;*
      Scarlatti: *2 Sonatas*). Angel CDC-47517 (CD)
   Chopin: *Sonata 3; Barcarolle; Nocturne,* Op. 27/2; *Mazurka,* Op. 50/3.
      Columbia ML 4721
   Enesco: *Sonata 3* (+ Ravel: *Alborada del gracioso;* Liszt: *Sonetto del
      Petrarca 104;* Schubert: *Impromptus,* Op. 90/2 & 3; Brahms:
      Waltzes, w/ Boulanger). EMI 1C 049-01811 M
   Schumann: *Concerto* (cond. Ansermet). London STS 15176
   Schumann: *Concerto* (+ Grieg: *Concerto,* cond. Karajan). Columbia
      YT 60141 *
   Recital (Bach: *Partita 1;* Mozart: *Sonata 8;* Schubert: *Impromptus,*
      Op. 90/2 & 3; Chopin: 13 *Waltzes*). Angel 3556 B

LIVELY, David
   Busoni: *Concerto* (cond. Gielen). Koch Schwann MSI 311 160 H1
      (CD)
   Fauré: 13 *Nocturnes.* Etcetera KTC 1082 (CD)
   Stravinsky: *Petrouchka; Tango; Piano Rag Music* (+ Ravel: *Le Tom-
      beau de Couperin*). DGG 2535009

LONG, Marguerite
   Beethoven: *Concerto 3* (w/ Weingartner). Koch 3-7128-2 HI (CD)
   Beethoven: *Concerto 5* (w/ Munch). Columbia LFX 679/83 #
   Chopin: *Concerto 2* (w/ Cluytens). Pathé FC 25010

Chopin: *Barcarolle.* Columbia LFX 325 #

Chopin: *Fantasy.* Columbia 17018/9-D #

Fauré: *Piano Quartet 1* (w/ Trio Pasquier); *Piano Quartet 2* (w/ Thibaud, Vieux, Fournier). EMI 2C 051-12815

Mozart: *Violin Sonatas,* K. 378 & 526 (w/ Thibaud). EMI GR-70101

Ravel: *Concerto* in G (cond. Ravel [actually, Freitas-Branco]) (+ Milhaud: *Alfama; Paysandu; Concerto 1,* cond. Milhaud; Debussy: *Arabesques 1 & 2; La plus que lent; Jardins sous la pluie*). EMI GR 2171

Ravel: *Concerto* in G (cond. Tzipine) (+ Fauré: *Ballade,* cond. Cluytens). EMI GR 2132

LORIOD, Yvonne

Albeniz: *Iberia* (excerpts). Adès ACD-14071-2 (CD)

Mozart: *Sonata,* K. 331; *Fantasias,* K. 394, 396, 475, 397; *Rondo,* K. 485. Adès OR 13.204-2 (CD)

Messiaen: *Oiseaux exotiques; Reveil des oiseaux* (cond. Neumann); *La Bouscarole.* Candide CE 31002

Messiaen: Complete piano works. 8-Erato OME 1

Messiaen: *Turangalîla-Symphonie* (cond. Ozawa). RCA ARL-2 1.143

Schumann: *Novelette 8.* Pathé PD 117/8 #

LORTAT, Robert

Chopin: *Etudes,* Opp. 10 & 25. Columbia LFX 135/42 #

Chopin: *Sonata 2; Waltz* in E minor, Op. Post. Columbia D 15092/3 #

Chopin: 14 *Waltzes.* Columbia LFX 214/8 #

LOYONNET, Paul

Beethoven: *Sonatas,* Opp. 13, 27/2, 53, 57. Janus JA 19005/6

Couperin: *Sixième Ordre.* Concert Hall-B 14 #

Fauré: *Theme & Variations; Nocturne 7; Barcarolle 1.* Concert Hall CHC-16

Haydn: *Flute Sonata* in G (w/ Le Roy). Concert Hall CHS 1082

Schumann: *Humoreske.* Concert Hall A-1 #

LUISADA, Jean-Marc

Chopin: 17 *Waltzes.* DGG 431 779-2 (CD)

Chopin: *Fantasy; Scherzo 4; Sonata 3; Polonaise-Fantasy.* Harmonic H/CD 8612 (CD)

Schumann: *Humoreske; Davidsbündlertänze.* Harmonic H/CD 8822 (CD)

MAGALOFF, Nikita

Chopin: *Preludes,* Op. 28. Philips 411 164-4 *

Chopin: *Etudes,* Opp. 10 & 25. Philips 420 705-4 *

Granados: *Goyescas.* London LL 954

Mendelssohn: Recital. Denon CO 73535 (CD)

Schumann: *Carnaval.* London LL 528

Stravinsky: *Concerto* for Piano and Winds; *Capriccio* (cond. Ansermet). London LL 1392

Weber: *Konzertstück* (cond. Davis). Philips 412 906-4 *

MALATS, Joaquin

Complete recordings (Malats, Chopin, Liszt, Wagner-Liszt). International Piano Library 109

MARIKA, Ina

Chopin: *Mazurkas,* Opp.41/3, 50/1 & 2, 56/1, 67/4. Chant du Monde 5028/9 #

Fauré: *Dolly* (+ Ravel: *Ma Mère l'Oye,* w/ Smadja). Philips N 00637R

Milhaud: *Concerto* for Two Pianos (w/ Joy, cond. Milhaud). Westminster XWN 19101

Stravinsky: *Les Noces* (cond. Boulez). Nonesuch H-71133

MARTY, Jean-Pierre

Brahms: *Hungarian Dances* (w/ Katchen). London CS 6473

Chopin: *Barcarolle; Fantasy; Berceuse; Polonaise-Fantasy; Tarantella; Fantasy-Impromptu.* EMI-VSM-FALP 504.

MERLET, Dominique

Brahms: *Handel Variations; 4 Ballades.* FY 077

Liszt: *Funérailles; Bénédiction de Dieu dans la solitude; Fantasy & Fugue on BACH; 2 Legends.* Quantum QM 1986 *

Ravel: Complete solo works. Circé 87125/6 (CD)

Schumann: *Symphonic Etudes; Arabesque; Humoreske; Davidsbündlertänze; Fantasiestücke,* Op. 111. Accord ACC 150.006

MEYER, Marcelle

Albeniz: *Navarra.* HMV D 1063 #

Couperin: 9 *Pieces.* Discophiles Français-DF A16 #

Debussy: *Preludes,* Books I & II; *Images,* I & II; *Masques; L'Isle joyeuse.* Discophiles Français DF 211/2

Mozart: *Concertos,* 466 & 488 (cond. Hewitt). Discophiles Français DF-37

Rameau: 11 *Pièces de Clavecin.* Discophiles Français DF-A14 #

Ravel: *Pavane pour une infante défunte; Jeux d'eau; Miroirs; Sonatine; Gaspard de la nuit; Valses nobles et sentimentales; Menuet sur le nom d'Haydn; Menuet antique.* Decca France DF 100/101

MICAULT, Jean

Beethoven: *Sonatas,* Opp. 13, 27/2, 57. Divertimento DVE 63508

Chopin: 4 *Ballades.* Collection Prestige SB-052

Chopin: *Sonatas 2 & 3.* Collection Prestige SB-043

MURANO, Roger

Messiaen: *Vingts Regards sur l'Enfant Jésus.* Art & Electronics AED2-10271 (CD)

Rachmaninov: *Sonata 2; Corelli Variations; 6 Moments musicaux.* Adès 14.186-2 (CD)

NAOUMOFF, Emile

Bach: *Well-Tempered Clavier* (complete). Thésis 2 THC 82025 and 26 (4 CDs)

Mozart: *Sonata,* K. 457; *Fantasias,* K. 396, 397, 474; *Rondo,* K. 511. EMI CDC 749 2742 (CD)

Poulenc: *Pastourelle; Suite française; Villageoises* (+ Debussy: *Images,* I; Fauré: *Nocturnes 7 & 13;* Naoumoff: *Impasse*). Wergo 60125-50 (CD)

NAT, Yves

Beethoven: 32 *Sonatas* (+*Variations* in C Minor). 8-Angel CDZH 62901 (CD)

Brahms: *Handel Variations; Rhapsodies,* Op. 79; *Intermezzi,* Op. 117. EMI 2C 051-16400

Chopin: *Sonata 2; Fantasy; Barcarolle.* EMI 2C 051-12005

Schubert: *Moments musicaux* (+ Schumann: *Faschingsschwank aus Wien*). EMI 2C 051-73033

Schumann: *Concerto* (cond. Bigot); *Kreisleriana; Humoreske; Kinderszenen; Toccata; Arabesque; Papillons; Etudes Symphoni-*

ques; Fantasy; 8 Novelettes; Fantasiestücke; Romances. 4-Angel
CDZD 67141 (CD)

NOVAES, Guiomar

Beethoven: *Concerto 5* (cond. Perlea). Allegretto ACD-8026 (CD)

Beethoven: *Sonatas,* Opp. 27/2, 81a, 111. Vanguard VCS-10014

Chopin: *Ballades 3 & 4; Polonaises,* Opp. 44 and 53; *Berceuse; 3
Ecossaises; Etudes,* Opp. 10/5 & 25/9. Vanguard VCS-10059

Chopin: *Etudes,* Op. 25; 3 Nouvelles Etudes. Vox PL 7560

Chopin: *Sonata 2; Preludes,* Op. 28 (complete). Vox PL 10.940

Schumann: *Carnaval; Kinderszenen; Papillons.* Turnabout TV 34164S

OUSSET, Cecile

Chopin: *Sonata 3; 4 Ballades.* Angel CDC-47707 (CD)

Liszt: *Sonata; 6 Paganini Etudes.* EMI DS-38259

Liszt: *Concerto 1* (+ Saint-Saëns: *Concerto 2* (cond. Rattle). Angel
CDC-47221 (CD)

Prokofiev: *Concerto 3* (+ Poulenc: *Concerto,* cond. Barshai). Angel
CDC-47224 (CD)

Ravel: *Gaspard de la nuit* (Mussorgsky: *Pictures at an Exhibition*).
EMI ASD 4281

PANTHÈS, Marie

Chopin: *Nocturne* in C-sharp minor (Posth.); *Mazurka,* Op. 17/4.
Columbia DF 1919 #

Chopin: *Nocturne* in B, Op. 62/1; *Mazurka,* Op. 33/4. Columbia DFX
216 #

Chopin: *Mazurkas,* Opp. 7/1-3 & 68/2. Pacific 6169 #

Mozart (attrib.): *Pastorale variée* (+ Albeniz: *Granada*). Columbia
DFX 169 #

PARASKIVESCO, Theodore

Beethoven: *Sonatas,* Opp. 31/2, 54, 57; *Bagatelles,* Op. 126. Calliope
CAL-9210 (CD)

Debussy: *Preludes,* Books I & II. Calliope CAL. 1831/2

Debussy: *12 Etudes.* Calliope CAL. 1836

PENNETIER, Jean-Claude

Brahms: *2 Viola Sonatas,* Op. 120 (w/ B. Pasquier). Harmonia
Mundi France HMC 1901092 (CD)

Jadin: *Sonatas,* Opp. 4/1-3 & 6/3. Harmonia Mundi France HMC 901189 (CD)

Schubert: *Sonatas,* Opp. 120 & 143. Harmonia Mundi France HM 1132

PERLEMUTER, Vlado

Chopin: 24 *Etudes,* Opp. 10 & 25. Nimbus 5095 (CD)

Chopin: *Fantasy; Tarantella; Scherzo 2; Barcarolle; Berceuse; Ballade 2; Etude,* Op. 10/12. Festival FC 453

Fauré: *Theme & Variations; Nocturnes, 1, 6, 7, 12, 13; Impromptu 2 & 5; Barcarolle 5.* Nimbus NI 5165 (CD)

Liszt: *Sonata* (+ Beethoven: *Eroica Variations*). Nimbus 2125

Ravel: Complete piano music; *Concerto* for the Left Hand (cond. Horenstein). Vox Box 410

Ravel: Complete solo works. Nimbus NI-5005 & 5011 (CD)

Schubert: *"Trout" Quintet* (w/ Pascal Qt.). Monitor MCS 2106

Schumann: *Kreisleriana; Symphonic Etudes.* Nimbus NI 5108 (CD)

PETIT, Annie

Ravel: *Violin Sonata* (w/ O'Reilly). Turnabout 34586

Saint-Saëns: Works for four hands (w/ Dosse). Vox SVBX 5476/7

French Piano Duos (Bizet, Chabrier, Fauré, Lalo, d'Indy, Massenet, Caplet, w/ Dosse). Pantheon D 106.99 (CD)

PETIT, Françoise

Bury: *Suites* for Harpsichord. Cybelia CY 880 (CD)

Durey: Piano works. Musical Heritage Society 3834

Roussel: Piano works. L'Oiseau-Lyre SOL 60052

PHILIPP, Isidor

Mozart: *Concerto,* K. 459 (cond. Marie). [unissued recording; copy in the International Piano Archive at the University of Maryland]

Saint-Saëns: *Scherzo* for Two Pianos (w/ Herrenschmidt). Polydor 561143-4 #

Saint-Saëns: *Violin Sonata,* Op. 75 (w/ Pascal). Pathé PAT15-17 #

Saint-Saëns: *Cello Sonata,* Op. 32 (w/ Bazelaire). Pathé PAT12-14 #

Early Italian Masters (Vinci, Rutini, Neghri, Pasquini, Caroso). Vox VL 1720

PLANÈS, Alain
  Beethoven-Liszt: *Symphonies 4 & 8.* Harmonia Mundi France HMC-
    901194 (CD)
  Debussy: *Preludes,* Books I & II. Harmonic H/CD 8506/7 (CD)
  Debussy/Ravel Recital. Denon DC 8008 (CD)
PLANTÉ, Francis
  Reissue of complete recordings (Schumann, Chopin, Gluck-Planté,
    Boccherini-Planté, Berlioz-Redon, Mendelssohn, Schumann-
    Debussy). International Piano Library 101
PLUDERMACHER, Georges
  Beethoven-Liszt: *Symphony 3.* Harmonia Mundi France HMC-
    901193 (CD)
  Brahms: *Handel Variations,* Op. 116. Lyrinx CD 093 (CD)
  Debussy: 12 *Etudes.* Lyrinx LYR 055
  Liszt: *Sonata* (+ Chopin: 24 *Preludes*). Lyrinx LYR 111 (CD)
POMMIER, Jean-Bernard
  Bach: *Inventions & Sinfonias* (complete). EMI 2 C 069-14155
  Bach: 7 *Toccatas; Italian Concerto: Capriccio on the Departure of a*
    Beloved Brother. EMI VSM C 167-14015/6
  Brahms: *Cello Sonatas 1 & 2* (w/ Rose). Virgin Classics VC 7 90750-
    2 (CD)
  Mozart: Complete sonatas (+*Fantasy,* K. 475). Virgin VC 7 91200-2
    (5 CDs)
  Schumann: *Kreisleriana; Carnaval.* Adda 581068 (CD)
  Schumann: *Quintet* (w/ Bernède Qt.). EMI VSM C 061-10687
POULENC, Francis
  Poulenc: *Mouvements perpétuels; Nocturne* in C; *Suite française*
    (Satie: *Descriptions automatiques; Gymnopédie 1; Sarabande 2;*
    Gnossienne 3; Avent-dernières pensées; Croquis et agaceries d'un
    gros bonhomme en bois). CBS Jap. 2OAC 1890
PUGNO, Raoul
  Reissue of complete recordings (Scarlatti, Handel, Chopin, Men-
    delssohn, Weber, Liszt, Massenet, Chabrier, Pugno). Opal 836

QUEFFÉLEC, Anne

Poulenc: *Clarinet Sonata* (+ Saint-Saëns: *Clarinet Sonata,* w/ Deplus). Cybelia CY-662

Ravel: *Miroirs; Le Tombeau de Couperin.* Erato STU 71038

Ravel: 2 *Concertos* (+ Debussy: *Fantasy,* cond. Jordan). Erato ECD-55041 (CD)

RAËS, Alain

Honneger: Complete solo works. FY 033

Pierné: *Concerto,* Op. 12; *Fantaisie-ballet* (cond. Vachey). Solstice SOCD 52 (CD)

Roussel: Piano works. Solstice SOCD 08 (CD)

REACH, Pierre

Alkan: *Grande Sonata,* Op. 33; *Menuet* in G; *Barcarolle* in G Minor; *Fantasy* in G. Musical Heritage Society 4875M

Messiaen: *8 Preludes; 3 Regards sur l'Enfant-Jésus.* Cybelia CY 830 (CD)

Roussel: Piano works. Solstice SOCD-08 (CD)

RICHEPIN, Eliane

Chopin: 4 *Ballades;* 4 *Mazurkas,* Opp. 30. REM 10983

Chopin: *Preludes,* Opp. 28 & 45. Variance VR 33.531

RIGUTTO, Bruno

Bach: *Concertos 1 & 2* for Three Pianos; *Concerto* for Four Pianos (cond. Wallez, w/ Collard, Tacchino, Béroff). Angel CDC-47063 (CD)

Debussy: *Violin Sonata* (+ Ravel: *Violin Sonata;* Fauré: *Violin Sonata,* w/ Wallez). PG 7174

Dvorak: *Concerto* (cond. Macal). Peters International PLE 102

RINGEISSEN, Bernard

Alkan: *Sonatine,* Op. 61; *Scherzo diabolico; Nocturne 2; Barcarolle; Saltarelle; Gigue; March 1.* Harmonia Mundi France HMA 190927 (CD)

Chopin: *Andante Spianato et Grande Polonaise; Barcarolle; Berceuse; Fantasy; Scherzo 4; 3 Ecossaises.* Adès 14.012

Stravinsky: Complete solo works. 4-Adès 7074

RISLER, Edouard
  Reissued Recordings (Beethoven, Weber, Chopin, Liszt, Rameau,
    Daquin, Couperin, Granados, Saint-Saëns, Chabrier, Godard).
    Symposium 1020
ROBIN-BONNEAU, Jacqueline
  Chabrier: *Trois Valses romantiques* (+ Bizet: *Jeux d'enfants,* w/ Joy).
    Pathé DT 1025
  Fauré: *La Chanson d'Eve* (+ Milhaud: *Poèmes juifs,* w/ Kolassi).
    Decca LXT 2897
  Milhaud: *Concerto 2* for Two Pianos & Percussion (w/ Joy, J.-C.
    Casadesus, Drouet, Masson, J.-C. François). Erato STU 70.224
  Mozart: *Sonata* for Two Pianos (+ Clementi, Couperin, W. F. Bach,
    J. C. Bach, w/ Joy). Musidisc RC 664
ROGÉ, Pascal
  Poulenc: *Les Soirées de Nazelles; 3 Mouvements perpétuels; 3 Novelet-
    tes; 9 Improvisations.* London 417438-2 LH (CD)
  Ravel: *Miroirs; Jeux d'eau; Ma Mère l'Oye* (w/ D. Rogé). London CS
    6936
  Satie: Piano works. London 421713-2 LH (CD)
ROGER-MICLOS, Marie
  Chopin: *Waltz,* Op. 64/1. Fonotopias 39254 #
  Godard: *Mazurka.* Fonotopias 39253 #
  Liszt: *Hungarian Rhapsody 11.* Fonotopias 39258 #
  Mendelssohn: *Spinning Song.* Fonotopias 39255 #
  Mendelssohn: *Rondo Capriccioso.* Fonotopias 39256 #
ROUVIER, Jacques
  Debussy: 12 *Etudes.* Denon CO 2200-EX
  Franck: *Violin Sonata* (+ Ravel: *Violin Sonata,* w/ Kantorow).
    Denon OF 7076-ND
  Ravel: *Miroirs; Sonatine; Valses nobles et sentimentales; Ma Mère
    l'Oye* (w/ Paraskivesco). Calliope CAL 7825 *
  Ravel: *Gaspard de la nuit; Jeux d'eau; Sonatine.* Musical Heritage
    Society 3252

SAINT-SAËNS, Camille

Saint-Saëns: Improvised cadenza from *"Africa" Fantasy,* Op. 89. French Gramophone and Typewriter 035506 #

Saint-Saëns: *Valse Mignonne,* Op. 104. French Gramophone and Typewriter 035507 #

Saint-Saëns: *Prelude* (arr. from *Le Déluge,* w/ Willaume). French HMV 037920 #

Saint-Saëns: *Elégie,* Op. 143 (w/ Willaume). French HMV 037921 #

SANCAN, Pierre

Chopin: *Nocturne,* Op. 9/2; *Waltz,* Op. 64/2. Victor France A-95001

Mozart: *Concertos,* K. 242 & 365 (w/ Pommier & Silie, cond. Chorofas). Nonesuch H 71028

Ravel: *Sonatine* (+ Debussy: *Preludes,* Book I, 8 & 12;   Book II, 3, 5, 6). RCA F-230003

Schumann: *Papillons* (+ Bach: 3 *Chorale Preludes*). RCA F-230004

SCHMITZ, E. Robert

Debussy: *Preludes,* Book I. Camden CAL 179

Debussy: *Preludes,* Book II. Victor Masterworks 1138 #

Debussy: *Rêverie* (+ Ravel: *Pavane*). Victor 12-0066 #

Debussy: *Suite Bergamasque* (1-3 only). Victor 11-8694 & 8240 #

SELVA, Blanche

Bach: *Partita No. 1.* Columbia D 15234/5 #

Beethoven: *Violin Sonata,* Op. 24 (w/ Massia). Columbia LFX 105/8 #

Franck: *Violin Sonata* (w/ Massia). Columbia DX 240 #

Franck: *Prelude, Chorale & Fugue.* Columbia GQX 10750/2 #

Séverac: *Baigneuses au soleil.* Columbia D 15142 #

SEVILLA, Jean-Paul

Roussel: *Sonatine; Trois Pièces,* Op. 49; *Suite* (+ d'Indy: *Thème varié, Fugue et Chanson*). Musica Viva MVCD 1024 (CD)

Schumann: *Symphonic Etudes* (+ Papineau-Couture: *Complementaire*). Radio Canada International RCI 384

STAUB, Victor

Chopin: *Waltz,* Op. 34/3. Parlophone R 3513 #

Debussy: *Golliwog's Cakewalk.* Parlophone R. 3544 #

Debussy: *Minstrels*. Odéon 166.048 #
Mendelssohn: *Spinning Song*. Odéon 166043 #
Schumann: *Des Abends*. Odéon 166.173 #

TACCHINO, Gabriel

Chopin: *Scherzo 2; Fantasy; Polonaise*, Op. 53; *Ballade 1; Berceuse; Fantasy-Impromptu*. EMI 2C 069-14144

Poulenc: *Concerto; Aubade; Concerto* for Two Pianos (w/ Ringeissen, cond. Prêtre). Angel CDC 47369

Poulenc: *Les Soirées de Nazelles; Villageoises; Thème Varié; Pièce Brève; 3 Intermezzi; Valse; Improvisation*. EMI 2C 069-73101

Prokofiev: *5 Concertos* (cond. Froment). Vox CD3X 3000 (3 CDs)

TAGLIAFERRO, Magda

Fauré: *Ballade* (cond. Coppola); *Impromptu 3*. Gramophone W984/5 #

Fauré: *Nocturnes 4 & 6; Ballade; Dolly* (w/ Varsano). CBS 37246

Hahn: *Concerto* (cond. Hahn) (+ Villa-Lobos: *Mômoprecoce*, cond. Villa-Lobos). EMI 2909621

Saint-Saëns: *Concerto 5* (cond. Fournet). Epic 3LC 3057

Schumann: *Sonata 1*. Ducretet-Thomson LA 1001

Schumann: *Carnaval* (+ Chopin: *Ballade 4*; Debussy: *L'Isle joyeuse*; Hahn: *Les Rêveries du Prince Eglantine*; Schumann: *Intermezzo*, Op. 26). Copacabana COLP 12.463

Recital (Falla, Granados, Albeniz, Franck, Fauré, Mompou, Ravel, Debussy, Poulenc). Echo 191 (CD)

THIBAUDET, Jean-Yves

Chausson: *Concert* (w/ Bell, Isserlis, Takacs Qt.) (+ Ravel: *Trio*). London 420860-2 LH (CD)

Franck: *Violin Sonata* (+ Debussy: *Violin Sonata;* Fauré: *Violin Sonata 1*, w/ Joshua Bell). London 421 817-2 (CD)

Liszt: *Concertos 1 & 2; Totentanz; Hungarian Fantasy* (cond. Dutoit). Decca 433 075-2DH (CD)

Ravel: *Le Tombeau de Couperin; Sonatine; Jeux d'eau*. Denon C37-7805 (CD)

THIOLLIER, François-Joël

Liszt: 3 *Sonetti del Petrarca;* 10 Songs (w/ Brewer). Thésis THC-82002 (CD)

Rachmaninov: Complete solo works. RCA RL 37.294 (9 LPs)

Rachmaninov: *Concerto 2* (cond. Bardon) (+ Debussy: 6 Piano works). Thésis THC-82040 (CD)

THYSSENS-VALENTIN, Germaine

Fauré: *Barcarolles* (complete). Ducretet-Thomson 300 C 022

Fauré: *Theme & Variations; Impromptu 3; Nocturne 4; Barcarolle 3.* Ducretet-Thomson 270 C 806

Franck: *Prelude, Choral & Fugue; Prelude, Aria & Finale.* Ducretet-Thomson LP 8716

TROUARD, Raymond

Saint-Saëns: *Carnaval des animaux* (w/ Devèze, cond. Lindeberg). Odéon OD 1003

Chopin: 14 *Waltzes.* Odéon XOC 104

Liszt: *Concertos 1 & 2* (cond. Bigot). Odéon ODX 161

Weber: *Perpetual Motion.* Odéon 123906 #

VALMALETE, Madeleine de la

Debussy: *Feux d'artifice.* Polydor 90033 #

Liszt: *Hungarian Rhapsody 11.* Polydor 90032 #

Liszt Collection. Ducretet LAP 1012

Ravel: *Le Tombeau de Couperin.* Polydor PO 5088/9 #

VARSANO, Daniel

Beethoven: *Diabelli Variations* (+ Bach: *Goldberg Variations*). CBS France 79231

Ravel: *Concerto* in G (+ Fauré: *Ballade; Fantasy,* cond. A. Davis). ProArte CDD 313 (CD)

Ravel: *Sonatine; Jeux d'eau* (+ Debussy: *L'Isle joyeuse; Feux d'artifice;* Fauré: *Barcarolles 6 & 9;* Chabrier: *Idylle; Scherzovalse*). Pro Arte PAD 165

VERED, Ilana

Beethoven: *Sonatas,* Opp. 13, 27/2, 53, 57. London 410282-4-LN *

Moszkowski: 15 *Virtuoso Etudes,* Op. 72. In Sync C 4040 *

VIEUXTEMPS, Jeannine

Lekeu: *Sonata* in G (+ H. & L. Vieuxtemps: Piano works). Pavane
ADW 7088

Stravinsky: *Les Noces* (cond. Hayrabedian). Pierre Verany PV
787032 (CD)

VIÑES, Ricardo

Reissue of recordings (Scarlatti, Gluck-Brahms, Albeniz, Borodin,
Debussy, Falla, Turina, Blancafort, Troiani, Lopez-Buchardo).
EMI 1731791

WAYENBERG, Daniel

Brahms: Piano Pieces, Opp. 116 & 76. Ducretet-Thomson 320 C 067

Chopin: *Scherzos 2 & 3; Nocturne 18; Fantasy; Barcarolle;* 4 *Impromptus.* Accolate CL 50003 (CD)

Rachmaninov: *Paganini Rhapsody* (+ Strauss: *Burleske,* cond. C. von
Dohnanyi). Ducretet 503

WEBSTER, Beveridge

Beethoven: *Sonata,* Op. 106. Dover HCR-ST-7008

Brahms: *Variations,* Opp. 9 and 21/1; *Piano Pieces,* Op. 119. Dover
HCR-5250

Debussy: Complete piano works. Desto DC-7111/5

Rachmaninov: *Etudes-tableaux,* Opp. 33 & 39. Dover HCR-ST-7284

Ravel: *Gaspard de la nuit; Le Tombeau de Couperin; Jeux d'eau.*
Dover HCR-5213

Schoenberg: *Piano Pieces,* Opp. 11, 19, 23 (+ Webern: *Variations;*
Berg: *Sonata*). Dover HCR-ST-7285

Schumann: 8 *Novelettes.* Dover HCR-ST-7002

APPENDIX III
PIANO PROFESSORS AT THE PARIS CONSERVATOIRE, 1795-1991

(Note: This list does not include professors of preparatory classes or of *étude de clavier*. Until 1916, classes were segregated by sex; thus, in this list M designates a men's class and W designates a women's class.)

Hélène Montgeroult: 1795-98 (M)
Antoine-Louis Granier: 1795-1800 (M)
Nicolas Séjan: 1795-1802 (M)
Benoît-François Mozin: 1795-1802 (M)
Louis Gobert: 1795-1802 (M)
Hyacinthe Jadin: 1795-1802 (W)
Ignace Ladurner: 1797-1802 (M)
Louis Adam: 1797-1842 (M, then W)
André Mozin: 1799-1802 (W)
François Nicodami: 1798-1800 (M)
François-Adrien Boieldieu: 1798-1809 (M)
Louis Pradher: 1800-27 (M)
Louis Jadin: 1802-15 (M)
Emilie Michu: 1816-27 (W)
Pierre Zimmerman: 1816-48 (M)
Louise Farrenc: 1842-72 (W)
Henri Herz: 1842-74 (W)
Adolphe Laurent: 1846-62 (M)
Antoine-François Marmontel: 1848-87 (M)
Marie-Anna Coche: 1851-66 (W)
Félix Le Couppey: 1854-86 (W)
Georges Mathias: 1862-87 (M)
Elie Delaborde: 1873-1913 (W)
Louise-Aglaé Massart: 1874-87 (W)

Alphonse Duvernoy: 1886-1907 (W)

Henri Fissot: 1887-96 (W)

Charles de Bériot: 1887-1903 (M)

Louis Diémer: 1887-1919 (M, then mixed)

Raoul Pugno: 1896-1901 (W)

Antonin Marmontel: 1901-07 (W)

Isidor Philipp: 1903-34 (M, then W, then mixed)

Edouard Risler: 1907-09 (M)

Alfred Cortot: 1907-23 (W, then mixed)

Victor Staub: 1909-40 (M, then mixed)

Santiago Riera: 1913-37 (M, then mixed)

Marguerite Long: 1920-40

Lazare-Lévy: 1923-53 (except 1940-45); previously was
    substitute-teacher for eight years (before 1919)
    and in 1920-23

Yves Nat: 1934-56

Magda Tagliaferro: 1937-39

Jean Batalla: 1941-58

Marcel Ciampi: 1941-61

Jean Doyen: 1941-77

Armand Ferté: 1942-53

Georges de Lausnay: 1943-52

Jules Gentil: 1947-75

Vlado Perlemuter: 1951-77

Yvonne Lefébure: 1952-67

Joseph Benvenuti: 1952-71

Lucette Descaves: c. 1953-76

Aline van Barentzen: 1954-67

Pierre Sancan: 1956-85

Jeanne-Marie Darré: 1958-75

Lélia Gousseau: 1961-78

Monique de la Bruchollerie: 1967-c. 1970

Yvonne Loriod: 1967-89

Monique Haas: 1968-70

Raymond Trouard: 1969-86

Germaine Mounier: c. 1970-87
Aldo Ciccolini: 1971-88
Pierre Barbizet: 1973-74
Dominique Merlet: 1974--
Gabriel Tacchino: 1975--
Reine Gianoli: 1976-78
Ventislav Yankoff: 1977-91
Jacques Rouvier: 1979--
Theodore Paraskivesco: 1980--
Jean-Claude Pennetier: 1985-91
Gérard Frémy: 1985--
Jean-François Heisser: 1986--
Bruno Rigutto: 1987--
Michel Béroff: 1989--

APPENDIX IV
SELECTED METHODS, EXERCISES, AND ETUDES

(Excluding Concert-Etudes)

A. Selected Early Publications (before 1821 and the patent for double-escapement action)

Adam, Louis. *Méthode de piano-forte du Conservatoire de Musique.* Paris: Imprimerie du Conservatoire, 1804.

Adam, Louis and Ludwig Lachnith. *Méthode ou principe générale du doigté pour le forte-piano.* Paris: Sieber, 1798.

Cazot, Félix. *Exercices préparatoires, Op. 2.* Paris: chez l'auteur, c. 1813.

Despréaux, Louis-Félix. *Cours d'éducation de clavecin ou piano-forte.* Paris: chez l'auteur, c. 1783.

Dourlen, Victor. *Méthode élémentaire pour le piano-forte.* Paris: J. Martinn et l'auteur, c. 1816.

Dreux, C. *Principes du clavecin ou piano.* Paris: Frère, c. 1796.

Hüllmandel, Nicolas Joseph. *Principles of Music, chiefly calculated for the Piano-Forte or Harpsichord, Op. XII.* London, c. 1790.

Jadin, Hyacinthe. *Vingts petites leçons.* Paris: Imprimerie du Conservatoire, 1798.

Kalkbrenner, Friedrich. *24 Etudes dans tous les modes majeurs et mineurs, Op. 20.* Paris: Sieber, c. 1816.

Levasseur, Jean-Pierre. *Nouvelle méthode de piano-forte, Op. VII.* Paris: chez l'auteur, c. 1817.

Momigny, Jérôme J. *La Première année de leçons de piano-forte.* Paris: chez l'auteur, c. 1802.

Montgeroult, Hélène de. *Cours complète pour l'enseignement du forte-piano.* Paris: Janet et Cotelle, c. 1820.

Pleyel, Ignace et Jean-Louis Dussek. *Méthode pour le piano-forte.* Paris: Pleyel, c. 1797.

Tapray, Jean-François. *Premiers éléments du clavecin ou du piano.* Paris: chez Bonjour, c. 1789.

Viguerie, Bernard. *L'Art de toucher le piano-forte, oeuvre V.* Paris; chez l'auteur, c. 1795.

B. Important Nineteenth- and Twentieth-Century Publications

Batalla, Jean. *Précis de technique du piano.* Paris: Lemoine, 1957.

Benoist, André. *The Virtuoso's Daily Dozen.* New York: Carl Fischer, 1924.

Bériot, Charles de. *Mécanisme et style, Op. 66.* Paris: Hamelle, n.d.

_____. *La Sonorité du piano, Op. 67.* Paris: Hamelle, n.d.

Bertini, Henri. *Fifty Selected Studies.* New York: Schirmer, 1919.

Boghen, P. *Exercices journaliers en double notes.* Paris: Heugel, 1924.

Cortot, Alfred. *Principes rationnels de la technique pianistique.* Paris: Salabert, 1928.

Diémer, Louis. *Méthode supérieure de piano* [in collaboration with Lazare-Lévy and Victor Staub]. Paris: Enoch, 1907.

Decombes, Emile. *Etude journalière des gammes et arpèges.* Paris: Heugel, 1902.

_____. *Petite méthode élémentaire de piano.* Paris: n.d.

Descaves, Lucette. *Technique des gammes* . . . . Paris: Billaudot, 1950.

Descaves, Lucette and Marie Claude. *Nouvelle méthode Le Couppey.* Paris: Billaudot, 1953.

Duvernoy, Alphonse. *Ecole du mécanisme.* Paris: Enoch, n.d.

Duvernoy, Jean-Baptiste. *Ecole primaire, Op. 176.* Paris: Schott, n.d.

_____. *Ecole du mécanisme, Op. 120.* Cincinnati: John Church, 1895.

Falkenberg, Georges. *Etudes-exercices.* Paris: Leduc, 1887.

_____. *Exercices progressifs et journaliers.* Paris, L. Grus, 1907.

Farrenc, Louise. *L'Ecole du pianiste.* Paris: Leduc, n.d.

Ferté, Armand. *Méthode de piano*. Paris: Schott, 1953.

Fétis, François Joseph and Ignaz Moscheles. *Méthode des méthodes*. Paris: Schlesinger, 1840.

Fournier-Rabaud, Ginette. *Doigtés d'exécution des gammes en tierces dans tous les tons majeurs et mineurs*. Paris: Henry Lemoine, 1952.

Garaudé, Alexis-Adélaïde. *Méthode complète pour le piano-forte* [with exercises by L. Jadin, J. Herz and L. Levasseur]. Paris: chez Ch. Laffilé, c. 1822.

Goria, Alexandre. *Etudes de style et de mécanisme, Op. 72*. Paris: Heugel, n.d.

Hanon, Charles. *The Virtuoso Pianist*. New York: G. Schirmer, 1900.

Herz, Henri. *Scales and Exercises*. Sherman Oaks, CA: Alfred, 1985.

_____. *Méthode complète de piano, Op. 100*. 4th American edition. Baltimore: W.C. Peters, 1850.

Jaëll, Marie. *La Musique et la psycho-physiologie*. Paris: F. Alcan, 1896.

_____. *Le Mécanisme du toucher*. Paris: A. Colin, 1897.

_____. *Le Toucher*. 3 vols. Paris: Costallat, 1899.

_____. *L'Intelligence et la rythme dans les mouvements artistiques*. Paris: Alcan, 1904.

_____. *Les Rythmes du regard et la dissociation des doigts*. Paris: Fischbacher, 1906.

_____. *Un Nouvel état de conscience: la coloration des sensations tactiles*. Paris: Alcan, 1910.

_____. *La Résonance du toucher et la topographie des pulpes*. Paris: Alcan, 1912.

_____. *Le Main et la pensée musicale*. Paris: Presses universitaires de France, 1927.

_____. *Un Nouvel enseignement artistique*. Paris: Presses universitaires de France, 1927.

_____. *Le Toucher musical par l'education de la main*. Paris: Presses universitaires de France, 1927.

Kalkbrenner, Friedrich. *Méthode complète de piano*. Paris: Heugel, n.d.

_____. *Méthode pour apprendre le piano à l'aide du Guide-Mains, Op. 108*. Paris: J. Meissonnier, 1830

Kartun, Léon. *Synthèse de la technique quotidienne du piano*. Paris: Les Editions Ouvrières, 1965.

Lack, Théodore. *Méthode de piano*. Paris: Leduc, n.d.

_____. *The Art of the Piano, Op. 289*. Philadelphia: Presser, 1919.

Lacombe, Louis. *Six études de style et de mécanisme, Op. 10*. Paris: Heugel, n.d.

Le Couppey, Félix. *Cours de piano*. Paris: Hamelle, n.d.

Leduc, Alphonse. *Ecole élémentaire du piano*. Paris: Leduc, n.d.

Lemoine, Henri. *Méthode pratique pour le piano*. Paris: chez l'auteur, c. 1827.

Logier, Jean-Bernard. *Le Compagnon de Chiroplaste, ou Méthode de piano*. Paris: Gambaro, c. 1822.

Long, Marguerite. *Le Piano*. Paris: Salabert, 1959.

_____. *La Petite méthode de piano*. Paris: Salabert, 1963.

Loyonnet, Paul: *Les gestes et la pensée du pianiste*. Montréal: Louise Courteau, 1985.

Marmontel, Antoine François. *Ecole de mécanisme et d'accentuation*. Paris: Heugel, n.d.

_____. *Le Mécanisme du piano*. Paris: Heugel, n.d.

Mathias, Georges. *Etudes speciales de style et de mécanisme, Op. 28*. Paris, 1862.

Morhange-Motchane, Marthe. *Le Petit clavier*. 2 vols. Paris: Salabert, 1954.

Morpain, Joseph. *Comme il faut jouer du piano*. Paris: Heugel, 1922.

_____. *Les Gammes*. Paris: Henri Lemoine, 1936.

Panthès, Marie. *La Semaine du pianiste*. Paris: Leduc, 1932.

Parent, Hortense. *L'Etude du piano*. Paris: Hachette, 1872.

_____. *Les Bases du mécanisme*. Paris: J. Maho, 1886.

Philipp, Isidor. *Exercices pratiques*. Paris: Durand, 1897.

_____. *Exercices quotidiens tirés des oeuvres de Chopin, avec préface de G. Mathias*. Paris: Hamelle, 1897.

_____. *Exercises for Independence of the Fingers*. New York: Schirmer, 1898.

_____. *School of Octave-Playing*. New York, G. Schirmer, 1901.

_____. *Gammes en double notes*. Paris: Durand, 1904.

_____. *Etudes techniques*. Paris: Ricordi, 1904.

_____. *Exercices pour développer l'indepéndence des doigts*. Paris: Heugel, 1908.

_____. *Complete School of Technique*. Bryn Mawr: Presser, 1908.

_____. *Dix Exercices-études en double notes*. Paris: Leduc, 1910.

_____. *Ecole des arpèges*. Paris: Heugel, 1923.

_____. *Une demi-heure de préparation technique*. Paris: Heugel, 1925.

_____. *Exercises on the Black Keys*. New York: G. Schirmer, 1944.

_____. *Etude technique des gammes*. Nice: Delrieu, 1955.

_____. *Etudes choisies de Ch. Czerny*. Paris: Heugel, n.d.

_____. *Etudes de vélocité*. Paris: Heugel, n.d.

_____. *Etudes en octaves d'après J.-S. Bach*. Paris: Heugel, n.d.

_____. *Une heure d'exercice*. Paris: Costallat, n.d.

_____. *179 Exercices d'extension*. Paris: Leduc, n.d.

_____. *Exercices d'Antoine Rubinstein*. Paris: Heugel, n.d.

_____. *Exercices de moyenne force*. Paris: Heugel, n.d.

_____. *Exercices de virtuosité*. Paris: Heugel, n.d.

_____. *Exercices techniques*. Paris: Hamelle, n.d.

_____. *Exercices de tenues*. Paris: Heugel, n.d.

_____. *Exercices préparatoires de Ad. Henselt*. Paris: Heugel, n.d.

_____. *Exercices journaliers de J.-N. Hummel*. Paris: Heugel, n.d.

_____. *Exercices progressifs de Pischna*. Paris: Heugel, n.d.

Pugno, Raoul and Charles Bresselle. *L'Art de travailler le piano*. Paris, C. Pugno, 1908.

Ravina, Henri. *Etudes harmonieuses, Op. 50*. Paris: Leduc, n.d.

Rie, Bernard. *Ecole moderne du pianiste*. Paris: Leduc, n.d.

_____. *L'Indépendence des doigts, Op. 36*. Paris: Leduc, 1877.

Riera, Santiago. *Nouvelle école du trille*. Paris: Leduc, 1917.

Schmitz, E. Robert. *The Capture of Inspiration*. New York: C. Fischer, 1935.

Selva, Blanche. *Le Travail technique du piano — d'après Safonoff.* Paris: B. Roudanez, 1919.

_____. *L'Enseignement musicale de la technique du piano.* Paris: Rouart, Lerolle & Cie., 1919.

Stamaty, Camille. *Le Rythme des doigts, Op. 36.* Paris: Heugel, n.d.

_____. *Melody and Execution, Opp. 37 and 38.* London: Augener, 1920.

Staub, Victor. *Etudes pour la main gauche.* Paris: Heugel, n.d.

_____. *Cours de piano en trois années.* Paris: E. Gallet, 1922.

Thalberg, Sigismund. *L'Art du chant appliqué au piano, Op. 70.* Leipzig: Breitkopf & Härtel, n.d.

Vieuxtemps, Jeannine. *Les Livres du pianiste.* 2 vols. Paris: Billaudot, 1991.

Zimmermann, Pierre. *Exercices techniques.* Paris: Heugel, n.d.

_____. *Célèbres gammes, exercices et préludes.* Paris: Heugel, n.d.

_____. *Encyclopédie du pianiste-compositeur.* Paris: chez l'auteur, n.d.

_____. *Méthode pratique pour piano.* Paris: chez l'auteur, c. 1827.

SELECTED BIBLIOGRAPHY

A. BOOKS AND ARTICLES

Archimbaud, Michel, ed. *Le Guide du piano*. Paris: Mazarine, 1979.

Bachmann, Alberto. *Le Piano* (typescript, dated 1955, Paris, Bibliothèque nationale: Rés. Vma 142).

Bailbé, Joseph-Marc, *et al. La Musique en France à l'époque romantique: 1830-1878*. Paris: Flammarion, 1991.

Barbier, Jean-Joël. *Au piano avec Erik Satie*. Paris: Editions Garamont, 1986.

Bargauanu, Grigore and Dragos Tanasescu. *Dinu Lipatti*. French translation by G. Bargauanu. Lausanne: Editions Payot, 1991 (orig. Bucarest: Editura Muzicale, 1971). (For English language edn. see Tanasescu & Bargauanu, below.)

Barli, Olivier. *La Facture française du piano de 1849 à nos jours*. Paris: La Flûte de Pan, 1983.

Barli, Olivier, *et al. Le Piano français au XXe siècle* (Vol. 15 of *Revue internationale de musique française* [November 1984]).

Bauer, Harold. *His Book*. New York: Norton, 1948, reprinted New York: Greenwood Press, 1969.

_____. "The Paris Conservatoire: Some Reminiscences". *The Musical Quarterly*, October 1947: 533-542.

Bellamann, Henry. "Isidor Philipp". *The Musical Quarterly*, October 1943: 417-425.

Belt, Philip R., *et al. The Piano* (The New Grove Musical Instruments Series, ed. Stanley Sadie). New York: W. W. Norton, 1988.

Benoist, André. *The Accompanist... and Friends*. Edited by John Maltese. Neptune City NJ: Paganiniana Publications, 1978.

Bernac, Pierre. *The Interpretation of French Song*. New York: Norton, 1970.

Bidal, Denise. *Technique du piano*. Lausanne: Foetisch Frères, 1947.

Bie, Oscar. *A History of the Pianoforte and Pianoforte Players*. Translated and revised by E. Kallet and E. Naylor. London: J. Dent & Sons, 1899, reprinted New York: Da Capo Press, 1966.

Bloom, Peter, ed. *Music in Paris in the Eighteen-Thirties*. Stuyvesant, N.Y.: Pendragon Press, 1987.

Blum, David. *Casals and the Art of Interpretation*. London: Heinemann, 1980.

Boissier, Madame Auguste. *Liszt Pedagogue*. Edited and translated by Elyse Mach in *The Liszt Studies*. New York: Associated Music, 1973.

Bongrain, Anne. "Advanced Musical Studies in France". *The Juilliard Journal,* May 1991: 4.

Boschot, Adolphe. *Chez les musiciens*. Paris: Plon-Nourrit, 1922.

Brody, Elaine. *Paris: The Musical Kaleidoscope, 1870-1925*. New York: George Braziller, 1987.

Brower, Harriette. *Modern Masters of the Keyboard*. Freeport, N.Y.: Books for Libraries Press, 1969 (reprint of the 1926 edition).

_____. *Piano Mastery*. New York: Frederick A. Stokes, 1915.

Casadesus, Gaby, with Jacqueline Muller. *Mes noces musicales*. Paris: Buchet-Chastel, 1989.

Casella, Alfredo. *Music in My Time*. Translated and edited by Spencer Norton from the original 1941 edn. Norman: University of Oklahoma Press, 1955.

_____. *Il Pianoforte*. Milan: Ricordi, 1954.

Chasins, Abram. *Speaking of Pianists*. 2nd ed. New York: Alfred A. Knopf, 1961.

Closson, Ernest. *Histoire du piano*. Brussels: Editions universitaires, 1944. (New ed., *History of the Piano*. Translated by Delano Ames and edited and revised by Robin Golding. New York: St. Martin's Press, 1974.

Comettant, Oscar. *Francis Planté*. Paris: Heugel, 1874.

Conservatoire impérial [royal/national] de musique . . . Distribution des prix. Paris: Imprimerie nationale, annual issues consulted for 1844-1938.

Cooper, Martin. *French Music from the Death of Berlioz to the Death of Fauré.* New York: Oxford University Press, 1951.

Cortot, Alfred. *La musique française de piano.* 3 vols. Paris: Presses universitaires de France, 1948.

_____. *Studies in Musical Interpretation.* Set down by Jeanne Thieffry and translated by Robert Jaques. London: George G. Harrap & Co., 1937.

Couperin, François. *L'Art de toucher le clavecin.* Paris: chez M. Couperin, 1717; new edition, Wiesbaden: Breitkopf & Härtel, 1933.

Dandelot, Arthur. *Francis Planté: une belle vie d'artiste.* Paris: Edouard Dupont, 1921.

Debussy, Claude. *Monsieur Croche, antidilettante.* Paris: Dorbon aîné, 1921.

(Debussy, Claude.) *Debussy on Music.* Collected and introduced by François Lesure, translated and edited by Richard Langham Smith. New York: Alfred A. Knopf, 1977.

(Debussy, Claude.) *Letters.* Selected and edited by François Lesure and Roger Nichols, translated by Roger Nichols. Cambridge: Harvard University Press, 1987.

Deschaussées, Monique. *L'Homme et le piano.* Paris: Editions Van de Velde, 1982.

Dietschy, Marcel. *A Portrait of Claude Debussy* (originally *La passion de Claude Debussy* [1962]). Edited and translated by William Ashbrook and Margaret G. Cobb. Oxford: Clarendon Press, 1990.

Dolge, Alfred. *Pianos and their Makers.* Covina: Covina Publishing Co., 1911. Reprint. New York: Dover, 1972.

Dorian, Frederick. *The History of Music in Performance.* New York: W. W. Norton, 1942.

Dumesnil, Maurice. "Coaching with Debussy". *The Piano Teacher,* September-October 1962: 10-13.

_____. "Music Study in France: An Interview with Maurice Dumesnil". *The Piano Teacher,* May/June 1960: 11-13.

Dunoyer de Segonzac, Cecilia. *Marguerite Long.* (forthcoming book from Indiana University Press).

_____. "The Paris Conservatoire: Its Political and Musical Climate in the Nineteenth Century". *American Music Teacher*, June/July 1986: 10-12; and September/October 1986: 24 and 41.

Ehrlich, Cyril. *The Piano: A History*. London: J.M. Dent & Sons, 1976.

Eigeldinger, Jean-Jacques. *Chopin vu par ses élèves*. Neuchatel: la Baconnière, 1979. (New ed., *Chopin: Pianist and Teacher, As Seen By His Pupils*. Translated by Naomi Shohet and edited by Roy Howat. New York: Cambridge University Press, 1986.)

Elder, Dean. *Pianists at Play*. Evanston: The Instrumentalist, 1982.

Falkenberg, Georges. *Les pédales du piano*. Paris: n.p., 1892.

Fauquet, Joël-Marie, *et al. La Musique à Paris en 1830-1831*. Edited by François Lesure. Paris: Bibliothèque nationale, 1983.

Favre, Georges. *La Musique française de piano avant 1830*. Paris: Didier, 1953.

Fétis, François-Joseph. *Curiosités historiques de la musique. Paris: Janet et Cotelle, 1830*.

Fleury, Louis. *"Souvenirs d'un flûtiste: le Conservatoire à l'époque de son centenaire (1895-1900)"*. *Le Monde musical,* January 31, 1925: 10-12 and February 28, 1925: 44-46.

Friedland, Bea. "Louise Farrenc (1804-1875): Composer, Performer, Scholar". *The Musical Quarterly,* April 1974: 257-274.

_____. *Louise Farrenc, 1804-1875*. Ann Arbor: UMI Research Press, 1980.

Gat, Jozsef. *The Technique of Piano Playing*. Translated by Istvan Kleszky. 5th ed. London: Collet's, 1980.

Gavoty, Bernard. *Alfred Cortot*. Geneva: Kister, 1955.

_____. *Alfred Cortot*. Paris: Editions Buchet/Chastel, 1977.

_____. *Anicroches*. Paris: Editions Buchet/Chastel, 1979.

_____. *Clara Haskil*. Geneva: Kister, 1963.

Gerig, Reginald R. *Famous Pianists and their Technique*. New York: Robert B. Luce, Inc., 1974.

Gold, Arthur and Robert Fizdale. *Misia*. New York: Alfred A. Knopf, 1980.

Gottschalk, Louis Moreau. *Notes of a Pianist.* Edited by Jeanne Behrend from the orig. ed. of 1881. New York: Alfred A. Knopf, 1964.

Grover, David S. *The Piano.* New York: Charles Scribner's Sons, 1976.

Gubisch, Nina, ed. "Le Journal inédit de Ricardo Viñes". *Revue international de la musique française,* June 1980: 154-248.

Hambourg, Mark. *The Eighth Octave.* London: Williams and Norgate, 1951.

_____. *From Forte to Piano.* London: Cassell & Co., 1931.

Harding, James. *Saint-Saëns and His Circle.* London: Chapman & Hall, 1965.

Harding, Rosamond. *The Piano-forte: Its History Traced to the Great Exhibition of 1851.* 2nd rev. ed. Cambridge: University Press, 1978.

Heidsieck, Eric. "Dynamics or Motion?" Translated by Charles Timbrell. *The Piano Quarterly,* Winter 1987-88: 56-58.

Helffer, Claude and Catherine Michaud-Pradeilles. *Le Piano.* Paris, Presses universitaires de France, 1985.

Heller, Stephen. *Lettres d'un musicien romantique à Paris.* Edited by Jean-Jacques Eigeldinger. Paris: Editions Flammarion, 1981.

Hildebrandt, Dieter. *Pianoforte: A Social History of the Piano.* Translated by Harriet Goodman. New York: George Braziller, 1988.

Herz. Henri. *My Travels in America.* Transl. by Henry Bertram Hill. Madison: University of Wisconsin Press, 1963.

Hipkins, Alfred J. *A Description and History of the Pianoforte.* 3rd ed. London: Novello, 1929.

Imbert, Hughes. *Médaillons contemporains.* Paris: Librairie Fischbacher, 1902.

Jean-Aubry, Georges. *French Music of Today.* Translated by Edwin Evans from the 1919 ed. Plainview: Books for Libraries Press, 1976.

Kaemper, Gerd. *Techniques pianistiques.* Paris: Alphonse Leduc, 1968.

Kehler, George. *The Piano in Concert.* 2 vols. Metuchen NJ: Scarecrow Press, 1982.

Kendall, Alan. *The Tender Tyrant: Nadia Boulanger.* London: Macdonald and Jane's, 1976.

Kochevitsky, George. *The Art of Piano Playing.* Evanston: Summy-Birchard, 1967.

Labat, Jean-Baptiste. *"Zimmermann et l'école française de piano"* in *Oeuvres littéraires-musicales.*Paris: J. Baur, 1883.

La Grange, Henry-Louis de, *et al. Dans le souvenir d'Yvonne Lefébure.* Paris: Bibliothèque musicale Gustav Mahler, 1987.

_____. *Exposition Alfred Cortot.* Paris: Bibliothèque musicale Gustav Mahler, 1988.

Laloy, Louis. "Marie Jaëll". *La Revue musicale,* May 1925: 139-143.

Landowska, Wanda. *Landowska on Music.* Edited and translated by Denise Restout and Robert Hawkins. New York: Stein and Day, 1964.

Laurent, Albert. *"L'Enseignement du piano". Le Guide du concert,* 11 November 1949: 49-51.

Lavignac, Albert and Lionel de la Laurencie, eds. *Encyclopédie de la musique et dictionnaire du Conservatoire.* Paris: Librairie Delagrave, 1931.

Lazare-Lévy. "E. R. Blanchet". *Le Monde musical,* 31 May 1936: 158-59.

_____. *"La fièvre interprétative". Revue internationale de musique,* April 1939: 895-898.

Le Couppey, Félix. *De l'enseignement du piano.* Paris: Hachette, 1882.

Lefébure, Yvonne. *"Cortot au Conservatoire: Souvenirs d'enfance d'-Yvonne Lefébure".* Unpublished manuscript, dated 1955, given to the author.

_____. "Cortot, le poète du clavier". *Revue internationale de musique,* April 1939: 903-06.

_____. *"Le piano". Le Guide du concert et du disque,* 19 April 1969: 9-11.

Lenoir, Auguste and Jean de Nahuque. *Francis Planté.* Hossegor: Librairie D. Chabas, 1931.

Locard, Paul and Rémy Stricker. *Le Piano.* Paris: Presses universitaires de France, 1974.

Lockspeiser, Edward. *Debussy: His Life and Mind.* 2 vols. New York: Cambridge University Press, 1978.

Loesser, Arthur. *Men, Women and Pianos*. New York: Simon and Schuster, 1954.

Long, Marguerite. *Au piano avec Claude Debussy*. Paris: Julliard, 1960.

_____. *Au piano avec Gabriel Fauré*. Paris: Julliard, 1963.

_____. *Au piano avec Maurice Ravel*. Paris: Julliard, 1971.

Loyonnet, Paul. *Beethoven: "ce mal connu"*. Paris: Editions de l'Epargne, 1967.

_____. *Les gestes et la pensée du pianiste*. Montréal: Louise Courteau, 1985.

_____. *Paradoxes sur le pianiste*. Ottawa: Leméac, 1981.

_____. *"Souvenirs"*, manuscript sent to the author, dated 1986.

_____. *Les 32 sonates pour piano: Journal intime de Beethoven.Beethoven* Paris: R. Laffont, 1977.

Marmontel, Antoine-François. *Conseils d'un professeur sur l'enseignement technique et l'esthétique du piano*. Paris: Heugel, n.d.

_____. *Les Pianistes celèbres*. Paris: A. Chaix, 1878.

_____. *Virtuoses contemporains*. Paris: Heugel, 1882.

Mathias, Georges. *"Préface"* to Isidor Philipp's *Exercises quotidiens tirés des oeuvres de Chopin*. Paris: Hamelle, 1897.

Méreaux, Amédée. *Variétés littéraires et musicales*. Paris: Calmann Lévy, 1878.

Merlet, Dominique. *"Enseignement et carrières du piano"*. *Le Guide du piano*. Paris: Mazarine, 1979.

Methuen-Campbell, James. *Catalogue of Recordings by Classical Pianists (Vol. I: Pianists born to 1872)*. Chipping Norton: Disco Epsom, 1984.

_____. *Chopin Playing*. New York: Taplinger, 1981.

_____. "Edouard Risler and Louis Diémer," liner notes for Symposium 1020 (LP recording).

Monsaingeon, Bruno. *Mademoiselle. Conversations with Nadia Boulanger*. Translated by Robyn Marsack. Manchester (England): Carcanet Press, 1985.

Morpain, Joseph. *Comment il faut jouer du piano*. Paris: Heugel, 1922.

Moszkowski, Moritz. "Methods and Customs of the Paris Conservatoire". *The Etude,* February 1910, 81.

_____. "The Paris Conservatory of Music," *The Etude,* January 1910: 9-10.

Murdoch, William. *Chopin: His Life.* New York: Macmillan, 1935. (Reprint, New York: Greenwood Press, 1971.)

Nat, Yves. *Carnet.* Paris: La Flûte de Pan, 1983.

Nectoux, J.-Michel. *Fauré.* Paris: Editions du Seuil, 1972.

Neuhaus, Heinrich. *The Art of Piano Playing.* Translated by K. A. Leibovitch. New York: Praeger Publishers, 1973.

Newman, William S. *The Sonata in the Classic Era.* 2nd ed. New York: W. W. Norton, 1972.

_____. *The Sonata Since Beethoven.* 2nd ed. New York: W. W. Norton, 1972.

Nichols, Roger. *Ravel Remembered.* New York: W. W. Norton, 1987.

Novaes, Guiomar. "Technic and Beauty in Piano Playing". *The Etude,* August 1927: 565-66.

Orenstein, Arbie. *Ravel: Man and Musician.* New York: Columbia University Press, 1975.

_____, ed. *A Ravel Reader.* New York: Columbia University Press, 1990.

Pâris, Alain. *Dictionnaire des interprètes.* Paris: Robert Laffont, 1982.

Perkins, John F. and Alan Kelly. "The Gramophone & Typewriter Ltd Records of Camille Saint-Saëns". *Recorded Sound,* January 1981: 25-27.

Perlemuter, Vlado & Jourdan-Morhange, Hélène. *Ravel According to Ravel.* Transl. bu Frances Tanner; ed. by Harold Taylor. White Plains NY: Pro/Am Music Resources, 1988.

Perlis, Vivian. *Two Men for Modern Music: E. Robert Schmitz and Herman Langinger.* Brooklyn: Institute for Studies in American Music (Brooklyn College), 1978.

Philipp, Isidor. "Advice on Pianoforte Playing". *Musical Courier,* 3 January 1931: 7

_____. "*Causeries sur l'enseignement du piano*". *Musica*, November 1902: 31-32.

_____. "*Conservatoire national de musique et d'art dramatique*". *Le Monde musical et théatral*, January/February 1940: 20-21.

_____. "The French National Conservatory of Music". *The Musical Quarterly*, April 1920: 214-26.

_____. *Le Piano et la virtuosité*. Paris: Heugel, 1931.

_____. *Quelques considérations sur l'enseignement du Piano*. Paris: Durand, 1927öö.

_____. *Réflexions sur l'art du piano.*Paris: Heugel, 1931.

_____. "*Souvenirs sur Anton Rubinstein, Camille Saint-Saëns et Busoni*". *Revue internationale de musique*, April 1939: 907-12.

Piano Quarterly, Fall 1982 (includes articles on Robert Casadesus by Cone, Eves, Johannesen, Owings, Silverman, and Tolson)

Pierre, Constant. *B. Sarrette et les origines du Conservatoire national de musique et de déclamation*. Paris: Delalain Frères, 1895.

_____. *Le Conservatoire national de musique et de déclamation*. Paris: Imprimerie nationale, 1900.

_____. *Les factures d'instruments de musique*. Paris: E. Sagot, 1893, reprinted Geneva: Minkoff, 1971.

Pistone, Danièle. *La Musique en France de la Révolution à 1900*. Paris: Honoré Champion, 1979.

_____, ed. *Revue internationale de musique française*, November 1984 (issue entitled *Le piano français au XXe siècle*.)

Place, Adélaïde de. *Le Piano-forte à Paris entre 1760 et 1822*. Paris: Aux Amateurs de Livres, 1986öö.

Pueyo, Eduardo del. "*Autour de la Méthode de Marie Jaëll et de son apport à l'enseignement du piano*". *Revue internationale de musique*, April 1939: 929-38.

Pugno, Raoul. *Les Leçons écrites de Raoul Pugno: Schumann*. Paris: Librairie des Annales, 1911.

Rameau, Jean-Philippe. *Complete Theoretical Writings*, ed. Erwin R. Jacobi. [n.p.]: American Institute of Musicology, 1969.

_____. "*De la mechanique des doigts sur le clavessin*", in *Pièces de clavecin*, ed. by Erwin R. Jacobi. Kassel: Bärenreiter, 1958.

Rattalino, Piero. *Da Clementi a Pollini*. 2nd ed. Florence: Ricordi/Giunti Martello, 1984.

_____. *Pianisti e Fortisti*. Florence: Ricordi/Giunti. 1990.

Riemann, Hugo. "J. Ph. Rameau als Klavierpädagoge". *Der Klavier-Lehrer*, 1 August 1893: 197-99; 15 August 1893: 209-10; 1 September 1893: 221-23.

Rohozinski, Ladislas, ed. *Cinquante ans de musique française de 1874 à 1925*. 2 vols. Paris: Les ditions musicales de la Librairie de France, 1925.

Rolland, Romain. *Musicians of Today*. Translated by Mary Blaiklock. New York: Henry Holt, 1915.

Rorem, Ned. *Setting the Tone*. New York: Coward-McCann, 1983.

Rosenstiel, Léonie. *Nadia Boulanger: A Life in Music*. New York: W. W. Norton, 1982.

Rougier, Philippe. "Magda Tagliaferro: A Discography". *American Recorded Sound Collections Journal*, Fall 1991: 180-90.

Rougnon, Paul. *Souvenirs de 60 années de vie musicale* . . . . Paris: Editions Margueritat, 1925.

Rubinstein, Arthur. *My Many Years*. New York: Alfred A. Knopf, 1980.

_____. *My Young Years*. New York: Alfred A. Knopf, 1973.

Saint-Foix, Georges. "*Les premiers pianistes parisiens*". *Revue musicale*, August 1922: 121-36; April 1923: 194-205; June 1924: 187-98; June 1925: 209-15; August 1925: 105-09; November 1925: 43-46; February 1926: 102-10; August 1928: 321-32.

Schick, Robert D. *The Vengerova System of Piano Playing*. University Park: Pennsylvania State University Press, 1982.

Schmitz, E. Robert. *The Capture of Inspiration*. New York: Carl Fischer, 1935.

_____. *The Piano Works of Claude Debussy*. New York: Duell, Sloan & Pearce, 1950. Reprint. New York: Dover Publications, 1966.

_____. "A Plea for the Real Debussy". *Etude*, December 1937: 781-82.

_____. "Technique Must Release Music!" *Etude,* March 1949: 158, 194.

Schonberg, Harold C. *The Great Pianists.* New York: Simon and Schuster, 1963.

Schwarz, Boris. *Great Masters of the Violin.* New York: Simon & Schuster, 1983.

Schwerké, Irving and Harry L. Anderson. *Francis Planté,* booklet accompanying International Piano Library 101 (LP recording).

Shattuck, Roger. *The Banquet Years.*Revised ed. New York: Vintage, 1968.

(Shaw, George Bernard). *Shaw's Music,* 3 vols., ed. Dan H. Laurence, 2nd rev. ed. London: The Bodley Head, 1989.

Spycket, Jérôme. *Clara Haskil.* Lausanne: Payot, 1975.

_____. *Scarbo: le roman de Samson François.* Lausanne: Van de Velde/Payot, 1985.

Tagliaferro, Magda. *Quase tudo.* Rio de Janeiro: Nova Fronteira, 1979.

Tanasescu, Dragos and Grigore Bargauanu. *Lipatti.* White Plains NY: Pro/Am Music Resources, 1988 (orig. Bucarest: Editura Muzicale, 1971). (For French lang. edn. see Bargauanu & Tanasescu, above.)

Taylor, Karen M. "A Bridge Across the Rhine: In Memoriam, Edouard Risler (1873-1929)". *Journal of the American Liszt Society,* December 1980: 25-43.

_____. *Alfred Cortot.* (forthcoming book from Indiana University Press).

Thomson, Virgil. *Music Reviewed, 1940-1954.* New York: Vintage Books, 1967.

Timbrell, Charles. "Alfred Cortot: His Life and Legacy" (with a discography). *The Piano Quarterly,* Fall 1984: 19-31.

_____. "The French School of Pianism: A Talk with Gaby Casadesus". *Keyboard Classics,* May/June 1990: 8-9.

_____. "An Interview with Paul Loyonnet". *Journal of the American Liszt Society,* June 1986: 112-21.

_____. "Liszt and French Music".*Journal of the American Liszt Society,* December 1979: 25-33.

_____. "Ravel's *Miroirs* with Perlemuter". *The Piano Quarterly,* Fall 1980: 50-52.

Tocco, James. "Magda [Tagliaferro] as Muse," *Musical America,* February 1980: 34-35, 40.

Tranchefort, François-René, ed. *Guide de la musique de piano et de clavecin.* Paris: Fayard, 1987.

Vianna da Motta, José. "I. Philipp". *Der Klavier-Lehrer,* October 1903: 289-92.

Vitale, Vincenzo. *Il Pianoforte a Napoli nell'Ottocento.* Naples: Bibliopolis, 1983.

Walker, Alan. *Franz Liszt. Vol. I: The Virtuoso Years, 1811-1847.* New York: Alfred A. Knopf, 1983.

Weill, Janine. *Marguerite Long: une vie fascinante.* Paris: Julliard, 1969.

Weitzmann, C. F. *A History of Pianoforte-Playing and Pianoforte Literature.* New York: G. Schirmer, 1897. Reprint. New York: Da Capo, 1969.

B. SCORES (by editor)

Béroff, Michel and Michael Stegemann, eds. Debussy: *Preludes,* Book I; *Deux Arabesques.* Vienna: Wiener Urtext/Universal, 1985.

Casadesus, Gaby, ed. Debussy: *Pour le piano.* New York: Schirmer, 1987.

_____. Ravel: *Miroirs, Sonatine, Gaspard de la nuit, Jeux d'eau.* New York: Schirmer, 1985-90.

Ciampi, Marcel, ed. Beethoven: *Concerto* in G, Op. 58. Paris: Choudens, 1950.

Cortot, Alfred, ed. Major works by Chopin, Liszt, Mendelssohn, Schumann, and Weber. Paris: Salabert, 1915 ff. Works by Brahms and Franck. Milan: Curci, 1950-57.

Debussy, Claude, ed. Chopin: Complete Piano Works. Paris: Durand, 1915-16.

Delaborde, Elie and Isidor Philipp, eds. Alkan: Selected Works. Paris: Costallat, c. 1903.

Diémer, Louis, ed. Beethoven: *Sonatas* (complete). Paris: Lemoine, 1915-16.

_____. Chopin: Piano Works (complete). Paris: Lemoine, 1915-18.

_____. Couperin: *Pièces de clavecin*. Paris: Durand, n.d.

_____. Mozart: *Sonatas* (complete). Paris: Lemoine, 1915.

_____. *Les vieux maîtres*. Paris: Heugel, n.d.

Ericourt, Daniel and Robert P. Erickson, eds. *Masterclasses in Debussy*. Chapel Hill: Hinshaw, 1978.

_____. *Masterclasses in Spanish Piano Music*. Chapel Hill: Hinshaw, 1984.

Falkenberg, Georges, ed. Mendelssohn: Complete Piano Works. Paris: Heugel, 1924.

Farrenc, Aristide and Louise, eds. *Le Trésor des pianistes*. 20 vols. Paris: A. Farrenc, 1861-72. Reprint. New York: Da Capo, 1977.

Ferté, Armand, ed. Bach: *Well-Tempered Clavier*(complete). Paris: Choudens, 1953.

_____. Beethoven: *Sonatas* (complete). 3 vols. Paris: Choudens, 1931.

_____. Liszt: *2 Legends*. Paris: Choudens, n.d.

_____. Liszt: *Sonata*. Paris: Lemoine, 1924.

Helffer, Claude, ed. Debussy: *Douze Etudes*. Paris: Durand-Costallat, 1991.

Helffer, Claude and Roy Howat, eds. Debussy: *Preludes,* Books I and II. Paris: Durand-Costallat, 1985.

Kartun, Léon, ed. Scarlatti: *36 Sonatas*. Paris: Les Editions ouvrières, 1954.

Lack, Théodore, ed. Bach: *Inventions and Sinfonias*. Paris: Lemoine, 1915.

_____. Liszt: Selected Works. 3 vols. Paris: Lemoine, 1919.

Lazare-Lévy, ed. Bach: *English Suites; French Suites*. Paris: Choudens, n.d.

_____. Chopin: *Mazurkas* (complete). Paris: Senart, 1918.

_____. Chopin: *Polonaises* (complete). Paris: Senart, 1919.

_____. Schubert: *Impromptus*, Op. 142. Paris: Salabert, 1954.

_____. Schumann: *Sonatas*, Opp. 11 and 22. Paris: Choudens, n.d.

Long, Marguerite, ed. Mendelssohn: *Songs without Words*. Paris: Senart, 1918.

_____. Mozart: *Sonatas* (complete); *Concertos*, K. 450, 466, 488 and 491. Paris: Choudens, c. 1935.

Loyonnet, Paul and Lucien Capet, eds. Beethoven: *Sonatas* for Piano and Violin (complete). Paris: Senart, 1927.

Marmontel, Antoine-François, ed. Beethoven: *Sonata*, Op. 111. Paris: Heugel 1916.

Morhange-Motchane, Marthe, ed. Albeniz: *Iberia*. New York: International, 1982-3.

_____. Couperin: Selected Works. Miami: Belwin-Mills, 1968.

_____. Ravel: *Sonatine*. New York: International, 1982.

_____. Scarlatti: *39 Sonatas*. Miami: Belwin-Mills. 1968.

Philipp, Isidor, ed. Albeniz: *España*. New York: International, ë 1950.

_____. Bartók: *For Children*. New York: International, 1951.

_____. Beethoven: *Concertos 1 & 2*. Paris: Heugel, 1925.

_____. English Virginalists. Paris: Heugel, 1925.

_____. Fauré: Selected Works. New York: Schirmer, 1944.

_____. Liszt: *Variations on* "Weinen, Klagen, Zorgen, Sagen". New York: Schirmer, 1946.

_____. Mozart: *Concertos*, K. 459 and 595. New York: Schirmer, 1945.

_____. Mozart: *Concertos*, K. 488, 466, and 491. Paris: Heugel, 1926.

_____. Scarlatti: *9 Sonatas*. New York: International, 1943.

_____. Scriabin: *Fourth Sonata*. New York: International, 1942.

Pugno, Raoul, ed. Chopin: *Ballades; Impromptus; Etudes; Mazurkas; Waltzes*. Vienna: Universal, n.d.

_____. Chopin: *Nocturnes*. Leipzig: Hofmeister, 1909.

Ravel, Maurice, ed. Mendelssohn: Complete Piano Works. Paris: Durand, 1915-18.

Riera, Santiago, ed. Liszt: *Harmonies poétiques et réligieuses*. Paris: Durand, 1920.

_____. Liszt: *Paganini Etudes*. Paris: Durand, 1919.

_____. Liszt: *Sonata*. Paris: Durand, 1919.

Risler, Edouard, ed. Liszt: *Hungarian Rhapsodies* (complete. Paris: Heugel, 1924.

_____. Mozart: *Sonatas* (complete). Paris: Société française d'Edition des Grandes Classiques musicaux, 1917.

Risler, Edouard and Vincent d'Indy, eds. Beethoven: *Sonatas,* Opp. 2/2, 2/3, 7, 10/1, 10/2, 10/3, 13, and 53. Paris: Senart, 1920.

Riss-Arbeau, Marie-Jeanne, ed. Chopin: *Mazurkas* (complete). Paris: Société français des Grandes Classiques musicaux, 1918.

_____. Chopin: *Polonaises* (complete). Paris: Société français des Grandes Classiques musicaux, 1917.

_____. Mendelssohn. Selected Works. Paris: Heugel, 1925.

_____. Weber. *4 Sonatas*. Paris: Société français des Grandes Classiques musicaux, 1920.

Saint-Saëns, Camille, ed. Beethoven: *5 Piano Concertos*. Paris: Durand, 1916.

_____. Mozart: *Sonatas* (complete). Paris: Durand, 1915.

_____. Rameau: *Pièces de clavecin*. Paris: Durand, 1895.

Schmitz, E. Robert, ed. Bach: *15 Two-Part Inventions*. New York: Carl Fischer, c. 1938.

_____. Chopin: *Etudes* (complete). New York: Carl Fischer, 1938.

_____. Prokofiev: *Seventh Sonata*. New York: Leeds, 1945.

_____. Ravel: *Alborada del gracioso.* New York: Associated Music, 1942.

Selva, Blanche, ed. Clementi: *Sonatinas.* Paris: Editions français de musique classique, 1916.

_____. Froberger: *Toccata* in D Minor. Paris: Senart, n.d.

_____. Séverac. *Cerdaña.* Paris: Rouart-Lerolle, 1911.

_____. Séverac. *Sous les lauriers roses.* Paris: Rouart-Lerolle, 1920.

Selva, Blanche and Vincent d'Indy, eds. Rust: *12 Sonatas.* Paris: Rouart-Lerolle, 1913.

Staub, Victor, ed. Haydn: *Sonatas,* 3 vols. Paris: Heugel, 1926.

Webster, Beveridge, ed. Chabrier: *Pièces pittoresques.* New York: International, 1962.

_____. Prokofiev: *Concertos 1 and 2.* New York: International, 1963.

NOTES

I. THE NINETEENTH CENTURY

[1] *(page 1)* Issue of 12 September 1768, 581, translated from Adélaïde de Place, *Le Piano-forte à Paris entre 1760 et 1822* (Paris: Aux Amateurs de Livres, 1986), 153.

[2] *(page 1)* Place, 9; Constant Pierre, *Les facteurs d'instruments de musique* (Paris: E. Sagot, 1893; reprinted Geneva: Minkoff, 1971), 139-40.

[3] *(page 1)* Voltaire, *Correspondence* (Banbury: Voltaire Foundation, 1975), XLI, 215; Arthur Loesser, *Men, Women and Pianos* (New York: Simon and Schuster, 1954), 317.

[4] *(page 2)* Alfred Dolge, *Pianos and Their Makers* (New York: Dover, 1972), 259; Alfred J. Hipkins, *A Description and History of the Pianoforte* (London: Novello, 1929, reprinted Detroit: Information Coordinators, 1975), 20.

[5] *(page 3)* Jean-Jacques Eigeldinger, *Chopin: Pianist and Teacher, As Seen by his Pupils*, trans. Naomi Shohet, ed. Roy Howat (New York: Cambridge University Press, 1986), 26.

[6] *(page 3)* The recordings referred to here are: Electrola 1C 065.99.199 (Chopin's Berceuse played on an 1845 Pleyel by Jörg Demus); Oryx EXP 64 (various Chopin works performed on an 1840 Erard by Ernst Gröschel); and Pandora PAN 107 and 109 (various Liszt and Chopin works performed on an 1851 Erard by Martha Goldstein). Earlier French pianos made by Pascal Taskin in 1788 and 1790 may be heard on Arion ARN 68028 (various Mozart works played by Nadine Palmier and Joël Rigal) and on Attacca Babel 8843-1 (works by Hüllmandel and his contemporaries played by Hilbrand Borkent).

[7] *(page 5)* *Racine et Shakespeare* (Paris: Michel Lévy, 1854), 20.

[8] *(page 5)*   Loesser, 386.

[9] *(page 6)*   The Conservatoire was originally located in the Hôtel des Menus-Plaisirs in the Faubourg Poissonnière. In 1911 it moved to premises at 14 rue de Madrid, a former Jesuit school. After World War II, the division of drama (*déclamation*) became a separate institution and moved back to the original location. In September 1990 a dance division was added to the Conservatoire, and the newly organized school — today officially known as the Conservatoire National Supérieur de Musique et de Danse de Paris — moved to the north-eastern part of the capital, in the Cité de la Musique in the Parc de la Villette. For the history of the Conservatoire, its divisions, regulations, faculty, and prize winners before 1900, the principal source is Constant Pierre, *Le Conservatoire national de musique et de déclamation* (Paris: Imprimerie nationale, 1900). For more recent curricular developments, see especially Dominique Merlet, *"Enseignement et carrières du piano"* in *Le Guide du piano*, ed. Michel Archimbaud (Paris: Mazarine, 1979), 100-15.

[10] *(page 6)*   René Dumesnil, *"L'Enseignement"*, in *Cinquante ans de musique française de 1874 à 1925*, ed. Ladislav Rohozinski (Paris: Les Editions musicales de la Librairie de France, 1925), 191-92; Merlet, 110.

[11] *(page 7)*   This figure does not include assistant-teachers or professors hired to teach at the preparatory level. See below.

[12] *(page 9)*   The *accessits*, which by Morpain's time had been reduced from three to two (and today are discontinued entirely), allowed students to remain in class provided they won a progressively higher one at least every other year. Exceptional students, however, could skip *accessits* as well as lower medals and prizes. Thus Robert Casadesus, who entered the preparatory level in 1909, received just two piano awards: a first medal in 1911 and a first prize in 1913.

[13] *(page 9)*   For interesting observations about these competitions see: Hector Berlioz, *Evenings with the Orchestra*,

trans. Jacques Barzun (Chicago: University of Chicago Press, 1956), 215-19; journal entries by Ricardo Viñes, in Elaine Brody, *Paris: The Musical Kaleidoscope, 1870-1925* (New York: George Braziller, 1987), 178-80; an article by Claude Debussy for *Le Figaro*, in *Debussy on Music*, ed. François Lesure, trans. Richard Langham Smith (New York: Alfred A. Knopf, 1977), 236-39; and Harold Bauer, *His Book* (New York: Norton, 1948, reprinted New York: Greenwood Press, 1969), 111-17.

14 *(page 9)*　The narrow curriculum at the Conservatoire is in marked contrast with the requirements of many of the world's other leading music schools. For example, during the 1920s, when advanced-level pianists at the Conservatoire were only required to pass an examination in solfège, the advanced pianists at the Vienna Academy of Music were required to take two-year courses in harmony, sight-reading, history, and counterpoint, and a one-year course in Italian. (Information from an interview in 1991 with the Austrian pianist Gustav Heintze.)

In the Soviet Union, musical education was even more comprehensive. According to the system in use in the 1970s and 80s, talented children were identified at age six or seven and sent to a special music school for beginners, where the seven-year curriculum included instrumental study, theory, and history. After receiving a diploma from this school, the student could then attend a four-year Music College that included a broad curriculum in music as well as the sciences and literature. After completing this school, the student could take conservatory entrance examinations. (An alternate route to conservatory study was possible by starting the child in a different kind of special music school that only trained students to enter conservatories. That curriculum took ten years rather than the total of eleven just described.) The conservatory entrance examinations included tests in theory, harmony, and Russian history and literature, as well as extremely competitive performance auditions. In 1989 the five-year curriculum at the Moscow Conservatory included the following required courses: accompanying (four years), music history (four years), chamber music (three years), applied pedagogy (three years), harmony (one year), analysis (one year), counterpoint (one year), history and literature of the piano (one year), and courses in Marxism, political economics, and Scientific Communism (five years). The graduation requirement was a full-length recital as well as a concerto performance (with a second piano). A higher diploma, approximately equivalent to a doctorate, could be obtained after two further years of study and assistant-teaching, two additional recitals, and two written papers. The total length of musical studies to this point was, typically, eighteen years. (Information from an interview in 1991 with the Russian pianist Oleg Volkov.)

[15] *(page 13)* *Curiosités historiques de la musique* (Paris: Janet et Cotelle, 1830), 145.

[16] *(page 14)* See modern edition (Wiesbaden: Breitkopf & Härtel, 1933), 11-12.

[17] *(page 14)* Author's translation from the reprint (Kassel: Bärenreiter, 1958), 17.

[18] *(page 14)* Author's translation from the reprint in Rameau's *Complete Theoretical Writings*, ed. Erwin R. Jacobi (n.p.: American Institute of Musicology, 1969), IV, 35.

[19] *(page 14)* *Der Klavier-Lehrer*, XVI (August and September 1893), 197-99, 209-10, 221-23; James Methuen-Campbell, *Chopin Playing* (New York: Taplinger, 1981), 163.

[20] *(page 16)* Gottschalk, *Notes of a Pianist*, ed. Jeanne Behrend after the original edn. of 1881 (New York: Alfred A. Knopf, 1964), 221.

[21] *(page 17)* Harold Schonberg, *The Great Pianists* (New York: Simon and Schuster, 1963), 180.

[22] *(page 18)* 31 October 1846, 2.

[23] *(page 18)*   Jaëll's main ideas, explained in detail in *La Musique et la psycho-physiologie* (1896) and *Le Toucher* (1899), were that the movements which transmit musical expression to the keyboard are capable of being classed and explained; that tactile sensibility must be directly related to musical sensibility through the mental imagining of movements and muscular tension; that practicing circular and sliding motions of the fingers on the keys guarantees a continuity of movement after one attack and before the next; and that different surfaces of the finger produce different sounds from the piano. Most of her ideas were developed after her study with Liszt in the 1880s and have no relation to her study with Herz. Although Jaëll's concepts never gained wide acceptance in France during her lifetime, they were promoted by her students at the Ecole Marie Jaëll in Paris and by the late pianist Eduardo del Pueyo at the Brussels Conservatory. More recently they have influenced several leading Parisian teachers, including Pierre Sancan.

[24] *(page 20)*   For a full account of this duel, see Alan Walker, *Franz Liszt. Volume I: The Virtuoso Years* (New York: Alfred A. Knopf, 1983), 232-240.

[25] *(page 21)*   See Madame Auguste Boissier, *Liszt Pédagogue* (Paris: Honoré Champion, 1927) and the translation by Elyse Mach in *The Liszt Studies* (New York: Associated Music, 1973).

[26] *(page 21)*   Eigeldinger, 170. In Clara's letter to her father of 19 March 1839, she identifies Mathias as "a pupil of Chopin." Yet Mathias stated sixty years later (in his preface to Philipp's *Exercices quotidiens tirés des oeuvres de Chopin*) that his study with Chopin was from 1840-45.

[27] *(page 23)*   Chopin's words as translated in Eigeldinger, 195.

[28] *(page 23)*   Chopin's page of exercises is reproduced and transcribed in Eigeldinger, 35-36.

[29] *(page 23)*   Loesser, 372.

[30] *(page 27)* Bea Friedland, *Louise Farrenc, 1804-1875: Composer— Performer—Scholar* (Ann Arbor: UMI Research Press, 1980), 22.

[31] *(page 27)* *Shaw's Music*, ed. Dan H. Laurence, 2nd rev. ed. (London: The Bodley Head, 1989), II, 887.

[32] *(page 28)* *Virtuoses contemporains* (Paris: Heugel, 1882), 164-65.

[33] *(page 29)* *From Forte to Piano* (London: Cassell & Co., 1931), 162.

[34] *(page 30)* *Music in My Time*, trans. and ed. Spencer Norton, from the original 1941 edn. (Norman: University of Oklahoma Press, 1955), 39-40.

[35] *(page 30)* Jérôme Spycket, *Clara Haskil* (Lausanne: Payot, 1975), 247.

[36] *(page 33)* Robert Lortat and Magda Tagliaferro, who completed their training just after the turn of the century, will be mentioned at the end of this section. Excluded from consideration throughout this survey are recordings made from piano rolls and recordings by pianists who were active primarily as accompanists or chamber musicians.

[37] *(page 35)* *Chez les musiciens* (Paris: Plon-Nourrit, 1922), 140.

[38] *(page 35)* During his brief appointment as piano instructor at the Ecole Niedermeyer, from 1860 to 1863, Saint-Saëns taught piano to two future composers, Gabriel Fauré and André Messager. Otherwise, he is known to have coached Isidor Philipp and Leopold Godowsky, although it has not been determined to what extent.

[39] *(page 37)* Planté, who only taught privately, had at least one noted student, Alfonso Thibaud, who performed as a soloist and with Saint-Saëns and the violinist Pablo de Sarasate prior to moving to Buenos Aires around 1885.

[40] *(page 37)* See Methuen-Campbell, *Chopin Playing*, 76.

[41] *(page 41)* Arbie Orenstein, ed., *A Ravel Reader* (New York: Columbia University Press, 1990), 219; François Lesure and Roger Nichols, ed. and trans. *Debussy Letters* (Cambridge: Harvard University Press, 1987), 222n.

[42] *(page 43)*   As translated in Karen M. Taylor, "A Bridge Across the Rhine: In Memoriam, Edouard Risler", *Journal of the American Liszt Society*, VIII (December 1980), 25-26.

[43] *(page 43)*   *My Many Years* (New York: Alfred A. Knopf, 1973), 159. Rubinstein also refers to the pleasure of performing two-piano recitals with Risler in Buenos Aires and Montevideo in 1920.

[44] *(page 44)*   *Le Piano* (Paris: Salabert, 1959), 2.

[45] *(page 45)*   Marguerite Long, *Au Piano avec Maurice Ravel* (Paris: Julliard, 1971), 143.

[46] *(page 49)*   Nat's other recordings are mentioned in Chapter Three.

II. LEADING ARTIST-TEACHERS, 1900-1940

[47] *(page 55)*   Although Nadia Boulanger often coached pianists, including Idil Biret, Julius Katchen, and Emile Naoumoff, the only official appointment she ever had as a piano professor was at the Conservatoire Femina-Musica. Subsequently, she taught keyboard harmony and accompanying at the Conservatoire; accompanying, harmony, and counterpoint at the Ecole Normale; and composition at the American Conservatory.

[48] *(page 63)*   This concept was perhaps easiest to put into practice on turn-of-the century Erard pianos, on which one felt a pronounced resistance prior to the second escapement. According to Marthe Morhange-Motchane, who practiced on these instruments as a student, no other pianos then or since have had such a pronounced resistance.

[49] *(page 68)*   It has sometimes been claimed that Long was the first woman professor of a *classe supérieure* at the Conservatoire, but this not accurate. Louise-Aglaé Massart taught a *classe supérieure* until her retirement in 1887. Before her, Louise Farrenc and Hélène de Montgeroult taught upper-level classes, although they had not yet been designated *classes supérieures*

(as opposed to *classes préparatoires* or, before that, *étude de clavier* [keyboard study].)

[50] *(page 77)* Gavoty, *Alfred Cortot* (Paris: Editions Buchet/Chastel, 1977), 149.

III. MAJOR FIGURES OF THE POSTWAR PERIOD, 1945-1985

[51] *(page 118)* The American pianist Robert Lurie, who studied with Gentil from 1947 to 1951, recalled in an interview three types of exercises he worked on with Gentil. First, for independence of the fingers, Gentil assigned original exercises in which up to four different rhythms were to be played in the two hands simultaneously while holding down one finger in each hand. (These exercises were to be repeated with different combinations of fingers and rhythms.) Secondly, Gentil stressed, through the use of free-fall exercises, the need for suppleness in all the joints except the last phalange of the playing finger, in which a feeling of resistance was developed. A third type of exercise developed wrist flexion.

[52] *(page 126)* Other recollections of Casadesus's teaching are found in the interview with Grant Johannesen in Chapter IV.

IV. INTERVIEWS

[53] *(page 142)* The exercises referred to are found in her *Ecole de l'indépendence des doigts* (Paris: Heugel, 1896).

V. CODA: THE FRENCH SCHOOL, PAST AND PRESENT

[54] *(page 188)* *Le Piano* (Paris: Salabert, 1959), ii.

[55] *(page 189)* *Monsieur Croche, antidilettante* (Paris: Dorbon aîné, 1921), 79-80.

[56] *(page 189)* *Musicians of Today,* trans. Mary Blaiklock (New York: Henry Holt, 1915), 237, 242-43.

[57] {*page 189*) *The Interpretation of French Song* (New York: W. W. Norton, 1970), 35.

[58] (*page 190*) Gunnar Asklund, "Technique Must Release Music! A Conversation with E. Robert Schmitz", *The Etude*, March 1949, 158.

[59] (*page 190*) Bauer, "The Paris Conservatoire: Some Reminiscences", *The Musical Quarterly*, October 1947, 540.

[60] (*page 190*) *My Young Years* (New York: Alfred A. Knopf, 1973), 128-34.

[61] (*page 192*) Pierre Kostanoff (c. 1890-1962), reputed to be a student of Busoni, lived in France for much of his life. André Krust, who studied with him for six years, summed up his approach in an interview: "Kostanoff's teaching was based mainly on the use of the arm and forearm, including rotation and natural weight; on cultivating a beautiful sound; and on legato. He used the Brahms Exercises as the basis of his teaching, and he talked a great deal about how Busoni and Rachmaninov had played. Kostanoff's teaching was considered revolutionary in France at the time, for it was contrary to some ideas that had prevailed here since the nineteenth century."

[62](*page 193*) *Les Livres du pianiste,* (Paris: Gérard Billaudot, 1991, two vols.)

[63] (*page 194*) Mention should also be made of three professors of the previous generation who have not received attention in this book: Joseph Benvenuti, primarily a chamber musician, who studied with Diémer and Ferté and whose students included François-René Duchâble and Annie Petit; Germaine Mounier, who studied with Riera and Tagliaferro and whose students included Erik Berchot, Michelle Roy, and Yves Rault; and Raymond Trouard, a Liszt specialist who studied with Staub and Sauer and whose students included Michel Dalberto.

[64] (*page 194*) "*La Villette, aujourd'hui et demain*", *Le Monde de la Musique,* April 1992, 90-91.

PHOTO CREDITS

All photographs courtesy of the artist, except:

Jean-Joël Barbier: Photo Véronique Marmouset, Paris
Robert Casadesus: Sony Classical
Marcel Ciampi: Courtesy John-Paul Bracey
Jean-Philippe Collard: Photo Tony Frank, Paris
Alfred Cortot: Courtesy Robert Lurie
Louis Diémer: Dover Publications
Brigitte Engerer: Photo Irmeli Jung, Paris
Louise Farrenc: Courtesy Bea Friedland
Armand Ferté: Bibliothèque Nationale, Paris
Jacques Février: Roger-Viollet, Paris
Jules Gentil: Courtesy Judith Steck Gentil
Henri Herz: University of Michigan Museum of Art
    (Acc. No. 1956/1.55)
Grant Johannesen: Photo Meg Otto, New York
Lazare-Lévy: Roger-Viollet, Paris
Marguerite Long: Courtesy Cecilia Dunoyer
The Paris Conservatoire (3): Photo Jeffrey Engel
Isidor Philipp: Dover Publications
Francis Planté: Dover Publications
Raoul Pugno: Dover Publications
Edouard Risler: Dover Publications
Camille Saint-Saëns: Dover Publications
Pierre Sancan: Photo Gabriel Martinez, St-Jean-de-Luz
Blanche Selva: Bibliothèque musicale Gustav Mahler, Paris

NAME INDEX

Other Music Titles Available from Pro/Am Music Resources, Inc.

| BIOGRAPHIES & COMPOSER STUDIES |

ALKAN, REISSUE *by Ronald Smith.* Vol. 1: The Enigma. Vol. 2: The Music.

BEETHOVEN'S EMPIRE OF THE MIND *by John Crabbe.*

BÉLA BARTÓK: An Analysis of His Music *by Erno Lendvai.*

BÉLA BARTÓK: His Life in Pictures and Documents *by Ferenc Bónis.*

BERNARD STEVENS AND HIS MUSIC: A Symposium *edited by Bertha Stevens.*

JANÁCEK: Leaves from His Life *by Leos Janácek. Edited & transl. by Vilem & Margaret Tausky.*

JOHN FOULDS AND HIS MUSIC: An Introduction *by Malcolm MacDonald.*

LIPATTI *(Tanasescu & Bargauanu):* see PIANO, below.

LISZT AND HIS COUNTRY, 1869-1873 *by Deszo Legány.*

MASCAGNI: An Autobiography Compiled, Edited and Translated from Original Sources *by David Stivender.*

MICHAEL TIPPETT, O.M.: A Celebration *edited by Geraint Lewis. Fwd. by Peter Maxwell Davies.*

THE MUSIC OF SYZMANOWSKI *by Jim Samson.*

THE OPRICHNIK: An Opera in Four Acts by Peter Il'ich Tchaikovsky. *Transl. & notes by Philip Taylor.*

PERCY GRAINGER: The Man Behind the Music *by Eileen Dorum.*

PERCY GRAINGER: The Pictorial Biography *by Robert Simon. Fwd. by Frederick Fennell.*

RAVEL ACCORDING TO RAVEL *(Perlemuter & Jourdan-Morhange):* see PIANO, below.

RONALD STEVENSON: A Musical Biography *by Malcolm MacDonald.*

SCHUBERT'S MUSIC FOR PIANO FOUR-HANDS *(Weekly & Arganbright):* see PIANO, below.

SOMETHING ABOUT THE MUSIC 1: Landmarks of Twentieth-Century Music *by Nick Rossi.*

SOMETHING ABOUT THE MUSIC 2: Anthology of Critical Opinions *edited by Thomas P. Lewis.*

A SOURCE GUIDE TO THE MUSIC OF PERCY GRAINGER *edited by Thomas P. Lewis.*

Other Music Titles Available from Pro/Am Music Resources, Inc.

THE SYMPHONIES OF HAVERGAL BRIAN *by Malcolm MacDonald. Vol. 2: Symphonies 13-29. Vol. 3: Symphonies 30-32, Survey, and Summing-Up.*

VERDI AND WAGNER *by Erno Lendvai.*

VILLA-LOBOS: The Music *by Lisa M. Peppercorn.*

THE WORKS OF ALAN HOVHANESS: A Catalog, Opus 1 – Opus 360 *by Richard Howard.*

XENAKIS *by Nouritza Matossian.*

ZOLTAN KODALY: His Life in Pictures and Documents *by László Eosze.*

GENERAL SUBJECTS

ACOUSTICS AND THE PERFORMANCE OF MUSIC *by Jürgen Meyer.*

AMERICAN MINIMAL MUSIC, REISSUE *by Wim Mertens. Transl. by J. Hautekiet.*

CLARINET, REISSUE *by Jack Brymer.*

A CONCISE HISTORY OF HUNGARIAN MUSIC, 2ND ENL. EDITION *by Bence Szabolozi.*

EARLY MUSIC *by Denis Stevens.* Orig. title: Musicology (reissue).

FLUTE, REISSUE *by James Galway.*

GOGOLIAN INTERLUDES; Gogol's Story "Christmas Eve" as the Subject of the Operas by Tchaikovsky and Rimsky-Korsakov *by Philip Taylor.*

THE MUSICAL INSTRUMENT COLLECTOR, REVISED EDITION *by J. R-Obert Willcutt & Kenneth R. Ball.*

A MUSICIAN'S GUIDE TO COPYRIGHT AND PUBLISHING, ENL. EDITION *by Willis Wager.*

MUSICOLOGY IN PRACTICE: Collected Essays by Denis Stevens *edited by Thomas P. Lewis. Vol. 1: 1948-1970. Vol. 2: 1971-1990.*

MY VIOLA AND I, REISSUE *by Lionel Tertis.*

THE NUTLEY PAPERS: A Fresh Look at the Titans of Music (humor) *by James Billings.*

PEACE SONGS *compiled & edited by John Jordan.*

PERCUSSION INSTRUMENTS AND THEIR HISTORY, REV. EDITION *by James Blade.*

THE PRO/AM BOOK OF MUSIC AND MYTHOLOGY *compiled, edited & with commentaries by Thomas P. Lewis.* 3 vols.

Other Music Titles Available from
Pro/Am Music Resources, Inc.

THE PRO/AM GUIDE TO U. S. BOOKS ABOUT MUSIC: Annotated Guide to Current & Backlist Titles *edited by Thomas P. Lewis. 2 vols.*

SKETCHES FROM MY LIFE *by Natalia Sats.*

VIOLIN AND VIOLA, REISSUE *by Yehudi Menuhin & William Primrose, with Denis Stevens.*

GUITAR

THE AMP BOOK: A Guitarist's Inroductory Guide to Tube Amplifiers *by Donald Brosnac.*

ANIMAL MAGNETISM FOR MUSICIANS: Making a Bass Guitar and Pickup from Scratch *by Erno Zwaan.*

ANTHOLOGY OF FLAMENCO FALSETAS *collected by Ray Mitchell.*

ANTONIO DE TORRES: Guitar Maker–His Life and Work *by José Romanillos. Fwd. by Julian Bream.*

THE ART OF FLAMENCO *by D. E. Pohren.*

THE ART OF PRACTICING *by Alice Arzt.*

CLASSIC GUITAR CONSTRUCTION *by Irving Sloane.*

THE DEVELOPMENT OF THE MODERN GUITAR *by John Huber.*

THE FENDER GUITAR *by Ken Achard.*

THE GIBSON GUITAR FROM 1950 *by Ian C. Bishop. 2 vols.*

THE GUITAR: From the Renaissance to the Present Day, REISSUE *by Harvey Turnbull.*

GUITAR HISTORY: Volume 1–Guitars Made by the Fender Company *by Donald Brosnac.*

GUITAR HISTORY: Volume 2–Gibson SGs *by John Bulli.*

GUITAR HISTORY: Volume 3–Gibson Catalogs of the Sixties *edited by Richard Hetrick.*

GUITAR REPAIR: A Manual of Repair for Guitars and Fretted Instruments *by Irving Sloane.*

GUITAR TRADER' VINTAGE GUITAR BULLETIN. 6 vols.

THE HISTORY AND DEVELOPMENT OF THE AMERICAN GUITAR *by Ken Achard.*

AN INTRODUCTION TO SCIENTIFIC GUITAR DESIGN *by Donald Brosnac.*

LEFT HANDED GUITAR *by Nicholas Clarke.*

Other Music Titles Available from Pro/Am Music Resources, Inc.

LIVES AND LEGENDS OF FLAMENCO, 2ND EDITION *by D. E. Pohren.*

MANUAL OF GUITAR TECHNOLOGY: The History and Technology of Plucked String Instruments *by Franz Jahnel. English vers. by Dr. J. C. Harvey*

MAKING MUSIC SERIES: THE GURU'S GUITAR GUIDE *by Tony Bacon & Paul Day. MAKING* 4-TRACK MUSIC *by John Peel.* WHAT BASS, 2ND EDITION *by Tony Bacon & Laurence Canty.* WHAT DRUM, 2ND EDITION *by Geoff Nicholls & Andy Duncan.* WHAT GUITAR: The Making Music Guide to Buying Your Electric Six String, 3RD EDITION. WHAT'S MIDI, 2ND EDITION *by Andy Honeybone et al.*

THE NATURAL CLASSICAL GUITAR, REISSUE *by Lee F. Ryan.*

THE SEGOVIA TECHNIQUE, REISSUE *by Vladimir Bobri.*

THE SOUND OF ROCK: A History of Marshall Valve Guitar Amplifiers *by Mike Doyle.*

THE STEEL STRING GUITAR: Construction and Repair, UPDATED EDITION *by David Russell Young.*

STEEL STRING GUITAR CONSTRUCTION *by Irving Sloane.*

A WAY OF LIFE, REISSUE *by D. E. Pohren.*

THE WELL-TEMPERED GUITAR, ENLARGED ED. *by Nicholas Clarke.*

PERFORMANCE PRACTICE / "HOW-TO" INSTRUCTIONAL

GUIDE TO THE PRACTICAL STUDY OF HARMONY *by Peter Il'ich Tchaikovsky.*

HOW TO SELECT A BOW FOR VIOLIN FAMILY INSTRUMENTS *by Balthasar Planta.*

IMAGINATIONS: Tuneful Fun and Recital Pieces to Expand Early Grade Harp Skills *by Doris Davidson.*

THE JOY OF ORNAMENTATION: Being Giovanni Luca Conforto's *Treatise on Ornamentation* (Rome, 1593) *with a Preface by Sir Yehudi Menuhin and an Introduction by Denis Stevens.*

MAKING MUSICAL INSTRUMENTS *by Irving Sloane.*

THE MUSICIAN'S GUIDE TO MAPPING: A New Way to Learn Music *by Rebecca P. Shockley.*

THE MUSICIANS' THEORY BOOK: Reference to Fundamentals, Harmony, Counterpoint, Fugue and Form *by Asger Hamerik.*

Other Music Titles Available from
Pro/Am Music Resources, Inc.

ON BEYOND C *(Davidson):* see PIANO, below.

THE STUDENT'S DICTIONARY OF MUSICAL TERMS.

TENSIONS IN THE PERFORMANCE OF MUSIC: A Symposium, REVISED & EXTENDED EDITION *edited by Carola Grindea. Fwd. by Yehudi Menuhin.*

THE VIOLIN: Precepts and Observations *by Sourene Arakelian.*

PIANO/HARPSICHORD

THE ANATOMY OF A NEW YORK DEBUT RECITAL *by Carol Montparker.*

AT THE PIANO WITH FAURÉ, REISSUE *by Marguerite Long.*

EUROPEAN PIANO ATLAS *by H. K. Herzog.*

FRENCH PIANISM: An Historical Perspective *by Charles Timbrell.*

GLOSSARY OF HARPSICHORD TERMS *by Susanne Costa.*

KENTNER: A Symposium *edited by Harold Taylor. Fwd. by Yehudi Menuhin.*

LIPATTI *by Dragos Tanasescu & Grigore Bargauanu.*

ON BEYOND C: Tuneful Fun in Many Keys to Expand Early Grade Piano Skills *by Doris Davidson.*

THE PIANIST'S TALENT *by Harold Taylor. Fwd. by John Ogdon.*

PIANO, REISSUE *by Louis Kentner.*

THE PIANO AND HOW TO CARE FOR IT *by Otto Funke.*

THE PIANO HAMMER *by Walter Pfeifer.*

PIANO NOMENCLATURE, 2ND EDITION *by Nikolaus Schimmel & H. K. Herzog.*

RAVEL ACCORDING TO RAVEL *by Vlado Perlemuter & Hélène Jouran-Morhange.*

SCHUBERT'S MUSIC FOR PIANO FOUR-HANDS *by Dallas Weekly & Nancy Arganbright.*

TECHNIQUE OF PIANO PLAYING, 5TH EDITION *by József Gát.*

THE TUNING OF MY HARPSICHORD *by Herbert Anton Kellner.*

See also above:

ALKAN *(Smith)* – LISZT AND HIS COUNTRY *(Legnány)* – PERCY GRAINGER *(Dorum)* – PERCY GRAINGER *(Simon)* – RONALD STEVENSON *(MacDonald)* – SOURCE GUIDE TO THE MUSIC OF PERCY GRAINGER *(Lewis)* – TENSIONS PERFORMANCE MUSIC *(Grindea)*

The illustrious FRENCH SCHOOL OF PIANO PLAY-
ING here receives its first thorough examination —
from its roots in the Baroque era through major
19th-century masters and methods... the early
20th-century recordings... and the teaching of
Alfred Cortot, Marguerite Long, Isidor Philipp,
and other leading (and sometimes legendary)
modern pianist/pedagogues.

The author has conducted dozens of personal
interviews, spanning more than a decade, to bring
a special immediacy and comprehensiveness to
this unique historical/analytical survey. The result
is a "must" for every pianist and — indeed — lover
of music featuring the piano.

Among the topics covered are: practice and
performance techniques ● development of (and
departures from) a distinctive "French" school of
playing ● personal accounts of and by major
figures such as Lazare-Lévy, Ferté, Nat, Ciampi,
Gentil, Lefébure, Robert Casadesus, Gaby
Casadesus, Février, Descaves, Loyonnet, Sancan,
Barbier, Johannesen, Barbizet, Collard, and
Engerer...

Numerous appendices (including a discography and catalog of methods, exercises, and
études) and a complete index of names round out
this lively — and revealing — work.